CONSPICUOUS GALLANTRY

Stories of the Men and Women of 8th (Co Tyrone) Battalion, Ulster Defence Regiment

Anthony Leask

Helion & Company

Helion & Company Limited
Unit 8 Amherst Business Centre
Budbrooke Road
Warwick
CV34 5WE
England
Tel. 01926 499 619
Email: info@helion.co.uk
Website: www.helion.co.uk
Twitter: @helionbooks
Visit our blog at blog.helion.co.uk

Published by Helion & Company 2020. Reprinted in paperback 2023
Designed and typeset by Mach 3 Solutions (www.mach3solutions.co.uk)
Cover designed by Paul Hewitt, Battlefield Design (www.battlefield-design.co.uk)

Text © Anthony Leask 2020
Images © As individually credited
Maps © Anthony Leask 2020, drawn by Silverless.co.uk

Every reasonable effort has been made to trace copyright holders and to obtain their permission for the use of copyright material. The author and publisher apologize for any errors or omissions in this work and would be grateful if notified of any corrections that should be incorporated in future reprints or editions of this book.

ISBN 978-1-804514-69-6

British Library Cataloguing-In-Publication Data.
A catalogue record for this book is available from the British Library.

All rights reserved. No part of this publication may be reproduced, stored in a retrieval system, or transmitted, in any form, or by any means, electronic, mechanical, photocopying, recording or otherwise, without the express written consent of Helion & Company Limited.

For details of other military history titles published by Helion & Company Limited contact the above address or visit our website: http://www.helion.co.uk.

We always welcome receipt of book proposals from prospective authors.

Contents

Illustrations		iv
Maps		v
Preface		vi
Acknowledgements		vii
Glossary		viii
Introduction		xi
1	Patrol Action	15
2	Defending the Police and Ourselves	31
3	No Hiding Place	54
4	Greenfinches	106
5	Our Towns Devastated	118
6	Searches and Rummages	127
7	Forever Vigilant	157
8	Vehicle Checks	183
9	More Off-Duty Attacks	198
10	All Pulling Together	221
Retrospective		237
Bibliography		240
Index		241

Illustrations

Killymeal House, Dungannon, 8 UDR's HQ and Main Base	xii
B Company Patrol (Private David Neill) inserted on to the Sperrins, Winter 1984-85	15
Lance Corporal Winston Wray and Buff	28
Captured M1 Garand Rifles	29
Pomeroy Police Station Front View	37
Pomeroy Police Station from RPG-7 Firing Point	39
PIRA Mortar and Bombs	41
PIRA's Mark 10 Mortar	42
3 Lakeview Cottages, Ardboe	65
Raymond Richardson's House and Van	96
Under Vehicle IED	97
Private Carol Watson 1983	106
Car Bomb Scotch Street Dungannon 18th June 1974	119
Car Bomb Scotch Street Dungannon 18th June 1974	120
RPG-7: Shoulder-launched, anti-tank rocket-propelled grenade launcher.	129
RUC Vehicle in Crater	131
Find of 1 Ton HME	138
M1 and Ruger Rifles	142
Find of 1,000 lbs of Explosives	155
Route of Command Wire – CWIED at Cappagh/Galbally	165
CWIED in Culvert	169
B Company Team with the Explosives	170
The Yellow Cortina	186
PIRA Drogue Bomb	192
G3 and AK Rifles	196
AK47s	213
James Gibson's Ulsterbus	225
Scene of James Gibson's Killing	226
Getaway Car	228

Maps

Contact with PIRA Terrorists outside Donaghmore	21
PIRA Attack on Pomeroy Police Station	33
PIRA Attack on 8 UDR Cookstown Base	44
Attack on Private Glen Espie	66
PIRA Landmine Attack Galbally	165
PIRA Attack on Patrol in Pomeroy	173
PIRA Operations in Coalisland Interdicted	190
Attack on Private Jeffrey Lamont.	201
Killing of Private John Hardy and Follow-Up	211
Killing of ex-Private James Gibson and Follow-Up	223

Preface

History records many larger and more intensive campaigns but few that were sustained for so long as 'The Troubles', some twenty-five years. For all this time men and women fought in their homeland without respite, every hour of every day, sustained by the bonds of family, friends and those with whom they served. The cumulative effect of the constant pressure is only now becoming apparent. It was my privilege to serve with the soldiers of 8th (Co Tyrone) Battalion Ulster Defence Regiment (8 UDR). These are a few of their stories.

Anthony Leask
11 April 2020

Acknowledgements

This publication would not have been possible without the contributions of the storytellers, and for many it has not been easy to relive the past; all have, however, wanted the next generation to know what happened so that they can learn from this history. Others who are mentioned have not hidden behind anonymity for the same reasons.

Collecting the stories so that they are told in the individual's own words and are factually correct has been a huge task. Beverley Weir and Jay Nethercott recorded and transcribed the stories and did much else. Others in the team were Dessie Gordon who took on responsibility for checking the personal information of most of those mentioned, Dr Simon Taylor who allowed the use of his media database, and the late Bryce Sands who did the preliminary work on the images.

The editorial advisors included:

General Sir Roger Wheeler GCB CBE GOC Northern Ireland, Colonel Royal Irish Regiment, and Chief of the General Staff

Viscount Brookeborough KG served in the British Army including the UDR, one of the Hereditary Peers in the House of Lords, and Lord Lieutenant County Fermanagh

Assistant Chief Constable Raymond White OBE BEM LLB Head of Special Branch and Criminal Investigation Department of the Royal Ulster Constabulary GC

Each has brought their own different perspective and advice.

Julia Lowdon helped with the detailed editorial work.

A number of people gave donations to help ensure the publication of this book; their support was invaluable.

To all the above mentioned and many others, and on behalf of the men and women who served in 8 UDR, thank you.

Glossary

ANFO	Ammonium Nitrate and Fuel Oil
ANNIE	Ammonium Nitrate and Nitrobenzene
ARF	Airborne Reaction Force
ASU	Active Service Unit
ATO	Ammunition Technical Officer
CGC	Conspicuous Gallantry Cross
CO	Commanding Officer
COIN	Counter Insurgency
COP	Close Observation Platoon
COS	Chief of Staff
CPV	Covert Patrol Van
CQMS	Company Quartermaster Sergeant
CW	Command Wire
DOB	Date of Birth
DMSU	Divisional Mobile Support Unit (RUC)
EOD	Explosives Ordnance Disposal
FFR	Fitness For Role
GOC	General Officer Commanding
GR	Grid Reference
HME	Home Made Explosive
HQNI	Headquarters Northern Ireland
IAAG	Improvised Anti-Armour Grenade
ICP	Incident Control Point
IED	Improvised Explosive Device
INLA	Irish National Liberation Army
MID	Mentioned in Despatches
MSM	Meritorious Service Medal
NCO	Non Commissioned Officer
NISR	Northern Ireland Search Record
ODS	Off-Duty Soldier
PIRA	Provisional Irish Republican Army
PPW	Personal Protection Weapon
PSI	Permanent Staff Instructor
PTI	Physical Training Instructor
PVCP	Permanent Vehicle Checkpoint
QCVS	Queen's Commendation for Valuable Service

QGM	Queen's Gallantry Medal
QRF	Quick Reaction Force
RBL	Royal British Legion
RESA	Royal Engineers Search Advisor
RIC	Royal Irish Constabulary or Reconnaissance Intelligence Centre (Air)
R Irish	Royal Irish Regiment
RPG	Remotely Projected Grenade
RUC	Royal Ulster Constabulary
SAM	Surface to Air Missile
SLR	Self Loading Rifle
SOCO	Scenes of Crime Officer
SPED	Scheme for Purchase of Evacuated Dwellings
TA	Territorial Army
TAOR	Tactical Area of Responsibility
TCG	Tasking and Coordination Group
TPU	Timer and Power Unit
UD	Ulster Decoration
UDR	Ulster Defence Regiment
USC	Ulster Special Constabulary
UVBT	Under Vehicle Booby-Trap
UVF	Ulster Volunteer Force
UVIED	Under Vehicle IED
VCP	Vehicle Check Point
VRN	Vehicle Registration Number
WIS	Weapons Intelligence Section
WPC	Woman Police Constable

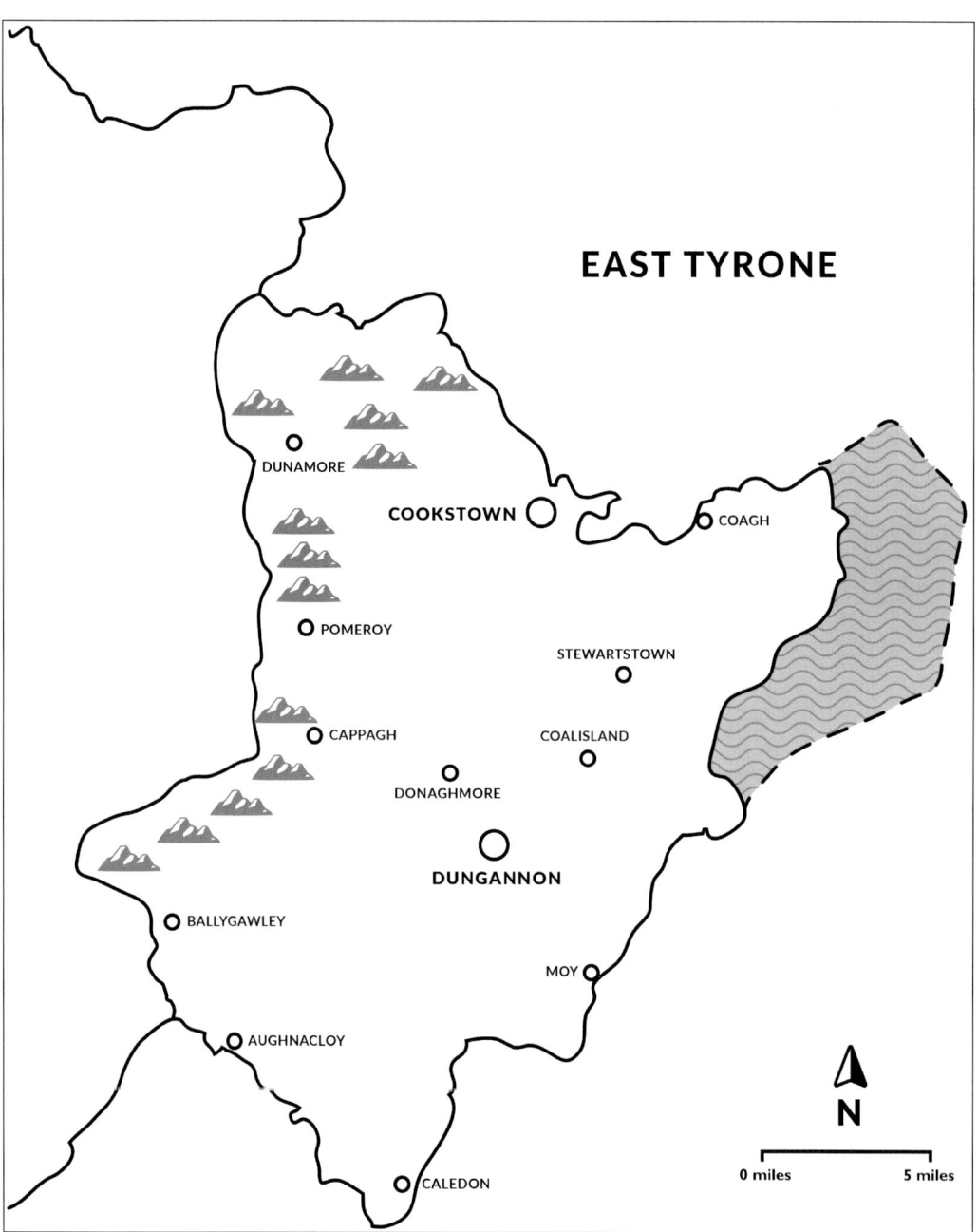

Introduction

US

Whenever the British Army has successfully countered an insurgency, locally raised forces have played a significant part. The Northern Ireland Campaign 1969-96 was no exception.

The Ulster Defence Regiment CGC (Conspicuous Gallantry Cross awarded by HM The Queen on 6th October 2006 as a mark of the Nation's esteem) was raised in 1970 and amalgamated into the Royal Irish Regiment in 1992. At its peak, the Regiment had eleven battalions with a total strength approaching 10,000. Throughout its existence, some 50,000 men and women served in the Regiment.

In the beginning the Regiment was used to support Regular Army battalions on static guard duties and patrols in relatively low risk areas. However, by 1981 most of Northern Ireland had become the responsibility of Ulster Defence Regiment battalions, some with Regular Army companies under their operational control.

8th (County Tyrone) Battalion (8 UDR) was recruited almost entirely in East Tyrone, the area in which it operated. There was a mix of permanent cadre (full-time) and part-time soldiers, eventually about 50:50; the former were similar to regular soldiers but lived at home and mainly operated during the week. Part-time time soldiers operated at night and at weekends. In 8 UDR both tended to work the same number of hours unless there was a particular operation or incident. All were under very considerable risk both on and off duty from the day they joined up, and this risk continued until the Campaign ended: for many it still does.

In the eighteenth century, military barracks were established in Dungannon and Altmore, in the pass above Cappagh, Both had long been abandoned. During 1970 the Regular Army established bases in Dungannon (Castle Hill) and Aughnacloy; they were fully occupied.

When 8 UDR was formed, by splitting 6 UDR which covered the whole of County Tyrone, it had five part-time companies. G and H were in Cookstown and in due course became C (Cookstown) Company, J and K were in Dungannon and became D (Dungannon) Company at Killymeal, and L in Aughnacloy became A (Aughnacloy) Company. New bases were found and secured. Battalion Headquarters was in Dungannon (Killymeal).

In 1981 8 UDR was given operational responsibility for East Tyrone, the area of the Province considered third highest risk; the other two remained the responsibility of Regular Army battalions until 1996. At this stage, the battalion had one full-time (B) and the three part-time operational companies. Headquarter Company was mainly permanent cadre. In addition it had one Regular Army company under its operational

Killymeal House, Dungannon, 8 UDR's HQ and Main Base

control. The total strength was about 600. From time to time other companies were deployed into East Tyrone for specific operations but the basic structure continued unchanged until 1992 when 8 UDR ceased to exist.

The Battalion operated in support of the police (RUC) who set the operational priorities. Tasks and resources were then allocated based on the available intelligence. All the time a balance had to be achieved between defensive operations, providing close protection to bases, business premises and individuals, and offensive operations that interdicted terrorist activities within Republican areas. Checking and searching people and vehicles, and the areas in which they lived and worked, provided the basis of all tactics, all the time trying to focus on the suspected terrorists while allowing the majority of the population to lead as normal a life as possible. Information was gathered both on and off duty and this was collated by the Intelligence Cell to help focus the operational effort more effectively. In the background were the men and women of Headquarter Company – armourers, vehicle mechanics, chefs, collators, signallers and many others without whom the Battalion would not have functioned.

East Tyrone is divided into three slices: in the west are the Sperrin Mountains, in the centre is the fertile farm land astride the Dungannon-Cookstown road, and in the east is the Lough shore – once very wet land but now drained. The west and east are predominantly Catholic and the centre Protestant. The two main towns are mixed. Boundaries are well defined but by no means straight. In the passes through the Sperrins are small Protestant enclaves, a factor of history. The northern boundary is the county boundary with County Londonderry and in the south that with County Armagh and the Republic of Ireland.

The population of East Tyrone is about 60,000 and evenly split. Initially Catholics joined 8 UDR but all but a few very brave men and women were intimidated out. So the Battalion had to recruit from a population of about 10,000 men and was increasingly reliant on women soldiers.

Many books have been written about the Regiment, some by men and women who have not experienced life in the front line. This is not a repeat of the excellent battalion history that was written some years ago but brings together the stories of men and women who served in 8 UDR; they tell their experiences in their own words. These remarkable men and women put their lives on the line for many years in order that their children could have a better future. Forty-four were killed by terrorists; many more were wounded.

One final word; the reader will soon realise the closeness of the family that was and still is 8 UDR. Like any family they knew each other very well indeed and provided close support to their men and women at every stage, from enlistment and through the stresses and strains of fighting every day for their lives and those of everyone else.

Them

The history of the IRA and the Republican cause in East Tyrone can be traced back well into the nineteenth century. In the 1920s the East Tyrone Brigade was organised in a hierarchical, military structure of units called battalions and companies; their size varied but were never much more than twenty strong. Such units existed in Dungannon, Donaghmore, Cappagh, Pomeroy, Dunamore, Ardboe and Coalisland.

This structure still existed in 1970 and the early attacks were carried out by these units. They suffered from several weaknesses: poor training, lack of arms and explosives, poor direction, limited intelligence and weak security were just some of them. As a consequence many of the units were ineffective, easily penetrated, and many men and weapons were captured. One of the biggest problems was leadership. A local unit did not always have a leader but imposing one carried big risks. Whilst the community might not inform on their own, that was not always the case with an outsider whom they did not know and who did not know them.

By 1972 the Brigade stabilised, increasing its attacks against off-duty soldiers and economic targets. Furthermore its capability against Security Forces' patrols also improved and it mounted two flying column attacks against their bases in this period, one against RUC Pomeroy and the other against 6 UDR in Clogher.

Despite this, East Tyrone PIRA by the end of the decade was being severely curtailed by enhancements in the Security Forces. PIRA reorganised. A Northern Command was set up to direct operations in Northern Ireland and the border counties of the Republic of Ireland, and to establish greater control of 'brigades'. A smaller cell structure replaced units to give greater security. Active Service Units (ASUs) were established, consisting of the most experienced men and the most effective weaponry, and prepared to act under Northern Command orders.

Northern Command kept control over Brigades and ASUs through the re-supply of weapons and explosives. The major dumps were in the Republic of Ireland but their allocation and movement forward was Northern Command's responsibility and one that gave them influence and control. PIRA now focused on the 'Long War' strategy which prioritised security over immediate offensive action.

The structure at the bottom did not disappear; indeed it was essential to provide support for the ASUs and the wider cause. It, however, remained a weakness.

1983 was a critical year. In order to be effective an ASU depended on leadership, technical expertise, individual experience, a willingness to engage in operations, and access to weaponry. Collapsed legal cases, prisoner releases and jail escapes meant that a number of highly experienced individuals returned to East Tyrone PIRA around this time. They transformed East Tyrone PIRA and in doing so entered the folklore of Irish Republicanism. Combined with the promotion of former brigade commander Kevin McKenna to be Chief of Staff, this ensured that by the end of that year East Tyrone PIRA had access to the very top of the organisation.

East Tyrone Brigade PIRA killed over 80 serving and former members of the Security Forces, and a further eleven civilian contractors working for them. Their biggest success was killing eight regular soldiers near Ballygawley in 1988; they were travelling in a bus and returning from leave to Omagh. Another success, also in Ballygawley, was in December 1985 when they attacked the RUC Station in the village, killing two policemen and destroying the station. There were many others.

Their biggest disaster was when eight of their own were killed in an attack on Loughgall RUC Station in May 1987. Again there were many others. This was never a one-sided fight.

So-called loyalist terrorist groups also operated in East Tyrone; they were mainly ineffective and dealt with by the RUC. Security Forces did recover a considerable quantity of their weaponry and ammunition but most was old and of little use. However, these groups did pose a threat to the Catholic community, one that was never ignored.

In the beginning large numbers of men and women were recruited into the UDR and the security vetting process was inadequate; the consequences were inevitable and a small number of men and women with paramilitary sympathies were enlisted. The vetting process duly improved, team work developed at every level (platoon, company and battalion) with zero tolerance and no place for divided loyalty; anyone suspected of such sympathies was discharged very rapidly. There were security breaches and it did not matter that the numbers were quite small in proportion to the huge number who served in the Regiment; each one tarnished the reputation of the Regiment as a whole and that of everyone who served in it.

8 UDR had its share but most were in the early years. By 1980 the Battalion was much reduced in size and its operational commitment great; letting down the Battalion and family and friends who served in it was not to be contemplated or tolerated. Countering 'them', any enemy within, was taken very seriously indeed by all ranks, as was any hint of loyalist paramilitary groups active within the Battalion area.

Perception more than reality dominated but it did make the Catholic community feel threatened and so provide propaganda for Sinn Fein and encourage support for PIRA. In East Tyrone it was never enough. PIRA failed to drive the Security Forces back to their bases or out of East Tyrone and failed to prevent the RUC making progress towards normality.

1

Patrol Action

Patrols were the bread and butter of operational life. They were carried out by day and night on foot and in vehicles. Some were defensive covering potential targets and some were offensive operating in the terrorists' heartlands. All were planned and co-ordinated with the Royal Ulster Constabulary (RUC). Tasks included the gathering of information, rummages (light searches), vehicle check points (VCPs) and route clearance, as well as target protection. Patrols varied in size but by 1982 a foot patrol of 12 (three 'bricks' or 'teams' each of four men) was the usual while a vehicle patrol was two vehicles (each with four men). Often they worked together to increase unpredictability.

B Company Patrol (Private David Neill)[1] inserted on to the Sperrins, Winter 1984-85

Chance encounters were rare because the patrols were in uniform and vehicle noise could be heard a very long way off, especially at night. However, sometimes a degree of cunning such as lurking in a dark spot or going back quickly over the same route did

---

1   LCpl David George Neill: 1964-: 8 UDR 1982-87.
    (Notes on 8 UDR men and women contain final rank, full name (used first name in brackets), post nominals, year of birth (and year of death if relevant), years of service in 8 UDR, awards, other Service, and occupation if part-time.)

catch the terrorists out. Later it was possible to deploy and recover patrols by helicopter, which further increased unpredictability and reduced risks.

Patrols, called Quick Reaction Forces, were deployed in the follow up to an incident. A difficult balance had to be struck between speed and caution. If the follow up was too slow the trail had gone cold, but the terrorists were well able to work out the routes to be used and mount a secondary attack should they wish to do so.

PIRA engaged the Security Forces on operations outside their bases in East Tyrone with small arms 169 times in the years 1970-92. The Security Forces opened fire on 66 similar occasions.

Donaghmore 11th and 12th August 1973

Donaghmore, with its population of about 1,000, stands beside the Torrent River on the road between Pomeroy in the Sperrins to the west and Dungannon two miles to the east. The village in 1973 was, and still is, predominantly Catholic and many supported the Republican cause. It also provided a bridge of support between the Catholic estates in west Dungannon and the Catholic communities in the Sperrins. Significant landmarks included St Patrick's Catholic Church which has direct connection with the arrival of Christianity in Ireland in 450 AD and the Brewer's House, one of the oldest pubs in Ulster. There was no RUC Station in the village; the old Royal Irish Constabulary (RIC) Barracks had been evacuated by the police in 1920 and then destroyed by the IRA. At that time a railway line ran from Dungannon through Donaghmore and Pomeroy to Omagh and Londonderry and was frequently interrupted by the IRA.

This is an outline report of an incident that occurred on 11th August 1973:

> At 2350hrs a mobile patrol of K Company 8 UDR was moving north on the Castlecaulfield-Donaghmore road. They had just stopped to do a snap VCP, and were dismounting from their vehicles, when they noticed a car moving towards them from the north. Two members of the patrol ran forward to intercept the car, which was about fifty metres in front of them, when it slowed abruptly and turned off the road to the east into the entrance of a house. Three men got out and ran behind the house; they were carrying rifles and were challenged. Meanwhile Lieutenant Maginnis[2] and Private Nethercott[3] ran round the south end of the building. The patrol opened fire on the gunmen, the noise of whose

---

2   Maj Kenneth (Ken) Wiggins Maginnis 1938-: 8 UDR 1970-82: Schoolmaster/Principal and Turkey Farmer: Dungannon District Council 1982-94: Member of Parliament for Fermanagh and South Tyrone 1983-2001: Later Lord Maginnis of Drumglass: (11 attempts have been made to kill him).
3   Maj William James (Jay) Nethercott MBE QGM 1952-: 8 UDR 1971-87: (5 UDR 1987-92, R Irish until 2000): MID.

escape could clearly be heard to the east. As Lieutenant Maginnis ran round the rear of the house he noticed a man lying on the ground holding a rifle. He apprehended the man who was Andrew Vincent[4] of Tullynure, Donaghmore. The rifle was a M1 Garand (No. 2413124) and loaded with a clip of eight .300 inch rounds. Three of the patrol followed the gunmen as far as a wood before discontinuing the follow up and returning to the road. Lieutenant Maginnis asked for additional troops to cordon the area.

These stories are about the men and women of 8 UDR as well as incidents they were involved in, so whenever possible an individual's background and experience is included. Jay Nethercott played a significant part in the Battalion for most of its existence. He sets the scene and describes an earlier incident on his first patrol:

Ken Maginnis, then serving as a Lieutenant in the UDR based in Dungannon, gave me my signing-on papers to join the Regiment as a part-time soldier. I never gave it a second's thought and signed up immediately in the autumn of 1971 when I was 18 years old and still at school. Ken had been my primary school teacher and also ran a small business rearing and processing turkeys for the local market and I had been doing seasonal work for him since I was 14. My recollection of Ken was that he was worldly wise and authoritative being a man of position in the local community, and quite handy with the cane.

After passing basic recruit training covering live firing exercises, anti-ambush drills and search skills I was posted to K Company 8 UDR based at Killymeal in Dungannon and joined my platoon in January 1972. I knew my Company Commander and the Second in Command, Ken was my platoon commander, and that was about it; everyone seemed quite old to me but experienced. I do not remember any other Privates my age, or anyone from my area of the town serving at that time. It was an exciting adventure for me and there was a great buzz in the Company; incidents were happening all the time, car bombs, shootings, and both Official and Provisional IRA (PIRA) were active throughout East Tyrone. The Battalion lost its first soldier in December 1971, Lance Corporal Denis Wilson[5] a farmer and like me part-time; he was murdered by the IRA while ill in bed at his home near the border village of Caledon. I did not know him nor had I ever been to Caledon but felt the grief of a family when our Company Commander called us on parade to hold a two minute silence

---

4 Andrew Hugh Vincent c1948-2015: Labourer: Donaghmore: Sentenced (1st May 1974) to six years' imprisonment for possession of two Garand rifles and 16 bullets with intent to endanger life on 23rd August 1973 (*Tyrone Courier* 15th May 1974).
 (Notes on suspect terrorists contain information about their activities which is in the public domain.)
5 +LCpl William Denis Wilson 1940-1971: 8 UDR 1970-71: Farmer: Killed 7th December 1971.

to remember him. To this day I see 8 UDR as my extended family and that is how we were.

I was eagerly looking forward to my first patrol, a mobile patrol using two Land Rovers. It was a winter's evening in early January 1972 and I was to report for duty at 1930hrs. In the late afternoon Ken called at our house and as he had an urgent order for turkeys to prepare that evening, he had organised with the patrol commander to draw my weapon and pick me up from his house slightly later at 2030hrs. I took my uniform and old clothes to work in, went with Ken to his house and worked flat out to finish the order and be ready on time for my patrol; nothing I felt was more important than completing my first patrol and I certainly was not going to let anyone down.

I did not take my work clothes off; preparing turkeys meant the odd feather and bit of blood was on them and being a slim and very fit young man thought the extra layer under my uniform would keep me warm on the winter's night. I put on my uniform over my work clothes, fitted my puttees over my boots, and immaculately dressed, prepared for my first operational patrol. The Land Rovers duly arrived at Ken's house on the outskirts of Dungannon, and the Section Commander gave me my rifle and a quick brief. I was to be cover man when carrying out vehicle check points and was in the back of the lead Land Rover with him. There was a bit of banter amongst the patrol, everyone was in a joyous mood as we moved off, here I was on my first operational patrol. Alert, jubilant, all the skills I had been taught fresh in my mind, the patrol moved down onto the main road and we turned left to go back into Dungannon. I had been on patrol for about a minute, long enough to catch the petrol fumes from the exhaust coming into the back of the open Land Rover doors and feel the chill of the night air, when the patrol was ambushed by gunfire from somewhere on the edge of the Lisnahull housing estate about two fields off the main Dungannon to Donaghmore road.

Our anti-ambush drills were to drive out of the kill zone, stop and engage the terrorists. Inside the front Land Rover, the section commander, a very capable NCO, directed the driver, who happened to be a trained rally driver, to 'Drive! Drive! Drive!' The acceleration was vicious and I was nearly thrown out of the open doors; immediately the section commander shouted 'Stop! Stop! Stop!' and the braking manoeuvre, equally vicious, meant I was catapulted into the Land Rover bouncing off everything from a spare wheel, jack and protruding bolts. Next I was out of the Land Rover on the road and I felt the jolt, something like a shock from the 240 volt mains, hit me on the right hand. The patrol commander was beside me returning fire with an automatic, and there was noise and confusion when Ken arrived at the scene; they knew that I was hurt too (*Jay had been hit in the right hand by a rifle firing from more than two hundred yards; a round went through another soldier's beret*). The shooting had all stopped and it was eerily quiet. A hasty follow-up was organised, some soldiers were whispering and some were shouting; Ken took my rifle and I kept telling him it was cocked with a live round in the breech and off they went across the field.

I went over to a nearby house with a small porch to take cover, a police vehicle was on the scene and one of the officers was beside me. The occupants of the house switched on the outside light and blood was everywhere; the lady opened the door, saw all this blood and promptly closed the door. The police officer realised I was hurt and he organised to get me to the local hospital with their patrol car. I was not sure what was hurting and patted myself down to feel if I was hurt anywhere else; I was concerned for myself now the adrenalin kick was over. The hospital was only a five minute drive away: they did it in two.

At the A&E Department of the South Tyrone Hospital they were already waiting for a gunshot casualty to arrive, the police having phoned in the details from the officer on the ground. We walked into the hospital, I was put on a trolley and taken into A&E where a very calm group of professional nurses and doctors took charge. Someone was dealing with my right hand and others started to undress me. I suddenly felt really embarrassed; once this uniform comes off, I thought, they will see the old clothes I was wearing when killing turkeys just an hour earlier; thankfully at least it was not my blood on these clothes underneath my uniform. I wasn't in any life threatening situation, and the nurses took a bit of a hand out of me as they sorted out my wound.

The patrol came back to the hospital to pick me up around 0100hrs, massive bandage, stitches and splints over my right hand, my rifle was there and it was decided that we should go back on patrol as it was good therapy for us all. Nothing had been found on the initial follow up so the terrorists had escaped; the daylight follow up found the firing point and the empty cases from a M1 Garand. Once the patrol had finished we signed in our weapons and debriefed; I managed to arrange a lift home, and tired and sore went to bed quite content with myself.

So much for Jay's first day on operations with 8 UDR in East Tyrone. That was in 1972; now eighteen months later Ken Maginnis and Jay were on patrol again. Ken was again the patrol commander and recalls:

While the UDR became, by the time PIRA was defeated in 1996, the epitome of efficiency in fighting terrorism that was not always the case. When it was formed and mobilised on 1st April 1970 – I was on duty that first day – it consisted of volunteers of all backgrounds, many of whom saw it as the only opportunity to pre-empt a civil war. This new and barely trained regiment was, initially, viewed with a mixture of relief among the Unionist community, suspicion among Nationalists, and nervousness among their professional uniformed colleagues.

But 'must do' is a great master and while the early years saw many die at the hands of terrorists, dire necessity, the need to survive, and development of a leadership from various walks of life saw some unusual successes occur.

Observation, efforts to interpret and to exploit information, often from the most unlikely sources, became a way of life for many as they pursued their day to day employment and then took to the highways and byways at night.

The patrol that night had been tasked into the area on the Dungannon side of Donaghmore where PIRA suspects had been sighted. The operation was planned on the basis that the two vehicle patrol would make its way slowly and deliberately from Castlecaulfield to Dungannon via Donaghmore. It would substitute one of its Land Rovers with an armoured Shorland (*Land Rover-based armoured car*) which would lead, and draw fire from the terrorists; the second vehicle would then, under cover from the sloping ground atop of which we had deduced would be the PIRA firing point, dismount and return fire (in the Shorland were the patrol commander, a Lance Corporal, Privates Symington[6] (stop man), McKenzie[7] (cover man), and one other; Lieutenant Maginnis (commander), Privates Nethercott (driver) and one other (cover man), were in the Land Rover behind.)

That's the background to the operation that developed entirely differently from what had been intended.

As we passed the grounds of Donaghmore Convent on our left and with a single semi-detached block on our right, an approaching vehicle deliberately swung off down the left hand driveway to the houses. As three soldiers from the Shorland pursued it, the car doors opened, the inside light came on and they were aware of three men emerging, each holding a rifle.

My men opened fire and those of us in the second vehicle, hearing a shouted alert from our front, moved on a right flanking movement to cut off whoever had caused our lead crew to open fire.

On reaching the right-hand rear of the houses but unable to proceed further because of the gunfire I was aware of a gunman about six metres away with his rifle pointing towards my men pursuing from the left.

Literally screaming 'Cease fire!' and obviously unable to fire for fear of hitting my own men I crossed to the gunman and struck him on the head with my rifle, then ran on still screaming 'Cease fire!' Nethercott following in my wake picked up the dazed terrorist and his rifle and we went into all round defence to the left rear of the building.

Beyond our location and much lower was the Gaelic pitch and beyond that a small stream. As my men from the lead vehicle briefed me we were aware of a splash and shout from the direction of the stream. I ordered two of my soldiers to open fire towards the sound.

---

6 Pte David Ivan Symington 1952-: 8 UDR 1973-74: Student.
7 Pte William (Billy) John McKenzie 1947-: 8 UDR 1972-74: Crop Researcher.

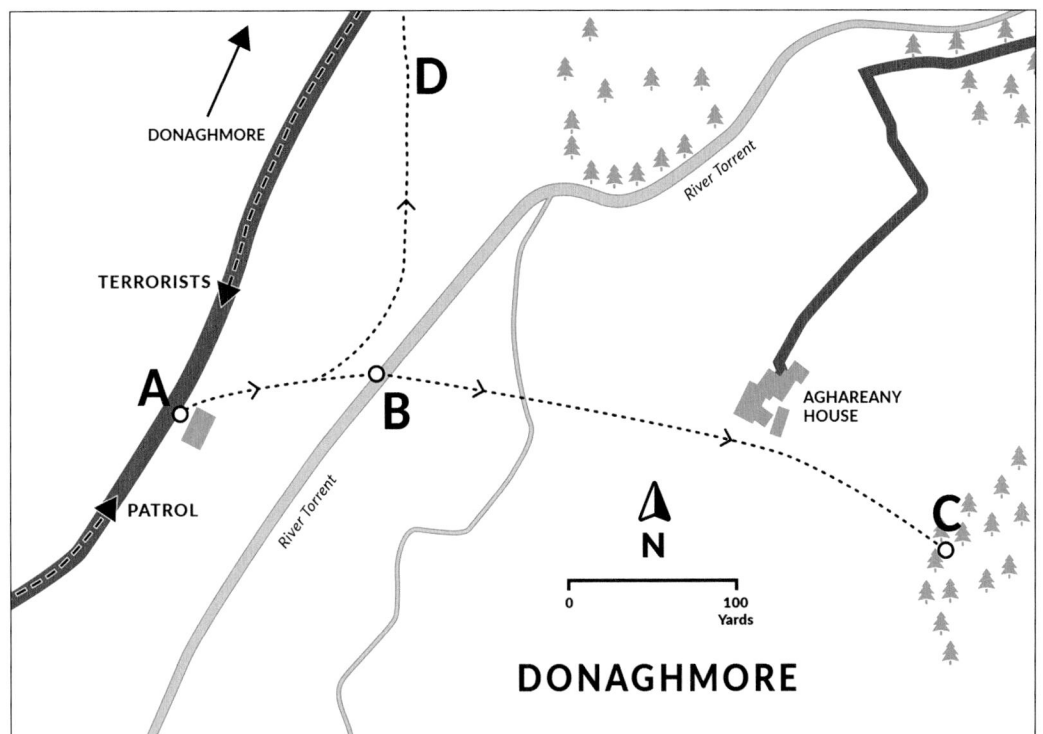

Contact with PIRA Terrorists outside Donaghmore
A: Contact/Vincent + Weapon captured, B: Weapon recovered,
C: McDonald captured, D: Terrorist escaped

Jay Nethercott's recollections and those of others provide the detail:

> By the time of this incident in Donaghmore in August 1973 I had completed hundreds of operational patrols as a part-time soldier in 8 UDR. It was a dangerous time in East Tyrone; terrorist incidents had increased significantly and I had witnessed violence against both the community and myself, and seen the effect this had in Dungannon town where I had grown up. Attempted murder, car bombs in the town, bodies blown to smithereens, and the killing of off-duty soldiers of the Battalion, all were common-place, and there was also now a significant division within communities too.
>
> I had grown up in a Nationalist housing estate on the north side of Dungannon and there had never been any time or event that I can recall during all the time I lived there when I was made to feel that as a Prod I was not welcome. Our neighbours, all of them, were the kindest, most honest and endearing families and friends anyone could have wished for, and it was a privilege to have lived and grown up there.
>
> However, the outside influence of other people can and does bring change and problems to communities like ours. In particular I can recall some young

Protestant boys from our estate during the period of the Civil Rights Campaign in 1969 were bullied by a gang from the south side of Dungannon who deliberately came to our estate, the White City, to beat them up. The ringleader was a slightly old teenager, a fellow McHugh[8] from the Donaghmore Road, and this went on until he picked on a young boy one evening who looked easy prey and McHugh came off worst having got his arm broke and ended up in hospital.

When the troubles started early in 1970 I was in the village of Coalisland one evening with friends and there was rioting outside the Police Station, very near to where I was visiting. I was watching events when I saw two men run from a factory near the village centre just as black smoke started to billow from the main building, and then very quickly it was engulfed in flames. Then two men came down the street, went into a house opposite the Police Station, and disappeared out the back and away. One of them was this man McHugh from the Donaghmore Road who I knew only too well.

Virtually all of our patrols were west of Dungannon covering up to the village of Pomeroy to the north, and PIRA gangs were active in this area. Our patrols did seem to be mostly two Land Rover mobile patrols carrying out vehicle check points and occasionally foot patrols were dropped off from these vehicles to check off-duty members' homes and search culverts for landmines. Donaghmore was an area of interest and we knew the ground around the village intimately. There was a part-time member of the Battalion living in the village and we would cover around his house occasionally. A few weeks before the incident on 11th August we were on foot patrol checking culverts and came across a couple of hundred metres of command wire secreted into the hedgerow of the Donaghmore to Castlecaulfield road leading up to a vantage point on high ground. This threw up the name, Andy Vincent, who I knew and I had been to his house a few times with friends some years before; he was a few years older than me and well known around Dungannon where his sister had a business.

On the Saturday evening I reported for duty at 1900hrs, at Killymeal House, our company base on the outskirts of Dungannon. Our Section Commander, a Corporal, told us we would be on a two vehicle mobile patrol (one Land Rover and one Shorland) and the Platoon Commander would be joining us, so no mucking about. I was to be the driver of the second vehicle so I drew the vehicle out, prepared it, checking petrol, oils and spares, and collected the Vehicle Check Point (VCP) kit, then loaded it all on the vehicle. Experience had taught me to check how I would exit the vehicle, where my rifle would be stored so I would have access to it at all times in the dark, and all the possible

---

8 Michael Joseph (Barry) McHugh c1951-: In his book *The Informer* Sean O'Callaghan PIRA writes 'Barry McHugh, also from Dungannon, was a quiet and unconvincingly committed IRA man.'

eventualities: I prepared myself mentally for my patrol and the role and function I was carrying out.

At the briefing the Platoon Commander, Ken, emphasised that terrorists were active and the patrol could be ambushed in the west area of Dungannon and Donaghmore. The plan was to start VCPs in the Castlecaulfield area then move to the west side of Dungannon carrying out snap VCPs en route, initiated by the front vehicle while our vehicle was to keep further back so we could follow up any attack, the logic being that the front vehicle would be the target of any terrorists.

I was happy to be with the soldiers on this patrol; they were experienced, dependable, very fit, competent and thoughtful, and there was a bond between us that comes from experience and trust. There was a wide range of working backgrounds, school teachers, civil servants, electricians, turkey pluckers, students and rugby players.

Late in the Saturday evening we were coming into the village of Donaghmore. It was now dark and we were driving slowly; there was not much traffic on the roads when the radio crackled into life, the lead vehicle indicating a snap VCP. We were blind to our lead vehicle slightly ahead of us and on a left hand bend when I stopped our Land Rover and got out; this was our standard drill. The stillness of the night gave way to shouting of voices and immediately gunfire. A quick couple of rounds then a heavy salvo of rounds were fired which seemed to go on for a long time followed by more shouting. The Platoon Commander quickly moved forward with our team shouting loudly 'Cease fire!' There was confusion as to what was happening: 'the car was just driving towards us when it turned off the road into a house on the same side of the road', 'three men with rifles jumped out of the car as it turned into the driveway of a house', 'a gunman with a rifle took up a firing position at the side of the garage' to 'there was a distinct sound of someone splashing in water in the area behind the house which leads out to open fields when the Section Commander's team had opened fire'.

The Platoon Commander took control, immediately tasking myself and one other soldier from our team to start a follow up through the fields in pursuit of two escaping gunmen (we knew one of the terrorists was apprehended by the garage). We were both very fit, excellent shots, and we knew the ground. We went forward into the fields at a fast running pace, our hastily put together plan was not to go to our right side (on the west), in which very few people would be likely to harbour fugitives, but to cross the river, go up onto the high ground and work our way along the hedgerows stopping at the edge of the village 30 mph zone on the Dungannon side of Donaghmore, working our way back to the scene of the incident and keeping within talking distance between us.

We did as best as we could in the fields, searching the hedgerows hoping we would find a gunman wounded or even dead. When I came back on the river on the Dungannon side of the village and was entering the water to search under a small bridge, there was a flurry of massive splashing going away from me. I was startled and fired instinctively, but those nesting ducks just kept on flying. I immediately radioed the Platoon Commander that it was a false alarm, explaining that it was a flight of ducks. We searched for a long time through the fields with no success. A helicopter with Nightsun gave excellent coverage of the area in the darkness; in the morning we were informed by radio that the Regular Army would take charge of the follow up and we were to return to the check point. The follow up search by the Regulars arrested one man (Eugene McDonald[9]) and recovered his rifle which he had thrown into the river during his escape.

The third man in the rear vehicle adds his memories:

I had joined 8 UDR as a part-time soldier in 1972 and was based at Killymeal House with K Company. My memory of those early days on night time patrols was very long hours, never home before 0500hrs, and very little rest before heading out to my work which was mostly in the Belfast and Portadown area.

It was a very dangerous and sad time in the country and the Dungannon area was particularly active; we were continually asked to do more patrols other than our Section's duty nights with K Company.

On one of these extra duties I went on a night time mobile patrol tasked to carry out vehicle checkpoints west of Dungannon.

I was travelling in the second vehicle of a two vehicle patrol and was in the back providing top cover to the rear of the patrol; there were three of us in the vehicle (I was able to use a hatch in the roof to stand out through). We had been on patrol for several hours carrying out snap VCPs when approaching the village of Donaghmore our vehicle slowed to a halt. I was standing in the hatch covering the rear able to hear voices shouting and immediately a volley of shots, more shouting, more firing, confusion; I had no idea who was shooting but knew instinctively the front team were engaged. We dismounted from our vehicle running forwards towards the other vehicle, the Platoon Commander shouting loudly 'Cease firing!' 'Cease firing!' Briefly it did. I joined up with the forward team on the road where someone shouted about a vehicle driving off, the section commander shouting about gunmen running into the fields, watch out for gunmen at the side of the house; it was a mass of information to make sense of in a split second, when splashing was heard from the darkness

---

9 Eugene Francis McDonald c1955-: Unemployed bricklayer: Dungannon: Sentenced (1st May 1974) to six years' imprisonment for possession of two Garand rifles and 16 bullets with intent to endanger life and for membership of the IRA (*Tyrone Courier* 15th May 1974 and *Dungannon Observer* 5th May 1974).

and we were ordered to fire. A terrorist was held at the scene and I was tasked to secure the rear and stop traffic from entering. Soon after local people looked out from their houses but no one approached us and time just seemed to stop, from seconds of mayhem and noise to hushed conversations, expectation of more shooting and waiting.

Back in Dungannon part of the section had to go and make statements at the police station and the rest of us put all the equipment away. The adrenalin stopped and tiredness took over; we had been on the go for 24 hours at this time. We were stood down; the other guys would be at the police station for a while and we went home; some of us were scheduled for duty again that night.

The Patrol/Section Commander, in the front vehicle, takes over and tells his story:

Having been born and reared in Dungannon I was from an early age very aware of the threat of violence to our community. Childhood memories of a bomb being exploded at the local Territorial Army barracks in the 1950s when attending a Sunday School party are memories I can recall as a child. Coming from a family with service both in the Home Guard and the Ulster Special Constabulary (see note), I felt the responsibility to do my bit when the opportunity arose. I decided to join the UDR shortly after it was formed to assist in countering the increasing threat to the community from IRA terrorists. Having good geographical knowledge of the East Tyrone area, I recall going out at times with Regular Army patrols in six-wheel Saracens to provide local knowledge.

This night I was the patrol commander; we were travelling in two vehicles on the road between Castlecaulfield and Donaghmore sometime around midnight. The roads were very quiet at that time and we had adopted a policy of driving slowly and stopping cars when we saw the approaching headlights. As we approached Donaghmore Convent School entrance I noticed car lights approaching from the direction of Donaghmore. I was in the passenger seat of the lead vehicle and myself and another soldier got out of the vehicle in order to stop the oncoming vehicle. As my colleague started to use the red torch light to stop the vehicle it sharply turned down a driveway leading to a house on the right hand side of the road as we faced Donaghmore. I ran forward about 30 yards to the entrance to the house and as I looked down the driveway towards the house I saw the car stopping at the gable wall of the house. The doors burst open and at least three men jumped out holding weapons. I shouted 'Halt!' and as the gunmen began to run I opened fire and fired several shots. By this time my colleagues had come running up and we went down towards the car. One gunman was found hiding behind the house and a rifle lay beside him on the ground. Despite searching the area we were unable to find any of the other gunmen. I had seen one gunman running across fields towards the direction of a large house. We were later joined by the police and Regular Army personnel. They also searched the area that night and later detained one of the gunmen hiding in the bushes. A helicopter with a searchlight was also used to search the area.

David Symington was also in the lead vehicle; he recalls:

> I was not attached to any particular section but 'floated' between them, going out with whichever section was doing foot or mobile patrol that evening. Sections varied in their keenness and efficiency; the section I was with this night was one of the sharper ones, so it was capable of doing not only static VCPs but also 'snap' stops at night. These involved two vehicles on a mobile patrol cruising steadily between locations showing only side-lights. If the patrol leader in the passenger seat of the front vehicle spotted the headlights of a vehicle approaching, and judged it was safe, he would shout 'Snap!' and the Land Rover would brake to standstill. As the 'Stop' man I would leap out of the back, race around to the front and swing the Bardic lamp switched to red, covered by my Corporal who had dismounted from the passenger seat with his rifle.
>
> However, because I needed to move quickly, and the difficulty of examining a stopped driver's licence with a Bardic in one hand, I would leave my own rifle in the back of the Land Rover (we were not issued with slings).
>
> On this night we had stopped in Castlecaulfield, I think to mount a VCP, then mounted up and proceeded on sidelights towards Donaghmore. As we approached the village there was thick mist across the bogs to our right. On a slight downhill near the Convent, headlights were spotted approaching, 'Snap!' was called and I leaped out and ran forward, swinging the lamp. I was aware of my Corporal behind me.
>
> The approaching vehicle slowed, then suddenly swung to its left into the short driveway of a house. I thought it was just someone arriving home but we both trotted forward, my Corporal slightly in front. The car had stopped at the left side of the house and silhouetted against the headlights shining into the mist was the driver leaping out with a long weapon in his left hand. The Corporal shouted 'Halt', cocked his rifle and loosed off a shot. The driver dodged to his right, behind the house. I went right flanking (I don't know if I told the Corporal – I think I did) and ran across the front of the house to the corner. At this point I remembered that I had no weapon, so stopped outside the inner porch to the front door.
>
> There was the noise of the patrol dismounting and rushing to the far end of the house. Firing began. At some point the front door opened and a shocked householder, lying on the floor, gasped 'What's going on?' I told him to stay under cover and he crawled backwards and closed the door.

I thought I would be better off armed, so ran back to the lead Land Rover and retrieved my rifle, then joined the patrol lying to the left side of the car (which still had its head-lights on) and banging off shots into the dark. I asked 'Big Willie' (McKenzie) what he was shooting at and learned that two men had leaped out of the left side of the car and sped off down the slope and into the night. This was news to me, which makes the point that during incidents you never know what the Hell is going on.

I could discern little in the dark, except the dim outline of a farmhouse across the valley, so I cocked my weapon but did not fire. Big Willie, having expended his 30 rounds, asked me tersely for my spare magazine, but I think I declined.

An officer, Ken Maginnis, who had been in the rear Land Rover, seemed to take command and part of the patrol was sent down the slope in pursuit of the runners. A search behind the house found that the driver had fallen over on building rubble and bashed himself, so he was captured.

At some point the (Regular) Army arrived and we were stood down. A helicopter searched the fields with a huge searchlight. We were told to unload, but shock was setting in and I was incapable of remembering the procedure. Mr Maginnis took my rifle, detached the magazine, cocked the gun to eject the round, and handed the rifle back to me. I learnt that night that a well-trained patrol could be proactive and aggressive, taking the fight to the enemy, not just sitting around a static VCP waiting to be ambushed. That time we got the drop on them.

Billy McKenzie adds:

This was one occasion the patrol had the essence of surprise instead of the terrorist. The two guys in the front Land Rover and I made good use of that, following the car into a 50 metre drive. It was all part of the plan for a quick call on an approaching vehicle, and it paid dividends.

My firing was to keep heads down at the right hand side of the house. Two other guys ran on and the next thing I hear a squeaky voice look out of the hedge saying, 'Who's shooting?' I don't want to be critical as I had borrowed some of his ammunition. It was noisy and when the rather bloodied Vincent was taken to the roadway I was told to guard him as he lay with hands across the bonnet. Later a police car called to collect him (and take him to South Tyrone Hospital).

A summary of the rest of the incident report (with its inevitable inaccuracies) brings a conclusion:

The Regular Army deployed a Nightsun helicopter to try and pin down the escaped terrorists. They then deployed the equivalent of four platoons in a large

Lance Corporal Winston Wray and Buff

cordon during the night. At first light on 12th August a search was mounted within the cordon assisted by Lance Corporal Wray[10] of 8 UDR and his tracker dog (Buff).

At 0602hrs Eugene McDonald was found and he was persuaded to retrieve his rifle (M1 Garand no. 2402459 – both weapons were made in USA 1943-44) from the bottom of the Torrent River where he had dropped it during his escape.

---

10 Cpl Winston Wray 1943-: 8 UDR 1971-77: (Buff enlisted in 1971 No. 2A23).

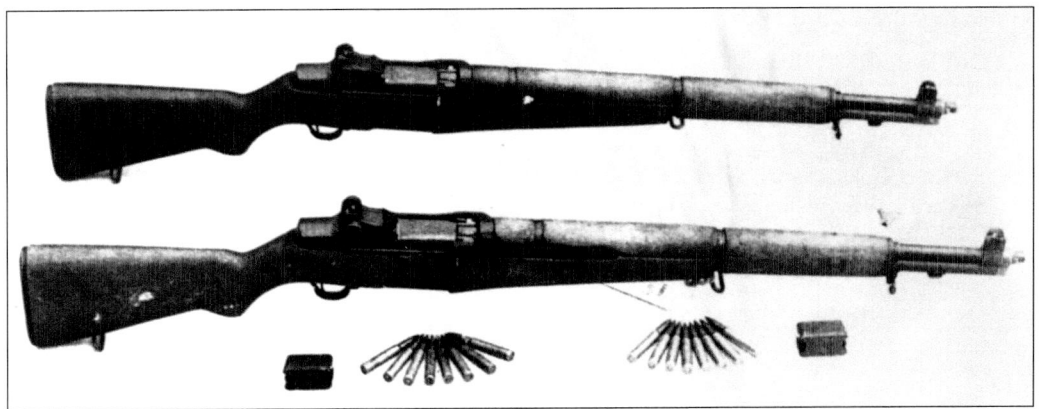

Captured M1 Garand Rifles

These three men were apparently on their way to take part in an attack on RUC Pomeroy. The capture of two of them and the flight of the third delayed and disrupted this attack which took place a few days later.

The patrol commander remembers the aftermath:

> I recall going to the Police Station in Dungannon after the incident to make a statement to the Detective Sergeant investigating. Whilst waiting to be interviewed an interview room door opened and one of the terrorists was in the room and able to see me. There was little protection given to me as I could have been easily identified. I also recall attending the High Court on the Crumlin Road in Belfast when the case against the terrorists was being heard. Myself and two other part-time UDR men were in Court as witnesses and after the terrorists were convicted we left the Court to travel home. Friends and family of the terrorists were in the car park and verbally and physically threatened us as we left. I recall them shouting and thumping the car, further evidence of how little protection was provided.

Ken Maginnis added:

> We were told that we would be giving evidence from behind a curtain. I said 'No, Vincent lives less than two miles from me and the IRA know exactly who I am'. We gave our evidence in open court and Vincent and McDonald were sentenced to six years' imprisonment.

At the time Ken Maginnis was serving in 8 UDR he was married with four children, the headmaster of a school, and running his turkey business producing 8000 birds in a good year. He averaged four hours sleep a night for much of this time.

A final word from him:

> I was lucky; in about 1986 I attended a Dungannon Council Meeting and would usually have gone home afterwards, about 11 pm. That night I decided to go to Fermanagh and visit RUC Stations and returned home at 4.30 am next day. It was only later that I was told that three men with rifles and a RPG had lain in wait for me from 10.30 pm to 2.30 am. Then the following year I came back home from Westminster midweek, again this was unusual. There was a parcel lying amongst the post, and for some reason I was suspicious of it; I knew who it was supposed to have come from but it was just too perfect. It was a bomb with several ounces of Semtex (*Soviet military explosive*). If I had not been home my wife, Joy, might have opened the parcel for me with the inevitable result.

<u>NOTE</u>: The Ulster Special Constabulary (USC) was a reserve special constable police force established in 1920. It consisted of A Specials who were full-time and paid; B Specials who operated in platoon size mobile groups mainly to release regular police when large numbers of them were required in one place – they were part-time and unpaid; and C Specials who were unpaid and non-uniformed reservists. The USC was disbanded in 1970 following the deployment of the B Specials in 1969 to deal with civil disorder for which they were neither prepared nor trained.

2

Defending the Police and Ourselves

Outnumbered and Outgunned

Guarding a RUC Station and 8 UDR's own bases was a necessary task but one that could easily become very tedious. Treating each one as an observation post and giving those guarding them clearly defined and worthwhile information gathering tasks was one solution.

The terrorists sniped at these places from long range on many occasions, rarely with any success. They planted devices at the gates and by the perimeters, again without any significant success. From time to time they did mount major attacks against bases but their difficulty was always breaking in and planting a device. The RUC stations received most attention with RUC Coalisland attacked 52 times, Pomeroy 18 and Stewartstown 11. The bases of 8 UDR, including the PVCP at Aughnacloy, were attacked 37 times.

The advent (1979) of the PIRA home-made Mark 10 mortar with a 20.5 kg bomb of Ammonium Nitrate and Nitrobenzene (ANNIE), and a multi-barrel and remote fire capability, made small and compact bases very vulnerable and several were totally destroyed. Later Marks of heavy mortar, up to Mark 15, further enhanced the terrorists' mortar capability. 8 UDR bases at Killymeal and Cookstown were both subjected to heavy mortar attacks.

Pomeroy 16th and 17th August 1973

The origins of the name Pomeroy can be traced back to the aristocratic families of the west counties of England who were of Norman descent. De la Pommerie and many other English servitors who later settled in this area of Ulster came from this region.

Situated in the high hills of County Tyrone along the spine of Ulster, the Sperrin Mountains, the village of Pomeroy is well known as the village with the highest elevation in Ulster. It was through this area that the main arterial routes linking the cities of Dublin, Armagh and Londonderry (Derry until 1613) passed and was of strategic importance to the Crown, having a garrison deployed in Cappagh (Altmore) just south of Pomeroy from 1602 to 1780s.

Under King James I in 1606, the Plantation of Ulster began when the first of more than 10,000 lowland Scots sailed into Ulster to form the basis of the new Ulster Scots community. They were mainly but by no means entirely Protestant and brought with them a culture and heritage still in evidence today.

Most came from southwest Scotland and the families who settled in Pomeroy with the names such as Adams, Somerville, Gilkeson, Symington, Whiteside, Moffatt, Irwin, Rainey, Johnston and Hamilton came from Lanarkshire. From Dumfriesshire and Kilmarnock came Dickson, Ellison, Bell and Boyd. It was from this influx of Scottish settlers the Lowry family arrived who had the most influence in forming the town of Pomeroy and subsequent work and trade in the area.

Sited on an area of moor, bog and mountain, a huge forested area covered most of the land as is evidenced by townland names such as Cappagh (land of tree stumps), Corkhill (round hill of Hazels), Gortavoy (field of Birch trees) and Goridarragh (little field of Oak). Some 50,000 Oak, 100,000 Ash and 10,000 Elm were harvested for building the City of Londonderry and other towns in Ulster. England and Scotland were the first countries in Europe to have their forests depleted and the woodlands of Ulster provided a much needed valuable resource, the Oak in particular for building ships. The deforestation allowed for farmland to be developed and tenant farmers brought to the land.

In 1750 King George II issued a charter granting the right to hold a weekly market and several yearly fairs in the town of Pomeroy and this was a pivotal development for trade supporting the farming community and the wider economy. The Reverend James Lowry was the first rector of the new parish.

Tenant farmers had a harsh life but were important to the financial prosperity of the area and neighbour helped neighbour at harvest time and in business generally. A close knit community from the Roman Catholic, Church of Ireland and other Protestant faiths, everyone worked together and their faith played a very important role in community and family life.

The Ulster Scots were expected to serve the Crown; it was and is a family tradition in Pomeroy. The men of Pomeroy, born of tenant farmers, volunteered to serve in the First and Second World Wars, during the civil war of the 1920s, the IRA campaign of the 1950s and the bloody conflict known today as 'The Troubles' starting in 1969.

The original police station, the Royal Irish Constabulary (RIC) Barracks, was probably built in 1824 when the Tyrone County Force was formed but it was first listed in 1840 (1st Constabulary Directory). It was on the high ground in the village to control the pass over the Sperrins and the village then grew up around it. In 1962 it was replaced with a new station built on the low ground to the east of the village and although on the road this station was dominated by the village. It was two storey and divided into two parts. At the eastern end, furthest from the village, was the Police House in which the Station Sergeant, his wife and two young children lived (they were on holiday in

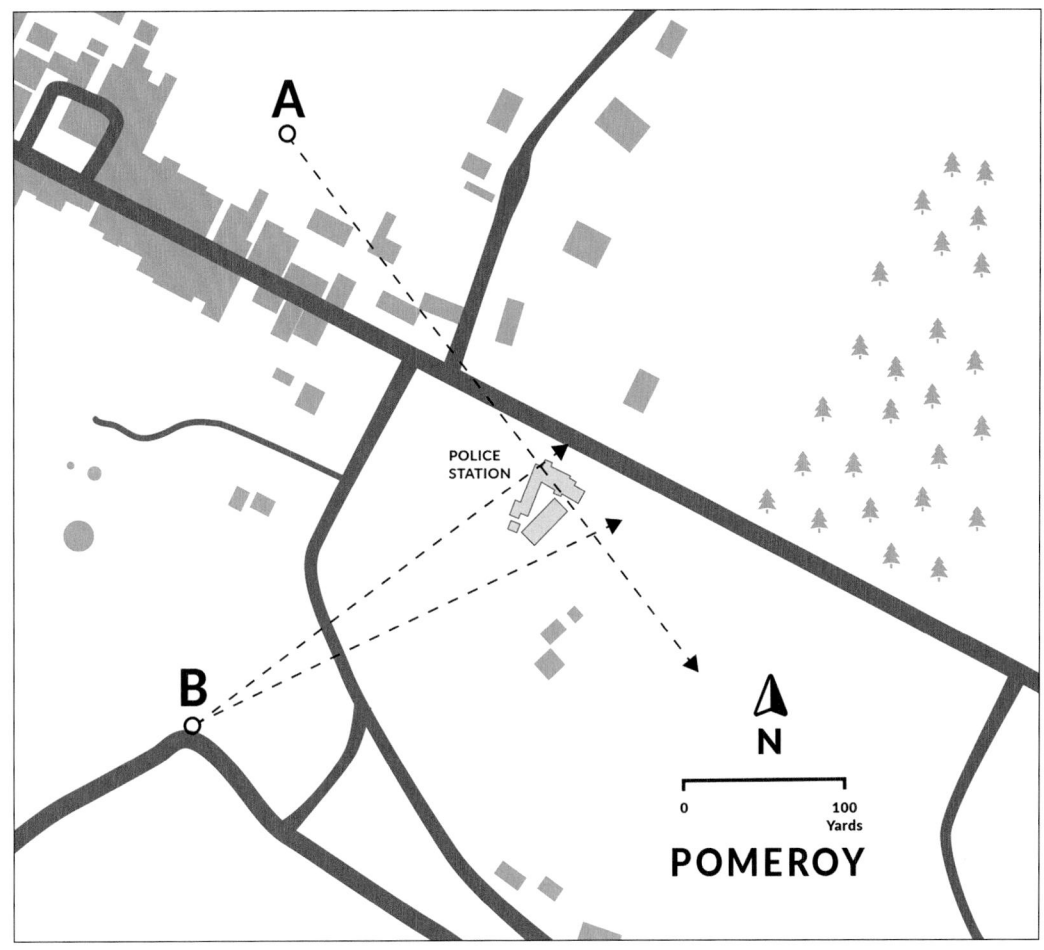

PIRA Attack on Pomeroy Police Station
A: RPG-7 Firing Point, B: Mortar Base Plate/Firing Point

the Isle of Man at the time of the attack in August 1973). The station had been built with little thought to defence but by 1973 this had been much improved. The police station consisted of the police office, interview room and cell, military guardroom and accommodation. Two constables manned the station with one on duty at any time: they had radio and telephone links.

At the front was a sangar (emplacement) at ground level to cover a man when he opened the main gate. On the roof was a large elevated sangar that could give all round observation and fire and was usually manned by two men. There was a further sangar on the roof for use as and when required. All the sangars were built of sandbags. Access to the elevated sangar was by ladder covered by corrugated iron so that men going to and from it had protection from view. The sangars were connected to the guardroom by intercom and the guardroom was connected to Battalion Headquarters 8 UDR by radio. Surrounding the station was a wire fence more than 12 feet high topped with barbed wire and with a gate at the front; it and the area outside the fence were lit at night.

The police station had been attacked many times before 1973. In the early years Civil Rights demonstrators attempted to storm the building. Small arms and bomb attacks were weekly events. An RPG-7 (*Soviet rocket propelled anti-tank grenade*) had been used on at least one previous occasion. In one attack the RPG-7 came through the corrugated sheeting around the ladder leading to the elevated sangar and took it out; no-one could then get up or down.

At 2230hrs on 16th August 1973, the police station at Pomeroy was attacked by simultaneous mortar, rocket and small arms fire. An RPG-7 round exploded in the sandbags protecting the sentry sangar on top of the building, blowing part of the corrugated iron roof off, and a hole through both the front and back walls. Four or five rounds of small arms fire hit the top row of sandbags in the second sangar. Corporal Irwin,[1] who was on duty at the time, was shaken but unhurt. A further six or seven rounds of small arms fire struck the wall and sandbags on the western side of the police station. Part of an exploding mortar bomb wedged itself in the grill of the kitchen window. There were no casualties. One hundred and twenty 7.62 mm rounds were returned by the guard. Flashes were seen from two firing points, one in the east and one in the west. The eastern one was probably mortar bombs exploding in the neighbouring field. At 2240hrs three red verey (signal) lights were fired and the attack ceased.

Vehicle Check Points (VCPs) were established by adjacent units. At 0300hrs the RUC at Omagh reported that a blue Ford Transit Van had been hijacked in Carrickmore. Two platoons of 1st Battalion Scots Guards were tasked to Pomeroy to start the follow-up. A Nightsun helicopter arrived from Omagh at about 0200hrs, and a search of the likely firing positions began.

Nothing was found that night and the search of the area was resumed at 0525hrs. At about 0600hrs the police in Dungannon received a report of two bodies lying at the side of a road. At 0625hrs the report was confirmed.

At 0620hrs the RPG-7 firing point was found. At 0642hrs the remains of a mortar bomb were found wedged in the grill of the kitchen window; there were no signs that it had exploded there. At 0721hrs impact craters from seven mortar bombs and a rocket motor were found in the field to the east of the police station. The motor was from the rocket that had hit the sangar. At about 0800hrs the mortar base plate position was found. Further investigation revealed tyre tracks belonging to a lorry and evidence of an explosion in the area, as there were glass and wood splinters lying about. A Colt .45 inch automatic pistol was also found at this point. Other searches in the Pomeroy area found three RPG-7 motors and tailfins on a hillside; these were from rockets that had missed the target and self-destructed beyond.

---

1 Cpl Norman William Thomas Irwin 1944-: 8 UDR 1970-92: (R Irish until 2001): Farmer.

The bodies found lying at the side of the road were identified as Patrick Joseph Quinn[2] and Dan McAnallen.[3] From their injuries it was apparent they had died as a result of an explosion. Shortly after they were found a report of a blood-stained vehicle was received. This proved to be a green Bedford truck which had been abandoned about a mile and a half north of the corpses. In the back was a mortar (2.5 inch home-made), the end of which had been split open by a bomb which had exploded prematurely. Also found in the truck were sixteen bombs, a Colt .45 inch automatic pistol and the remains of a transceiver. The roads between Pomeroy and the two locations were searched from the air and by vehicle for signs of unusual activity, but nothing else was found. Scenes of Crime Officer (SOCO) visited all locations. He removed the pistol from Pomeroy, and the pistol, transceiver and a quantity of ammunition and empty cases from the lorry. Ammunition Technical Officer (ATO) visited Pomeroy and ascertained there were no blinds (*unexploded bombs*). He removed the mortar and the bombs from the lorry and took them with him.

The rounds and empty cases found at Pomeroy were collected and given to RUC Cookstown (*a minimum of six rifles were fired by the terrorists that night*). The bodies were removed to the South Tyrone Hospital at Dungannon. By 1300hrs troops were clear of the locations. RUC Pomeroy continued the follow up with door to door visits in the area of the attack. A member of the UDR who lived near Pomeroy reported hearing a heavy truck drive past shortly after the attack. Someone in the vehicle was screaming loudly.

The Bedford had been hijacked by four armed men from the driver at 2130hrs on the 16th August. Three of the men were masked, but Patrick Quinn was not. The driver was told he would be shot if he reported it. The blue Ford Transit van was stolen in Carrickmore at about 2030hrs on the 16th August. Two men asked the owner where he kept it. They went to McGaughey's Garage, got the van out and put him in the back. They drove off and dropped him a short time later, saying that he would be shot if he reported it. At 0150hrs on 18th August, police from Cookstown found the van in the Kildress area. It is possible that it had only just been left there. The van was recovered at 0600hrs and taken to RUC Cookstown.

---

2   Patrick Joseph Quinn 1957-73: Dungannon: Unemployed: Volunteer PIRA: Killed 16th August 1973. (*Tyrone Courier* 22nd August 1973): Early in 1973 captured transporting an M1 Carbine, escaped from St Patrick's Training School, Juvenile Justice Institution: (Gerard Magee, *Tyrone's Struggle*).

3   Dan McAnallen 1946-73: Eglish: Plumber: Adjutant 1 East Tyrone Battalion PIRA: Killed 16th August 1973 (*Tyrone Courier* 22nd August 1973): According to Sean O'Callaghan in his book (*The Informer*) Kevin McKenna 1945-2019 was the unit's leader in the attack on RUC Pomeroy and later PIRA's OC Northern Command: McAnallen was his best friend: McKenna was OC PIRA's Tyrone Brigade 1972+ and COS PIRA 1983-1997 (Ed Moloney, *Secret History of the IRA* and *The Broken Elbow*, 26th June 2019).

Several days after the attack reports were received of a mine on the Pomeroy to Carrickmore road. It had been placed to cover the escape of the terrorists after their attack on the RUC Station and, since no Security Forces had ventured out to the west of the village, had served its purpose. Following two Beaver (light aircraft) photo reconnaissance missions, the device was located and the clearance was carried out on 25th and 26th August. The mine was buried in a bank that overlooked the road. It consisted of 400 lbs Home Made Explosive (HME), Ammonium Nitrate and Fuel Oil, with a Coop (*Sodium Chlorate and Sugar or Nitrobenzene*) booster. About 2 cwt (224 lbs) of farmyard scrap iron was placed in the front of the charge. At least two further terrorists must have been involved in this part of the attack making the total more than 14 (some reports say double this number).

As this report indicates, it was a well-planned and well-coordinated attack by PIRA on the police station in which a significant number of terrorists took part.

Eric Sinnamon's[4] section of 8 UDR was on duty at Pomeroy RUC Station on the night of 16th August. He recalls:

> It was my section, but, because they were short in Dungannon, I drove out and lifted Robert Johnston[5] that night and we went to Dungannon (so four instead of six men were on duty at RUC Pomeroy). We were coming up the bottom of Church Street in Dungannon and there was a bomb went off outside the wee pub (O'Neill's) that used to be opposite the church. And then we got up that length, and someone said where they went so we chased after them. That was one of the things that they had done – to maybe draw us. We went searching up round the Square and they were building Wellworth's at the time, I remember, and it just damaged round the door and there was someone slightly injured, and then we got word in that Pomeroy was hit and then of course we all wanted to go to Pomeroy and they wouldn't let us; we had to stay at Killymeal for a while till everything was cleared.

The record for this part of the incident states:

> At 10.35 pm on 16th August, ten minutes before the attack on RUC Pomeroy, and possibly timed to tie down the Security Forces in Dungannon, a bomb estimated between 15 and 20 lbs, exploded outside O'Neill's public house in Church Street. Four civilians were injured and taken to the South Tyrone Hospital.

---

4 Pte Eric Andrew Sinnamon 1955-: 8 UDR 1973-81: Teacher.
5 Pte Robert John Richard Johnston 1953-1982: 8 UDR 1970-72: Ambulance Driver.

Norman Irwin was in charge of the four man guard on RUC Pomeroy that night. He remembers:

> My father died when I was only eight years of age. My mother came down here to the old farmstead to live with three old sisters of the Johnstons. My mother came from Aghafad (between Omagh and Strabane) and she was sent down here to look after these three old ladies, so eventually, whenever they all passed on, she inherited this place here. There were four of us, two girls and two boys. Fifteen acres of ground we had, but sure we all survived. I farmed and worked too. I worked out, bits and pieces, here and there.
>
> I was in the B Specials of the Ulster Special Constabulary you see. I was maybe seven years in the B Specials before, and then they were disbanded and we all automatically signed up (for the UDR). I must have been about 24 then. It was a worry for my mum but it's like everything else. It was a fact of life, at that stage. Everybody did their bit.
>
> Pomeroy guard duties started in '72. There were two Constables and a Sergeant in the station. We worked three 12 hour shifts. Straight 12 hour shifts. We did straight 12 hour shifts for years. We hauled a lorry load of sandbags up and built the sangars. We done that all ourselves, we done all our own engineering.

Pomeroy Police Station Front View

> At the start, we got Compo (tinned) rations up from Dungannon, supplied every week but then as things progressed we were there that long, we started to

get fresh food. They brought us up fresh food. Whoever got to it first, ate well! There were bunk beds but I slept in the cell for years.

We were attacked several times before the big one. We had been hit with the RPG-7, I think, three times before. There was always some boy would have took a pot shot at you at the barracks (RUC Station). On that wall on the Pomeroy side, you could see the pepper marks on it. They would take a whack at you and clear off. They were coming from the top of Pomeroy, coming down the back gardens. Sure they came off North Street. All they had to do was go in off North Street. There was a lane, the back lane up North Street, and they were looking straight down on you.

It was on 16th August at 10.45 pm that the attack took place, and I was in the top sangar at that time (with Jack Johnston[6] and George Boyd[7] on the roof, and Mervyn Boyd[8] in the guardroom), and the first RPG-7, the first rocket, was fired (four were fired that night). I had heard them several times before because we got hit several times with the RPG. The first round went over the top of the sangar. I heard it goin' over. I heard the 'Whuss' goin' over the top of the sangar, but by the time I had alerted these boys down at the bottom the next round came straight through her. It came straight through her! I had the SLR picked up in my hand and it took the flash lighters off the SLR. So that's how close I was till it that night. So then, they started mortaring. I could see the mortars landin' out in Rectory field – comin' in, comin' in, and comin' in. They come down Station Road, they were firing off the lorry, and the other boys they were up the town. They were in a position up the town and they were firing down the town – two different angles, and then there was different positions of gunfire the men opened up.

They had a position in the plantin' – Micky Bann's Nissen hut – over in that area. And what we didn't know, but we know now, they must have had a two-way radio system in where Wilson Boyd[9] lived, down in the wee meadow you know, near where Geoffrey lives now. There were boys directin' it from there.

The range was … you know the old railway bridge at Pomeroy, there was a gap there, just as if it was facing up to Reid's house there, well they were firing over bushes that night. It would be a good 300 metres. I could see them

---

6 Pte John (Jack) Johnston 1912-1999: 8 UDR 1970-77: Farmer: His son Private Noel James (Jimmy) Johnston 1956-1984 was a porter working in the unit for the elderly at the South Tyrone Hospital in Dungannon; He was shot and killed there on his first day back to work after 8 UDR's summer camp.
7 LCpl George Raymond Boyd 1952-: 8 UDR 1970-77: Farmer.
8 Pte Thomas Mervyn Boyd 1935-2018: 8 UDR 1970-92: (R Irish until 1993): Tractor driver for Dungannon Council.
9 Cpl (Wilson) James Boyd 1938-: 8 UDR 1970-80: GOC's Commendation: Building Contractor.

Pomeroy Police Station from RPG-7 Firing Point

dropping off in the field. Eventually they were landin' in the back yard but that's when the mortar blew up.

There was three firing points, three locations. Their main firing point was up behind Fred Irwin's house there, up on the high ground. They were looking straight over. They were firing down from that big tree, and then there was Fred's hill – they were up on the high ground there. They were out at Donnelly's house. There was an old shed there that belonged to Donnelly's, the butchers. Whenever the thing went wrong, that's where the red flares went up from. Two red flares went up to call off the show and get the hell out. And I was at one time trying to fire flares, but the bloody oul' walls were too wide and the flares couldn't get over it.

The whole thing would have been over in twenty minutes. That night, I knew if I was going to be hit a second time, I'd had it. I knew that.

Dr Sharpe came to the police station that night to see if everybody was all right. He was the only one. I had sand in my eyes, I had sand in my mouth. I was … You don't know it at the time, but my back was injured. I was blew up against the back wall and my back was badly wrecked. From that one, it was never the same. Still have trouble today.

I served 21 years; I didn't do the 22 years exactly, because I was medically discharged. After Pomeroy I went to Cookstown for a while and later in the MT (Motor Transport) there. We done eight years up there.

George Boyd recalled:

My family is from Pomeroy – five or six generations. And believe it or not, where I am now, in the home place, there was five or six of the top stonemasons in Ireland born in our yard/house. In fact they built chapels in Meath, Louth and Cavan, all over and up here even. They were two of the top stonemasons in Ireland. I'm talking, back in 1850, they built Donaghmore chapel, Killeen chapel, out there 150 years ago. Over 160, coming 170 years.

I went to see the chapel in Donaghmore – it's only in the past 10 or 15 years I heard about it, the work they had done, the only two Protestant stonemasons, there were very few men. They built chapels; they couldn't get anybody else to do them. No mechanical tools. Just skill. Apparently they built a few along the border area – Cavan, Monaghan. Donaghmore chapel alone took seven years to build. You can see, in our yard, the wee house where they were born. They used to ride out on bicycles, there, and they stayed the whole week, that time. The workers all camped out along the side of the road in tents. They stayed there and worked there the whole week. They would have been great-great-uncles, probably. My grandfather's father and his brother.

I joined the B Specials at 18. The most of us were joining. My father was in the Specials. It was in the blood more or less. It was the done thing. I joined (8 UDR) in April 1970. I didn't start in Pomeroy for a wheen of years. I was part-time in Dungannon doing mobiles. Pomeroy guard duties started in '72. Well the full-time there was three shifts. 12 (hours) on 24 off, because there were three sections – six in a section. I kept my uniform and gun at home, drove along with a coat over the gun. You feared no man! Norman's father (Private Jack Johnston) there … the uniform on him, whistlin' away there, unconcerned. Like a thrush, you know. Back then it was no bother at all. I remember that well. We were paid £2.97 (a day); I always remember that. I was 22 or 23 years of age and lived with my parents. My mother would have been a wee bit worried, but it wasn't serious at that stage. You were young and care free. You were a young fella! Sleep – the next night – if you weren't up around Fivemiletown after a girl or something.

In all fairness, they weren't as ruthless … They can say what they like about East Tyrone, but they weren't as bad as the Fermanagh boys. They'd shoot you in the back of the head. East Tyrone hadn't the hardliners at that stage. They hadn't started the genocide thing. They could have wrote us all off; I remember in the early years, when I and my father would have been doin' the milking, out in the yard, at six o'clock in the mornin' and the same at night, in the dark …

> I remember the early days, going on duty, you wore your beret and all, and your SLR lying beside you on the seat. You were in uniform … or you worked and then you carried a wee coat, but sure you could see it underneath. They had no call to get us in there (police station); they could get us goin' in or out. They knew every man.
>
> We built a wall all round the building. There was no security at all, back then. I don't know whether we complained, or who complained, or whether they decided in Dungannon we needed more security, but they used to send us up rolls of that Army wire, you know. We put that wire up ourselves (*the high fence was put up later but before the August 1973 attack*).

Describing the incident, George Boyd goes on:

> We were on the roof; Jack and I were on the roof. He's deceased now. Only that tube (mortar) exploded, we wouldn't be here today. I says 'Jack, shoot away like hell and let them know we're here!' There was spoutins and slates all come down that night. Killymeal that night might as well have been a hundred miles away. We were on our own, like. They were well organised that night. It's just that the machinery did not work for them. If they got another ten to fifteen minutes on us that night we would not be here to tell the story.
>
> The mortar and bombs were all made up round Cappagh. They were all steel piping. They were well made – factory manufacturing. And then explosives were put inside the copper nose. They were drilled in the bottom and there was a .22 cartridge – that went down onto a firing point and that detonated the mortar. They would have a range of up to 300 metres anyway. Only that tube exploded, we wouldn't be here today.

PIRA Mortar and Bombs

I came off duty at 8 o'clock next morning and went home. My father had finished the milking. I suppose I was a bit late that morning, but I went home and changed my clothes and went on out and let him go in, and then I came in for breakfast. My mother had the breakfast ready… the news at nine. And she says: 'What were you at last night? That was an awful night they had in Pomeroy last night.'

I served until 1978, I think. I didn't stay that long, for we were kind of building up at home, work-wise. I was a Lance Corporal and I remember getting a letter to say I was promoted to Corporal; I think it was shortly after that that I quit.

8 UDR Base Cookstown 14th November 1988

On 14th November 1988 four armed men using sledgehammers to break down the door of a man's house, took the keys for his employer's van. He was driven to the home of his brother in law (who was already a prisoner of another three armed men) and took his car. Three mortar bombs were later fired from the van at the Cookstown UDR base. Two exploded causing extensive damage to offices. The third landed on the roof of the drill hall. (They were PIRA Mk 10 Mortars with a calibre of 165 mm and an explosive bomb weight of 20.5 kgs ANNIE). There were two casualties. The getaway car was found in Pomeroy.

PIRA's Mark 10 Mortar (employed in attack on RUC Newtonhamilton 1990)
© Cornwall's Regimental Museum

The Cookstown base had originally been Derryloran Primary School. It was on Main Street with houses on the other three sides; some were occupied by people who were unsympathetic if not hostile. When it became an 8 UDR base in 1971 this was both a security strength and a weakness. In 1988 the base consisted of the main school building including the assembly hall and original classrooms, and overflow offices in Portacabins attached to the main building, as well as some free-standing ones at the rear.

There had been two previous heavy mortar (PIRA Mark 10) attacks on the base in 1988. In May there had been a four tube mortar attack very similar to the one in November and then later there had been a single tube mortar attack. As a result the base had been strengthened with some overhead protection and a number of blast walls to confine any explosion. An elevated super sangar had been built which was now in addition to the front sangar, which controlled access, and another at the back. CCTV had been added which monitored the likely mortar base-plate positions. In addition, patrols were mounted at key times to specifically check likely base-plates, and all ranks were trained and practised in the actions to be taken when attacked.

The base was occupied by C Company, one platoon of B Company who provided the guard on the base and carried out operations from it and, from time to time, platoons and companies of the Regular Army.

Tom McKinney[10] recalls:

> I was a part-time officer in C Company in Cookstown and on duty that Monday morning 14th November 1988 at 0935hrs when the base was mortared. I was leaving the Company offices when the first explosion went off. I was hit by shrapnel and fell. When I got up there was another explosion which blew me down the corridor.
>
> I immediately got up and made my way to the sangar on Cemetery Road which is where I thought the base plate was. When I got to the sangar and spoke to the sentries, they had no information but the field telephone rang. Corporal Gates,[11] B Company Guard Commander, informed me and all his sangars that the base plate was at Conway's, as before. I left the sangar and made my way back to the main building for I thought that WO2 Gallagher[12] and Mrs McKenzie[13] were still in the offices.
>
> I then went to the Guard Room to arrange for evacuation of the base and check for blinds.

---

10 Capt Thomas (Tom) McKinney MBE 1940-: (Inniskillings/R Irish Rangers 1958-82 to WO1 (RSM 1 R Irish Rangers then 6 UDR)): 8 UDR 1983-92: (R Irish until 1997): GOC's Commendation (for his actions on 14th November 1988).
11 LCpl Hugh (Hughie) Gates 1951-: 8 UDR 1971-92: (R Irish until 1997): GOC's Commendation.
12 WO2 William George (Geordie) Gallagher 1938-: 8 UDR 1974-91: MID.
13 Mrs Sarah (Sadie) Ann McKenzie BEM: 1925-2016: Civilian Company Clerk 1975-89.

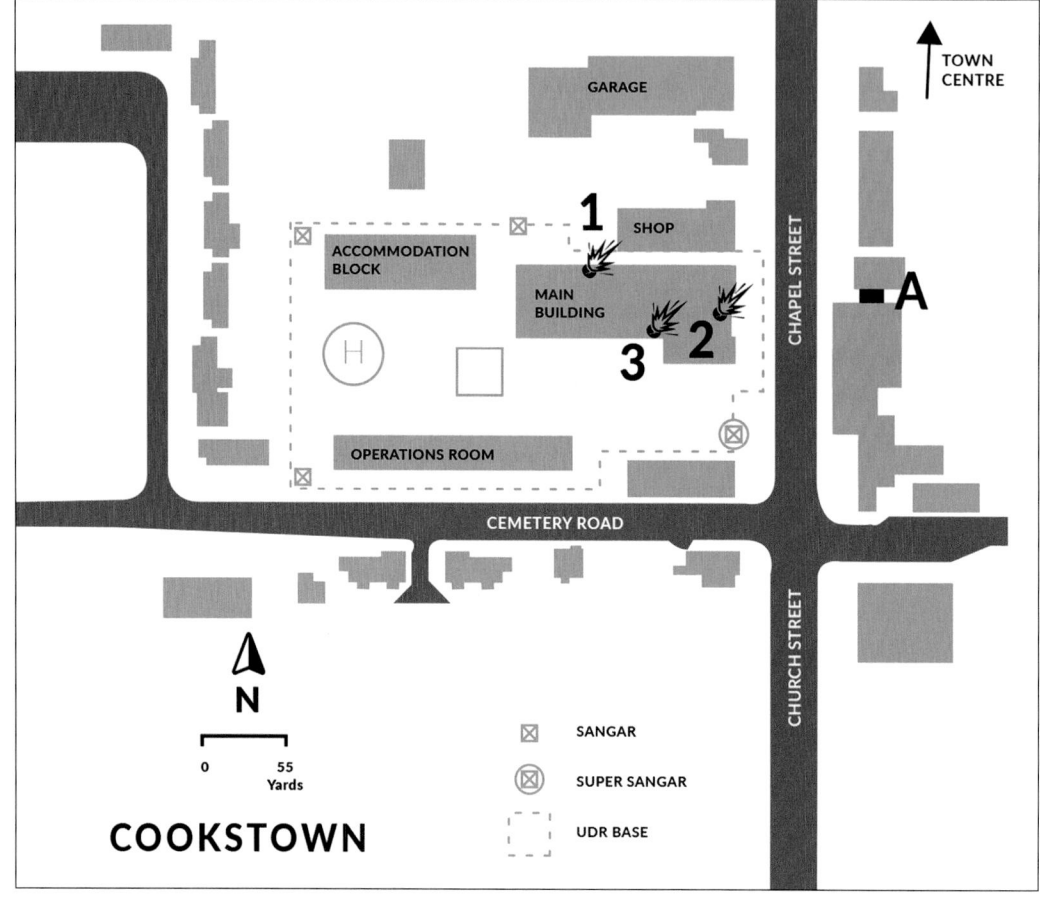

PIRA Attack on 8 UDR Cookstown Base
A: Mortar Firing Point/Base Plate, 1: 1st Round, 2: 2nd Round, 3: 3rd Round

I discovered that Corporal Gates had already carried out a quick recce of the roof of the armoury where he had heard something falling and thought there was a blind; he was engaged in organising the guard ready for evacuation and I made my way to the Ops Room.

Corporal Hugh Gates continues:

After the first attack, there was a lot more security put in. There was a new bomb bay built and a Super Sangar. They had cameras installed by that time, after the first attack. There were four cameras going at once so you could watch and zoom in which was a great help for the security of the camp. There was high fence wire round the front and the armoury was upgraded with a reinforced roof. That saved the Guardroom because there was one mortar went off very close and the dust came down into the Guardroom.

With the bank of cameras in the guardroom we were high up, looking down, which was an advantage. In the archway there across from the camp, the Conway family had started a TV business so their vans were coming in and out regularly. They had nothing to do with the attack. They were stopped up the road and the devices were put into one of their white TV vans. It was sitting in the archway, but it was there too long, so we were suspicious and we had the camera zoomed in on it. I think we had telephoned Dungannon at that stage for we were aware that there was something unusual going on.

On the day of the incident, I reported for duty at 7am and the attack took place just around 9.30am. There were eight men on the guard team. Big Chris McKnight[14] was on and young Maurice Murphy[15] and a wee boy Stewart.[16] He was away in the back sangar on his own. There was one man in the high front sangar. I was in the Guardroom, manning the cameras. Then I ran down the corridor, for I knew that three mortars had been launched but only two had exploded. We ran and got to the office door when the other one went off and it just blew me straight up the corridor again.

They all done well, especially McKnight. They took the whole thing in their stride. It was an experienced team and they all knew what to do and everyone did their own job without being told. Many of them had been there when there was an evening mortar attack previously, and they had been through the drills 'live'.

The Regulars were in the base. They'd only been there a week or so when the attack happened. There was an English officer who was lining up his men in front of the armoury in the corridor, and I told him not to line them up there because there was still one mortar that hadn't gone off and it was too dangerous. We were trained to count if there was an attack, to count how many were let off.

When the mortars were launched you could see the van shaking. It was top class work by the Provos. When they welded it in, the angle of that tube had to be accurate, so fair play to the IRA. They were coming from the width of the street away plus the distance across the fencing. The man in the top sangar would have seen the mortars coming in and there was a siren that he pressed to warn people. He had just a few seconds to do that. The whole thing took no more than five or six minutes from start to finish. The van had been hijacked, but it hadn't been reported as stolen, to my knowledge. If it had, then we'd have been prepared right away. We just had to react when it happened.

One of them landed on the mobiles out the back. Mrs McKenzie's office got a direct hit; she was the Company Clerk. There would have been twenty or thirty people in the base at the time and it was a complete miracle that nobody

---

14 Pte Christopher (Chris) Thomas McKnight 1959-: 8 UDR 1979-92.
15 Pte Maurice Elliot (Murph) Murphy 1960-: 8 UDR 1980-92: (R Irish until 1994).
16 Pte John (Jackie) Stewart 1933-2007: 8 UDR 1970-88.

was killed. In the Guardroom at that particular time there was no more than four of us and the others were posted round the sangars. There were two back sangars and the front sangar, so there would have been two men in the back sangars, two in the front sangar and four in the guardroom. The Regulars were down the corridor in the area opposite Mrs McKenzie's office. They used that area for their sleeping quarters. They weren't on duty with us on that day and I'm not sure what their duties were. We didn't ask.

The alarm was set off and that went straight to inform the Ops Room in Dungannon. After that, you do a head count, you ring the sangars to see that the men are all right and to give them a bit of confidence and tell them to stay there and the gate was locked to seal the area. That was routine. When we saw that there was nobody hurt we didn't call an ambulance. Anybody that needed to be checked over, such as Mrs Davison, was taken out in a minibus to the Health Centre before the gates were locked.

Then Tom McKinney came up and checked round the Guardroom and I think he checked the sangars at the back as well. I had sent Chris McKnight and young Murphy out round the back to look for anything that was maybe unexploded, to check round the base. I think Jackie Stewart was left in the guardroom and I went out with them to do the check. We then wrote down all the car registration numbers and then set up a VCP about 100 yards away, up at Harry Eastwood's. The police were there by then and ATO. We just stayed out there at the VCP cordon. So I don't know what they did inside the base after that.

The one that didn't go off was found in the area near where the regular soldiers were based.

Our training made us able to react to the situation. The mortars were welded into the back of the van at the just right angle to get them to drop accurately. There's the Ratheen estate just behind the base, right along the back fence and a shop and business beside the base. If they had gone 100 yards more, they'd have been into houses where several terrorist suspects and their sympathisers lived.

I joined the UDR on the 5th November 1971 aged 20 and served part-time in what was then G Company in Cookstown. I was working in the bacon factory during the day. On my first patrol in 1971, we were moving off from a VCP when the Land Rover came under attack from gunfire and was hit several times. A few months later, we were in the same area and came under gunfire attack from behind. The windscreen was shot out of the Land Rover. Some months after that, while we were on Land Rover patrol outside Coagh village, we topped the hill at Duff's crossroads and drove into a landmine. It blew a tree into the sky and clay came down on us. Another night, we were driving away from our VCP outside Stewartstown when our covert red van came under attack from gunfire. The van was hit and there were nine bullet holes between the next soldier's head and mine.

Then the bad times came in 1975 and the IRA were murdering soldiers and it was one funeral after another. Tommy Benson[17] came into the base one day; he had a green Morris Marina, and he had the window down and he had a cigarette with a big long end on it. I just happened to be on guard that day and Tommy came in (at that time everybody looked under the cars) and came down the yard and slid in round by the new bomb bay and I said: 'Tommy, get out of that effin' car and don't close the door!' At this stage, I was behind the MT wall! Anyway he got out and he was lucky that time. He hadn't seen it, an under-car device. They put a bomb in the fireplace in their wee cottage on the Dungannon road. Tommy was away to Bisley, shooting, and his sister went to light the fire and the whole thing went off. She took two weeks to die.

I went full-time to C Company in Cookstown and I was guard commander from 1988-1989. In 1990 I went to B Company in Dungannon and in 1993, I transferred from the UDR to the Royal Irish Regiment. I finished my time as a storeman in Armagh after 27 years' service and was given a medical discharge in 1997 because of post-traumatic stress.

George Gallagher was the full-time Administrative Warrant Officer of C Company and responsible for the base. The Sergeants' Mess was the backbone of the Battalion containing, as it did, many of those with long service and wide experience. They provided a steadying hand, especially in the toughest times. George Gallagher was one such man and tells his personal story before recalling the incident that morning:

I actually joined up when I was about 16 and I joined as a boy soldier. I was living in Coalisland and working in Derryvale factory at the despatch and I decided I wanted to join the Navy. I went and got the forms, went up to Belfast. I did all my exams and had a medical and whenever the doctor was finishing off, he said to me 'By the way, have you ever had any broken bones?' and I said 'Yes, I had a fractured femur whenever I was ten. I was carrying on with a couple of boys and one of them fell over my leg and snapped my femur'. Unfortunately it was decided that I had a pulled muscle and they lifted me up and made me walk and I threw myself to the ground and said, 'I can't do this'. So they sat me up on a bicycle to wheel me to the doctor!

Anyway the medical officer got me up on the table and measured my legs. Then he said: 'I'm sorry. You're not going to be able to join the Navy, because your left leg is an inch shorter than your right leg. I can't pass you'. I was down in the dumps and he said: 'By the way, it won't hold you back from joining the

---

17 WO2 Thomas (Tommy) Reginald Benson BEM 1933-2000: 8 UDR 1970-92.

Army or the Air Force'. So I walked out of that place on Donegall Street and went straight up to Clifton Street. I walked in and said: 'I want to join the Army'. The recruiting officer asked me which regiment I wanted to join. I had no idea but behind him there was a big photograph of the three Irish regiments, the Ulster Rifles, the Inniskillings and the Irish Fusiliers. So I said: 'I'm going to join them, in the middle' and that was the Royal Inniskilling Fusiliers. That was in 1954.

I served with the Inniskillings in Berlin, East Africa, Germany and England. I was also posted across here with the TA, the 5th Battalion Inniskillings. I was in charge of all the transport in Dungannon, Enniskillen, Magherafelt, Omagh and Limavady. When I finished with the Inniskillings, I joined the Ever Readies and had to do three years' reserve. If you were an Ever Ready at that time, if something broke out and news came on the radio, you had 24 hours to get to a particular destination. You had to do a fortnight's training every year to keep you up to date and you got more money. While I was doing that, I decided I might as well join the TA and by this time, the TA was known as the North Irish Militia. I was based in Omagh and travelled from home in Coalisland. The Troubles started around this time, the UDR had been formed and three of us were talking one night. It finished with the three of us transferring to 8 UDR in 1974.

When we arrived, full-time had just started and 8 UDR had the Ops Platoon, who were the first full-timers on the road. There was about ten of us and we were based in Killymeal. The powers that be realised that I had military experience and they started to send me on courses. I came in as a Lance Corporal and got rapid promotion. I went to J Company as PSI and stayed there for a while and then I was transferred to Aughnacloy. Ken Maginnis was the Company Commander.

I really enjoyed Aughnacloy. To see people who were really under pressure was a wake-up call for me. Every one of them in that Company, where they lived along the border and everything about them, you had to think of every one of them. But there was a great camaraderie about them all and the one man who held that place together was 'Dinger' Bell.[18] He knew every nook and cranny, where everybody lived, everything about them and he was invaluable. He had a great relationship with the police.

There was one big fella up there; he was a Corporal, but I can't remember his name. He had a farm (a lot of them were farmers) and he'd come to me and say: 'Where's your car?' and when I'd come home I'd find potatoes, vegetables, all sorts had been left. But it was a dangerous place to be if there wasn't much

---

18 WO2 Robert (Dinger) Bell 1946-98: 8 UDR 1970-92: (R Irish until 1998): GOC's Commendation (Twice).

happening and they opened up the bar. D'you see, trying to get home after that was a problem!

After Aughnacloy I came back to D Company and then Headquarter Company at Killymeal. From there, I was transferred to the Ops Room as Ops Warrant Officer. And I did seven years there, until Tim (Armstrong)[19] was shot in 1988. At that stage, I went to Cookstown. Albert Cooper[20] was the Company Sergeant Major, and Ronnie Nesbitt[21] was the Company Commander.

Cookstown was good. I enjoyed it. Good lads, and we had a couple of disasters there as well, the main one being Albert himself. Albert and I were very friendly and we and our wives used to go out together. We were out one night and I got a phone call to say there had been a shooting somewhere, and someone in the IRA had been shot. It was somebody that we all knew. As we were leaving, Albert said to me 'I wonder which one of us will go in retaliation'.

We were sitting in the mess and the word came through that there had been an explosion in Cookstown, in the Market Yard. I remember I said: 'Albert Cooper. Albert Cooper' and that hit me really hard. That was probably one of the hardest things that I had experienced. There was one that was worse, which was John Stewart.[22] I played bowls in Brackaville in Coalisland, in the Legion Club and John Stewart joined it after he left school. One night John came to me and said that he was going to join the UDR. I said: 'John, listen to me. You're living in the wrong place to be joining the UDR. Please, unless you're going to move house, don't join. Have you talked to your dad about this?' He said no. I told him to talk to his dad and to think about it. He came to me about a month later and asked me to act as referee for him. I asked if he had spoken to his father and he said he had. 'My father said the same as you', he said, 'but if you won't be my referee, I'll get another one. I'm going to join'. So John joined the UDR part-time and was in Killymeal and was a great fella.

He did gardens; he was a handyman. We were living in Belvedere Park and I wanted to have a place out the back where we could have a barbecue. I asked John to build me a patio area and to build a brick barbecue. He came round and discussed it and said his father was going to give him a hand. They arrived in his big minibus that he had all his stuff in, with his dog called Ruff, and they began to build. On the Friday night they hadn't it finished.

---

19 +Capt Timothy David Armstrong 1958-1988: 8 UDR 1986-88: Killed 16th January 1988.
20 +WO2 Albert David Cooper 1948-90: 8 UDR 1970-90: MID (posthumous): GOC's Commendation: Businessman: Killed 2nd November 1990.
21 Maj Ronald (Ronnie) Irwin Nesbitt UD 1947-: (10 UDR 1971-85): 8 UDR 1985-92: (R Irish until 1996): MID: Businessman/Driving Instructor.
22 +Pte William (John) Richard Stewart 1964-88: 8 UDR 1983-88: Landscape gardener: Killed 16th January 1988.

John went home that night, got changed and got something to eat and that was it (*John went on duty that night and was killed leaving his home*). That hit me hard. John's father came back to finish the job sometime later and I took a week off work to help him. He was driving John's minibus and when he opened the back door, Ruff came out like a shot, and down round the back, looking for John.

After the first mortar attack, the Regular soldiers' accommodation was mortar-proofed, with reinforced walls and the camera system was upgraded. The sangars at the front were reinforced by Henry Brothers. They were working in the base for ages. The cameras were all pointing out to the front of the base; there was no access from the sides. At the front entrance, there was a sort of air lock area for vehicles coming into the camp. There was a sangar looking out over a housing estate at the back of the base, but the view of the camp from the outside was restricted by a high wall.

Those reinforced walls started behind the Portacabins where our offices were. There was a space, a kind of a narrow alleyway, between the Regular Army accommodation and the back of our offices.

The morning of the mortar attack, I called in at Killymeal to pick up the mail and arrived in Cookstown around 9 o'clock. I went into the base and had a chat with the boys on guard, went round to my office, spoke to Sadie McKenzie, who was a clerk in the other office and walked round behind my desk and set some things down. I read some of them and eventually Tom McKinney arrived, came up and stood in the doorway directly in front of me. I was standing with my back to the window. Tom started to talk about something and all of a sudden we just heard 'Woof! Woof! Woof!' The two of us said together: 'Mortars!' and straight away 'Bang!' The window was right behind me and the whole lot blew in and a piece of concrete hit me on the ear on the way past. Tom McKinney was in the doorway and it hit Tom on the chest and knocked him off his feet. He fell on the ground. You couldn't have seen a thing with the stour. Tom gathered himself up and away.

My immediate concern was Sadie, next door. I shouted: 'Sadie! Are you OK?' No answer. I couldn't see but I went in and found her desk and there was just a pile of rubble on top of it. The dread I had looking behind that desk and climbing over and looking down behind it! And from underneath this desk a head appeared. I never was as glad to see anybody in my life. She looked up at me but her ears had gone. I says: 'Sadie, we've got to get you out of here'. She couldn't get out from where she was and I pulled things across from the front of the desk and got her out. We went down to the corridor. It was wrecked. I took Sadie into the Sergeants' Mess. As we went into the Mess, the second mortar went off and it went off with some authority, I can tell you. But I had heard three noises so I knew there was another one.

At this stage I started to wonder where everyone was. I knew that there was a room at the very end of the corridor where they used to peel potatoes to make dinner, and there was a girl in there on her own, Mavis Patterson.[23] And whenever the whole thing went off, she looked out, saw the corridor wrecked and she thought everybody was dead and she was in hysterics. So I got her out and Sadie immediately took over. Sadie was quite an elderly lady at that stage but she was absolutely fantastic. I said: 'Let's get into the Armoury. It's the most secure place' and we got Sadie and young Mavis into the Armoury. We stayed there for a bit and then I went out to go to look at the offices. There was no offices! The Portacabin where we were was wiped out. Sadie says: 'Right. Let's get the show on the road!' She meant we should start clearing up. I said: 'Sadie, there's nothing left to clear up. It's all gone!' She says: 'My coat's there!' But Sadie's coat wasn't there.

So the first mortar landed on the roof of our Portacabins, the second one landed in the alleyway and the detonator of the third one got caught on the overhead telephone wires so it didn't explode. The nose of that mortar came through the roof. I don't remember who actually found it; I think somebody who went into the big hall saw some plaster lying on the floor and looked up and saw the nose of the mortar sticking through the ceiling. That base plate area had to be secured and sealed. Once we discovered the unexploded mortar we got everyone out of the camp and up the street three or four hundred yards towards the furniture place.

At that stage they didn't know there was no detonator attached to it. So then it was a problem for ATO because he had to get up there. Getting up there was a problem.

We had no word of a threat at all against Cookstown. Naturally we had people manning the sangars all the time. But Conway's TV rentals van would have been round there all the time and it wouldn't have looked out of place. The IRA had reversed their van into the driveway directly opposite, so that it was nose on to the base. And they had taken the roof out of the van, so the three mortars came straight out. The van was hijacked but they had to do a bit of work to it beforehand.

When the attack happened, Tom (McKinney) just took off and I asked him afterwards where he went. He said he went to the sangar to see where it had come from.

We were only concerned with the security of the base. I was responsible only for the UDR people in the base and once I was satisfied that everyone in the building was safe, my job was done. I had to find out where everybody was and get them accounted for. I thought the Armoury was the most secure place, so my idea was to get everybody who wasn't being used into the Armoury and wait. We did that and Tom had been up to the sangars. The guard knew exactly what to do and they stayed in their places.

---

23 Pte Mavis Patterson 1964-: 8 UDR 1986-91: Chef.

The operation didn't get wrapped up till night time. I didn't get home till after tea time. We just had to stay around till the area was cleared.

Whenever the thing went off, I was standing with my back to the window. I was in civilian clothes, in a pair of flannels and if you had taken my trouser pockets and filled them full of grit and hammered the grit in as hard as you could, till it was completely solid, that's what my two pockets were like. It was set like concrete.

His wife, Florence, added:

He didn't come home till almost eight o'clock that night. He had phoned to say he was OK and told me not to worry about it. But when he came home I called him 'the grey man'. He had dark hair at that stage, but his hair was grey, his face was grey, the pockets of his waterproof jacket were full. His jacket fell on the floor with the weight of the stuff in the pockets. Friends explained that they were glad to see him alive. I didn't know what they meant. Then on the Sunday, George brought me over to Cookstown to show me. I nearly had a fit! He had played everything down and I couldn't believe how anybody got out alive.

Florence Davison[24] was also in the base that day:

I joined the UDR as a Greenfinch in February 1982 and served for almost fifteen years, until November 1996, because I was in the Royal Irish for a couple of years. I was married and had three children. When I joined, the youngest would have been two. My husband was on the UDR too. He was in one of the two platoons that went out at night and I was in the other, so we were able to alternate our duties.

At the time, you think it's going to be a night-time job and it's not going to affect you, but it's not easy when you weren't home from duty until maybe three in the morning. I always had the children in bed before I went out. Some days, I'd have been working in the kitchen until two in the afternoon and then go on UDR duty at seven that evening. I don't know how I did it!

I did basic training in Dungannon and was posted to C Company, in Cookstown. I went out on patrols sometimes, although not very often. I did a cookery course in Magilligan, so later on I worked in the kitchen as a cook during the day and then did duties at night. In the base at Cookstown, I would have prepared lunch for twenty or thirty people every day.

On the morning of the mortar attack on 14th November 1988, I was at work preparing to cook. Mavis, the other girl who worked in the kitchen, wasn't

---

24 Pte Margaret Florence Davison 1956-: 8 UDR 1982-92: (R Irish until 1996): Chef.

there when it happened. She was somewhere else in the building, so I was the only one in the kitchen area when it happened.

It was about half past nine and I had hung my coat up in the office, because there were no lockers back then, and went to the kitchen. Shortly afterwards, I left the kitchen to go to the store to get supplies. In the store there was a fluorescent light and it started to blink. I remember thinking that it was about to go and I ought to ask for it to be replaced. And just at that moment, 'Bang!' and the ceiling came down. I jumped in under a shelf, on top of the broken glass that was coming from the fluorescent tube. I had an apron on and I put the apron over my head and I just remember shaking. I looked out of the side of my eye and all I could see was a ball of dust. I thought to myself: 'Everybody's dead and I'm in here on my own'. I thought I was the only one still alive.

It seemed like ages but it was probably only a few minutes until there was a line of soldiers down that corridor where all the glass was broken and blew in and they came to get me. I don't know how they knew I was there. Our base was in Derryloran old school and there was a corridor which looked as if it was a mile long. They just formed a line along the corridor on top of the broken glass and they took me by the hand and led me out, up to the mortar-proof corridor. They kept saying: 'Mind the Glass'. There were shards of glass everywhere. Then they got a minibus and took us to the clinic. I can remember going to the clinic but everything seemed far away as if you were standing outside, watching in. I was shaking like a leaf. I had no serious injuries, apart from cuts to my knees from lying on the broken glass from the fluorescent tube, but about a week later my eye started to swell and to weep at the side, and then my whole face swelled up. It was like really bad conjunctivitis because the dust must have got into it. Then it moved to the other eye and my eyes were just throbbing.

It was tough going home that evening and trying to be 'normal'. In fact, I didn't do anything much for a few days afterwards.

My daughter had an exam that day in Maths. She heard the bang, because the school was just opposite, on Fountain Road, but she ended up getting 100 percent. It was hard to believe, because she was roaring and crying, thinking I was killed. She was running around saying: 'I want to go home', but Ivan, my husband, had gone to the school and reassured her that I was all right.

I was off work for six months, went back, and after the first day, I was off again, because there were doors banging and all of that and I couldn't cope with it. The area had been repaired but it still looked the same.

I still get flashbacks, even now. There was one day fairly recently, I was driving up the road beside where I live and there was a lorry approaching, with a load of wee fine stones. Suddenly there was a bang and I nearly crashed the car. A tyre had blown and all the stones scattered over my car, so it was like reliving those minutes in the storeroom, with all the dust. I don't like squeals and bangs. It does stay with you and you'll never forget it. Even flashing lights will trigger a flashback.

3

No Hiding Place

No Off-Duty

Almost all the 44 men of 8 UDR killed by the terrorists were killed off-duty. There were two main types of attack – shooting and under vehicle booby-trap. These attacks were carried out where the soldier's pattern of life was predictable, going to and from work or, in the case of certain workers such as bus drivers, farmers and postmen, at work.

Those living on the interfaces were especially vulnerable both because they were easier to attack and because they were considered a particular threat by the terrorists.

Many off-duty attacks were foiled by intelligence, by alertness of the man or woman, their family and friends, and by the courage of the individual soldier. Armed with only a personal protection weapon, they fought back on several occasions.

In total there were 115 attacks on off-duty members of the Battalion and those who had left it during the 22 years. In 12 cases they managed to return fire but two were still killed.

Franklin Kelly 25th February 1979

> I[1] was born in No 10 across the yard there, Tullyleek Road, on 27th February 1941 and I grew up there and went to school from there – Donaghmore Primary School. I had bad attendance because of my asthma and things like that. I missed out on the 11+ but I did the 'Review'. By that time I had went to the Technical College and made friends there and I passed the 'Review' all right but I hadn't the stomach then for changing over. So I stayed at the Tech. The Sale Yard was just outside; we used to go over and put bids on cattle and one thing and another. We were barred from going to the Sale Yard after that!
>
> I studied Metalwork, Woodwork, Maths, Chemistry and Physics and all that kinda stuff. Then after I'd done the Junior Tech in '56, Stanley Orr the boss

---

1 CSgt (Franklin) Hamilton Kelly BEM 1941-: 8 UDR 1970-92: (R Irish until 1994): Administrative Officer Health and Social Services.

man was looking for volunteers to do 'O' levels. There was eight of us volunteered to do this and we done Maths and Sciences and Geography and English Literature and English Language. We stayed there another couple of years – '57, '58. I then applied for a number of jobs – the Electricity Board was one of them – and I applied to the South Tyrone (Hospital) for a job there. It was unusual to have a clerical job in the hospital for there was no turnover there. So I was successful in that and I started on the 13th October and stayed there till 1973. I moved into Payroll and then to Accounts. Then we were reorganised and I was told I was being sent to Lurgan. So I put in for an Higher Clerical Officer (HCO) job (I was a CO, like) and they offered me the post of HCO in Administration and then a few years down the line they created a job SAO and I was there maybe a year when this other 'big event' happened (*the attack*). They were very good to me; I was off till the middle of June. I went back in June and tried for another promotion, back to the South Tyrone. No go.

I was in the Ulster Special Constabulary (USC) for nine years, from around '61. I was brought in for my clerical ability, I think, and I went up through the ranks until I become a Sergeant. And then on 2nd March 1970 I was duly enlisted in the UDR, up in Omagh, 6 UDR. And Snakebite McCauley (*Sergeant in 6 UDR*) was the man that took us for the first inspection in the drill hut down at Desertcreat (*between Cookstown and Dungannon*).

We were based here for a short time, first of all, up in Ballymacall (*between Donaghmore and Pomeroy*). They requisitioned this drill hall here, just up the road from the filling station. Then we moved to Northland Place for a short time; that was J Company, and then in November '71 they split Dungannon into J and K and I became K and we were sent to Killymeal. The first job over there was putting a perimeter fence around the place. The Aughnacloy boys were the main men about putting up fences – there was Percy Marshall[2] and Walter Devlin[3] and them men. They put up the fences and pickets. There was a knife rest across where the gate was eventually and red lamps on it and they dug in these sensor things. They weren't dug in deep enough and the jackdaws lit on them and the things went off all the time – it was an awful carry-on. And yer man that owned it (Killymeal House), he had a big Ford V8 and he left it – he just abandoned it so somebody went away and got a gallon of petrol and they went for a bit of a tour round the helipad in it. Somebody eventually took it away.

In October '71 we set up house here. I got married on 3rd September 1971, and this house was built, and we moved in on 1st October. That other house

---

2 CSgt Percival (Percy) Hamilton Marshall 1912-85: 8 UDR 1970-73: Farmer.
3 Lt Walter James Devlin 1917-1990: 8 UDR 1970-73: Clerk of Works.

and complex wasn't there (*his son's house next door*). There was just a bit of a whin hedge up at the top of the field.

Now, leading up to this 'event', there's a couple of things worthy of note. One is that we had a wee terrier dog, a barking dog, and it disappeared about three or four weeks before the event on 25th February 1979. It disappeared sometime before Christmas, and we toyed with getting another dog and we decided to wait till after Christmas. At the same time, there was a derelict house in behind us here belonging to the Quinn family of Killaharry. There was three families of them but at that time a lot of the young fellas were away in England.

Now, they were supposedly renovating the house and re-wiring it and putting in the electric. The house belonged to Cornelius Quinn, an old uncle. He died; he was got dead draped over a gate one morning, and these boys inherited but they couldn't agree. There was some dispute anyway. A repair job was going on and Mr PJ Loughran[4] (*suspect PIRA*) who was the taxi driver and pick up for this crew down here (*reference to the attack*), he was supposed to be helping to re-wire. Now that was only a smoke-screen, for they used it as a kind of a base to observe.

Now I had Close Observation Platoon (COP) teams in at different times up till that. There had been two or three COP teams and they would walk in and they would stay maybe a week and they would walk out. They usually walked in during the night and walked out during the night. But Paddy wasn't so slow. Paddy would have seen them out about, walking round the fields. They had been in a couple of times; there was the Queen's Own Highlanders and there was another crowd in too, once they stayed up in the yard here, once they stayed down in the bog there, in behind that tree-line, watching what was going on. So there was that important factor.

The other factor that comes into play was that after the second youngster was born in 1976, Nathalie had Post Natal Depression (PND) and then she got blood pressure problems. Her blood pressure was through the roof and they got her an ambulance and she went into the South Tyrone on the Sunday week before the event. She was admitted to C floor and the lad, Sam, had just started school and Norma was only about 18 months or so, and the mother-in-law moved in and there was blood pressure at home, never mind in the hospital. So, I brought him to school in the morning and some of the relatives brought him home at 2 o'clock.

---

4   PJ (Patrick Joseph) Loughran c1960-: Paul Williams in his book *Gangland* wrote, 'The leaders of this motley crew (The Athy Gang formed 1988) were IRA-trained PJ Loughran 29 originally from Dungannon in Co Tyrone: He had moved to live in Coolock, Dublin, to hide from the RUC, who wanted him in connection with terrorist offences in the North…he was normally the wheels man… during 1989 the gang was responsible for 32 heists…he was wounded and captured during a raid on the Bank of Ireland in Athy (1990): Because of his injuries he never stood trial'.

But he always craked about getting in to see Mammy. I says: 'Look, Mammy's not in a fit state to talk to you, son. I'll tell her you were asking about her and if you want to draw out a wee card, I'll take it in with me'. That was all right for the first three or four days; I always visited at night, because obviously I wanted to keep up the front going to work, and on the Sunday night he was determined he would get in. I says: 'You're going to school in the morning. There's not a chance. You've got to be realistic, you've to get to bed and Nanny will make you whatever you want for your supper'. He grudgingly agreed and I went in to the South Tyrone. Now, having worked there from 1958 till 1973, I knew a lot of the senior staff, but there was a lot of blow-ins about that time and one of them was this blade; she was an orderly on that floor.

Anyway, I went in on the Sunday night, and it was 7 till 7.45 or something like that. I left about 10 to 8 and on the way out, yer woman was standing in the corridor and she made sure that I seen her. I went out; I didn't go home, I went to Killymeal for there was a Fitness For Role (FFR) inspection starting on the Monday morning and I wanted to make sure that the platoon's weapons were all cleaned and blocks in them all, for at that time, for security reasons, we took the blocks home. I went in and I fell in with Joe Beggs[5] who was the Duty Armourer. We went down and checked the weapons and he was happy the weapons was all cleaned and the blocks were all in.

Anyway, I suppose about a quarter to nine, I decided it was time to head out the road and I thought in my mind: 'Which way do I go? The Cappagh road or the Pomeroy road?' I thought: 'Well, I've a right lively car, I'll go the Pomeroy road. It's the shortest road in'. I went the Pomeroy road, turned off there, and foot to the floor, always done a handbrake turn into the laneway, and just as I got into the first part of the laneway, the shooting started. Now, they had picked a bad firing point. They had a firing point at that tree on the other side of the lane but then they had another one up in the field on the hill, above the lane. Now the idea was that if I come the other road they were going to get me too, because there was a space in the hedge and they would have been shooting through it into the car. I put the shoe till her anyway, and the next thing there was this unmerciful racket and I seen stars; that was the boy that hit the roof. There was one round that hit the roof and that car was one of the big 1725cc Allegros and inside the roof there was a rib across her. Well the bullets hit the rib, one of them hit the rib and there was shrapnel come through and that's the thing that got me on the side of the head. No nerves there now. All cut. And the second one stuck in the roof, because the boys fished it out. And if I'd had Sam with me, he was dead as a maggot. For there was the loveliest group of three through the glove box. You couldn't have done any better if you had been

---

5 LCpl Joseph (Joe) Alexander Beggs 1938-: 8 UDR 1970-1992.

target shooting. And they shot under her and over her and even shot the brakes off her. I dived into the yard here and I didn't stop her, she just stalled. In fact, the flywheel flew off, busted the rivets and the studs on the flywheel, and they followed me up to the tree on the right there, and then they panicked because there was two cousins of mine here with my mother and they went out and the yard lights all went on.

But their lift was away. PJ was to lift them at a quarter past eight. He drove through, no boys, no nothing. He went away on about his business and they were seen by the neighbours high tailing there, carrying their guns. And they carried them on across Norman Burnside's[6] field and across the road below Gerry Dobson's concrete works and we lost track of them there. Now, they must have had a pick-up somewhere for the guns, and that night they slept in a hayshed in Tullnagall. Now the owner wouldn't have been a Nationalist or a Hibernian but the younger fry would have been a different kettle of fish. In fact one of the young ones might have been doing a line with one of these boys and that's how they knowed where to go. They stayed there till daylight and then they headed off across-country to the Cookstown road and that's where the Cookstown daylight patrol caught up with them. But they hadn't got briefed properly, they hadn't realised what had happened me the night before, stopped these gents, took their names and addresses and all, reported in to Killymeal and two or three minutes later Killymeal came back to them: 'Where is them boys? Oh, they're away on up the road'.

They went on ahead to Coalisland, got de-briefed, got a change of clothes, all clothes etcetera burned, and they didn't catch up with them for two days afterwards. And in the middle of it all, the Superintendent from Armagh, he says: 'No, it couldn't have happened in the South Tyrone (Hospital). You're wrong', he says, 'that's just a freak incident'.

I says: 'Sir, I know the set-up. I know the South Tyrone, I worked in it for twenty-one years'. I says: 'I know some of the people that come into it lately, and I know what happened the time the Civil Rights march was and the windows was lined with nurses watching it'. I says: 'I have no friends there'. Three months later, he was in briefing the Commanding Officer or something like that and he asked to see me. He apologised and he says: 'Colour, you were right. We checked the phone records; there was a call made from a phone box at five to eight'.

I was injured in my head and it cleaned the toe clean out of that shoe and took the top off the toe. We were lucky enough it didn't take bone; it just took the nail and the skin. There was twenty-two shells found and there was seventeen hits on the vehicle. They weren't just doing it for the fun of the thing.

---

6 Pte (Norman) Johnstone Burnside 1934-2016: 8 UDR 1972-74: Building Contractor.

The Army set up an ICP at the end of the Tullyleek Road and they brought the ambulance in from there. It was lucky the ambulance man was a local man, and at that time Devina Brodison and some other nurse were already here. I never came in here – they took me into my mother's; I was bleeding like a pig. But they got me patched up anyway and got me into the ambulance and they went in the ambulance too and Ronnie Brodison, that's Devina's husband, followed in the car. There was a mission on in Tullyaran Gospel Hall and they come out on the road, they heard the shooting – that's how they knew.

Well they got me into the ward and there was a consultant and he says: 'I can poke about and take them bits of shrapnel out of you but it'll leave your head a real mess'. He says: 'They'll work their way out over time', and that's what did happen. Over the next eight or nine years, you'd be combing your hair and you'd get this bit of a thing. I was very, very lucky. Mr Ward (the consultant) was a good man. And I was in there, you see, and that Sunday night, (Carnegie[7] was the RSM at the time), he insisted that he would do the guard himself. So he did do the guard and then Budgie[8] come in during the day and Carnegie come back the next night. By this time, some useful kind of a nurse had told the wife that her husband was downstairs and he'd had an accident. Well, she 'escaped' and made her way down and about half seven or eight o'clock that night, she walked in through the door into the room. Carnegie nearly busted a blood vessel. 'Who is this lady?' I says: 'Sir, don't worry. That is my wife'.

But they organised a discharge for both of us then on Wednesday morning. I said I wasn't content to be there; people looking in through the glass. If it had been anybody else only me, but I knowed the place and I knowed some of the 'clients' that was about it, and … you only have to look at Jimmy Johnston.[9] So I was glad to get home and I can still see that wee bush down the lane and that's where the boy was hiding. You see, (I suppose it depended on the amount of time they were going to have), when I got onto the lane, I was rising all the time so therefore by the time they got organised, that's why they were hitting the brake cylinder and the bottom of her, and they were firing upwards. But then these other boys in the field, they come down and joined in at the bank. That was the danger. They were firing from 50 yards.

At the time, I never thought anything of the dog disappearing; it was a wee bit of a rambler, but I maintain now, looking back on it, that the dog was 'removed'. I suppose if Nathalie hadn't been in hospital they were maybe going

---

7 Capt Sydney (Sid) John Carnegie Scots Guards 1938-: RSM 8 UDR 1979-81: GOC's Commendation.
8 CSgt Eric (Budgie) Cumberland 1940-2013: 8 UDR 1971-92.
9 +Pte Noel James (Jimmy) Johnston 1956-84: 8 UDR 1974-84: Hospital Porter: Killed in the grounds of South Tyrone Hospital 8th May 1984.

to mount a full attack on the house. Whether they knowed beforehand that she was in, I don't know, but there was rotten ones in the staff on all them floors.

Sam was old enough to know and he didn't see me till I come home out of the hospital, but the wee girl, Norma, was a bit confused. She didn't know what had happened. My mother, she was badly shook. And my mother-in-law was too; they never seen anything like this or never experienced anything like this. And this all landed on their doorstep. My mother in particular, she seen me coming in and the blood running out of me and of course, my mother-in-law, she couldn't contain herself; she paddled over and added to the confusion. She had a kind of an appreciation though, because one of her boys was in the Army. But to see someone like this in their own back yard is shocking.

The wee boy was in bed, and he got out of bed and then when we both come home he couldn't understand why the two of us was there and why I wasn't at work. I says: 'I'm not feeling well'.

I was off work and went back in June sometime. And I went back to camp in June as well. Now in the middle of this trouble, they wanted me to throw the whole thing in. Some of the powers that be wanted me to go full-time. I said: 'No, I can't afford that; I'm a public servant. I have a lot of years done and I have a pension worked up and I have probably another promotion and it definitely wouldn't be my idea'. So I said: 'Leave it with me' and we talked it over. Nathalie's final word on it was: 'Well, you know what you want to do, if you feel it's the right thing, you do that and I'm behind you'. My mother and mother-in-law were totally 'Get out when the going's good', but Nathalie stuck by me. So that's the way we left it and I don't think I was back on the road much after that. I was inside doing liaison work. I stayed then till July 1994. I would have stayed longer – I wanted to do my last two years, but the new Colonel that came in, he was thinking of the full-time boys and he wanted to get them up the ranks so that they would come out with a good pension.

Our Company Commander at that time, well, he had no loyalty to Dungannon anyway; he wanted me to go down to Local Sergeant. I was a Colour Sergeant. I listened to him and I said nothing. But then, the next thing, I got a phone call at work: 'You've a Commanding Officer's interview this evening at four o'clock'. So I invented a run to the bank and I headed to Killymeal and when I got to Killymeal I was told I had to be in uniform. Now I always kept my uniform in a holdall and I had been on the night before so the holdall was in the boot of the car. I changed into uniform anyway and went back in front of the CO and the Company Commander and the RSM was there.

And the Colonel introduced himself and he says: 'You've done a long period of service. I want to be loyal to the full-time men and I want to ask you would you think of reverting to Corporal?' I says: 'To be quite blunt Sir, I wouldn't. I nearly lost my life over the head of this outfit and against all things, I agreed to come back in'. And I says: 'I got my rank the hard way'. So he hummed and hawed a bit and I says: 'I'll solve your problem. If you want to be fair to the full-time boys, I'll sign off, for I'm going out on Colour Sergeant'. Well I come out with a head of steam; boys I was boiling! Being took out of work, told to get into uniform and then be asked to go to Corporal! So the last words he said, he said to the RSM: 'Make sure I see this Colour Sergeant before he leaves us'.

I went out and up the yard and I went to the OC's office and I says: 'Sir, what about that form I signed to revert to Sergeant?' 'Oh I don't know where it is'. I says: 'Better look for it there, for I want to see it.' So he hoked through this tray and I spotted it and pulled it out of the tray and I says: 'That's the form there we're talking about'. I says: 'There's what I think of that form' and I threw it at his feet. So we just parted at that; I didn't do any more arguing with him. This was June '94.

I was entitled to another two and a half years to take me to fifty-five. So that night, I was on duty, I was Watch-Keeper, and on into the night, when all was quiet, the wee medic came up to see me. He was a wee Captain, a Queen's Own Highlander. He says: 'When you came out of the OC's office this afternoon, you weren't in a great mood'. I says: 'If somebody asked you to go down three or four ranks after giving twenty-four years' service and nearly losing your life, what would you do?'

He seen me and he done the medical. He says: 'Your both knees is full of arthritis and it's going to spread on up and you'll get it in your hips as well. But before you go out, ask for a full medical. Insist on going to Armagh'. I asked to get an appointment for a full medical. I says: 'You know we all come in here FE, full employment, and I have been LE for the last couple of years, limited employment'. So they hummed and hawed about it but eventually I was took down to Armagh. I went into a room and there was this grey-haired man sitting behind the desk with a pile of brass on him. He says: 'You are Colour Sergeant Kelly, I take it?' He confirmed what the other boy said. He says: 'I'll put a report in and to tell you the truth, you have about fifteen years more in your joints than your age'.

So Helen Ferguson[10] was in the Welfare at that time, and she done a three-page dossier on my activity at the time we were attacked and all and sent it in to the Welfare people. So I got this letter then from the MOD to come to Marlborough House in Belfast on 22nd December.

So I went in and a girl took my particulars and I thought there'd be a whole panel of these boys, but there was only the one doctor, a youngish man, civil enough. He says: 'I hope you don't mind me asking these questions for you've probably answered them all already on this form'. I says: 'That's all right; carry you on'. He says: 'Hop up on that couch there'. I says: 'I wish I could hop on

---

10 Cpl Helen Ferguson 1947-: 8 UDR 1984-92: (R Irish until 2000).

it; I'll sit up on it and you can do the rest'. And he confirmed what the other boys had said.

So about the middle of March I got an award of 40%. So a couple of years down the line, the Welfare Officer was here one day and he says: 'Looking at your situation, I think you were short-changed. I'll give you a form and you fill it in and send it back to me'. That was round about April time and a call come then at the end of July or the beginning of August. Marlborough House again. Another doctor. He checked me and he says: 'According to my reading, if anything, you're worse than you were'.

After the incident, there was no Combat Stress or anything. Nobody asked you. You had to fight your own case in the court as well. Tony Irwin (*his solicitor*) got Reggie Weir to represent me and I got £11,000. But bear in mind, they wouldn't give any award to the youngsters or to the mother or the mother-in-law. So I divided it up like; they went through the mincer as well as me. But the final review, they put it up to 90% and back-dated to the date of the letter.

At the time they didn't increase the security. There was COP teams in and we had to spend a fortnight in Armagh. They had my car and they had her full of plates and so forth and after about ten days, they abandoned the car in the middle of the yard with the doors open. The mother got a message to me – at that time I had moved back and was living with an aunt and uncle in Moygashel.

In '93, they wanted to put rockets on the chimney but I says 'No'. So they put the armoured glass in and an alarm thing on the front doorbell. But I was left to my own devices. The most nerve-wracking thing was driving past that wee shrub down the lane. Every time I drove past it I seen shadows.

They never finished the renovation of the house next door. We thought it was genuine at the time but sure young PJ Loughran, who was the driver, he was picked up, the Guards (Garda Siochana – Irish Police) picked them up – he was caught in a bank raid down in the South. They fired on them in the robbery. The Guards come on the scene. You weren't playing with the RUC!

Glen Espie 22nd March 1978 and 19th March 1987

I[11] joined the Ulster Defence Regiment as a volunteer at eighteen years of age in January 1975 serving in G Company as a part-time soldier and was based at Cookstown in East Tyrone. There is a tradition of voluntary service by our family in the Security Forces and other members of our family had joined the UDR at the outset in 1970, and it was a natural step for me and one I was very keen to achieve and to follow in my father's footsteps.

---
11 Sgt Glen Espie BEM 1957-: 8 UDR 1975-89: MID: Plumber/Maintenance Manager NIHE.

As a fifteen year old I had applied to join the Junior Leaders for the Regular Army. However much to my disappointment, my parents did not consent to this and advised me to take up an apprenticeship first and when I turned eighteen then I could apply to join the Regular Army. On leaving school at fifteen I started an apprenticeship as a plumber based with a local firm in Cookstown.

We lived in a rural area to the east of Cookstown. My father was a farmer and a part-time member of the UDR. I grew up in a mixed area of Catholic and Protestant families who for the most part had strong neighbourly ties within our community. I had just become a teenager when the Troubles started in 1970 and this area of East Tyrone was particularly violent during the 1970s with IRA terror gangs carrying out murders, bombings and frequent attacks on the Security Forces both on and off duty and at their bases.

It was impossible, even as children, to be protected from what was happening in our community and even more so when a family member was serving in the UDR. One night my father's patrol was ambushed in a landmine attack in the Ardboe; often when my father was on duty we would listen in on the police radio net with our mother late into the night. You heard the bombs going off; if there was a suspicious car near our home I would go out around the fields checking that it was safe for my father to drive home alone from duty in the early hours.

On joining the Regiment I attended basic recruit training and on passing out joined my platoon in Cookstown. This was something I had eagerly wanted to do from an early age, to be a soldier. My Platoon Commander was Lieutenant Robin Smyrl[12] and he was to have, in the short time I served with him, a huge influence on my life. He saw potential in me, made me believe in myself, and I owe much to Robin for what I was to achieve in my civilian and military careers, and he gave me the tools that I drew on in times of great adversity. He had a charisma and character that made him stand out above all others. He was murdered by IRA terrorists on the morning of 13th September 1977 when off duty en route to his civilian place of work.

Being a part-time soldier was in reality a total commitment every minute of your day. It was common knowledge that you were serving and you were never off duty as far as a terrorist was concerned. On average I served 20 operational duties a month as a part-time soldier and worked as a plumber in my civilian job. At my civilian place of employment there was a small team of both Catholic and Protestant tradesmen and it was common knowledge that I was serving in the UDR. My work van was parked in the firm's yard and the first thing I would do is get down and religiously check the vehicle for an under

---

12 +2nd Lt Robert (Robin) George Smyrl 1950-77: 8 UDR 1972-77: MID (posthumous): Businessman: Killed 13th September 1977.

vehicle booby-trap bomb in full view of all. On occasions that a work colleague would have to use my van they told me they would look under the vehicle but did not really know what they were looking for and had a great sense of relief when they drove out of the yard without it blowing up; so did I really. I had a great respect for my work colleagues who told me never to acknowledge our association and friendship if I stopped them in a checkpoint as it would not go well with them especially if they were in a Republican area.

I covered all the Housing Executive rented properties from Pomeroy to the Ardboe following up planned maintenance schedules and repairs reported in to the office by the occupants. Visits were planned and an occupant would have notice when I would attend. You were an easy prey for the terrorist to target both your routes, your timings and they could choose the ground to ambush you in and make easy their escape. A Police Officer stationed in the village of Coagh warned me to be very careful when working in the Ardboe area as I was an easy target for an IRA attack and that even armed patrols were vulnerable such was the threat. The pressure that this can bring on you mentally could break you, however when you are twenty you do not back away, you believe in your ability to meet the challenge. We attended training sessions about personal security as a member of the Security Forces, videos showing how not to identify yourself as a member of the UDR, tips such as not hanging uniforms out to dry on washing lines. Yes, all relevant, however when your neighbour is a member of the IRA as was my case and everyone knows you were serving, you are kidding yourself if you think you can hide your identity as a member of the UDR. Incidents happen too when on operations resulting in you having to attend court as a witness and give evidence against known terrorists in public with your name and rank read out and using your own vehicle to go to a court held in your local town. You are now at a higher profile in the community as a result, however I joined to do the right thing and was prepared to accept the exposure.

I was ambushed by an IRA terrorist gang on 22nd March 1978 when off duty and working in my civilian job as a plumber in the Ardboe, about four miles east of the Police station in the town of Coagh, at number 3 Lakeview Cottages (Killygonlan) near to an area locally called the Diamond in the centre of the village. This was a Republican stronghold for the IRA and a number of attacks had been carried out against military patrols over the years; it was here that my father's patrol, a UDR mobile patrol, was attacked using a landmine under the road some years before.

That morning I left for work at my usual time just after 8 am. I followed a set routine rehearsed many times as part of my personal security objectives – I travelled alone. I was armed with an issue .22 Walther semi-automatic pistol for personal protection provided by the military. I noted that lecturers from the military who did our personal protection advice and training carried 9 mm semi-automatic pistols; the .22 was not recognised as a military operational weapon. My Commanding Officer carried a 9 mm. I had other objectives; debriefs from murders of off-duty members showed that maybe only three rounds of a barrage of 20 or 30 rounds had entered the target so it was vital that when ambushed I could keep even just one round out of my body. I was prepared mentally, alert to the situation, my gun attached to my body in the same place, rehearsed my 'actions on' many times.

I came back to the yard in Cookstown at lunchtime after completing a repair job in the town of Pomeroy, in a housing estate in the north of the town, again a Republican stronghold. On finishing my tea the foreman told me he had just received a call that there was a burst cylinder at number 3 Lakeview Cottages, Ardboe and to head out to the house and repair the burst.

The lough shore was active; a week earlier an attack had been mounted on a part-time member of the UDR commuting through the area, 23 rounds striking his car but no direct hits on him or disabling his car and he drove through the ambush and escaped. The Security Forces had killed a terrorist loading a bomb into a van three weeks earlier.

En route to the Ardboe I called at my home near Cookstown where my wife was trying to light the fire and look after our two children aged 9 months and a 2 year old. She wondered why I had called but I said I was heading to a job and

3 Lakeview Cottages, Ardboe – left end house with white door

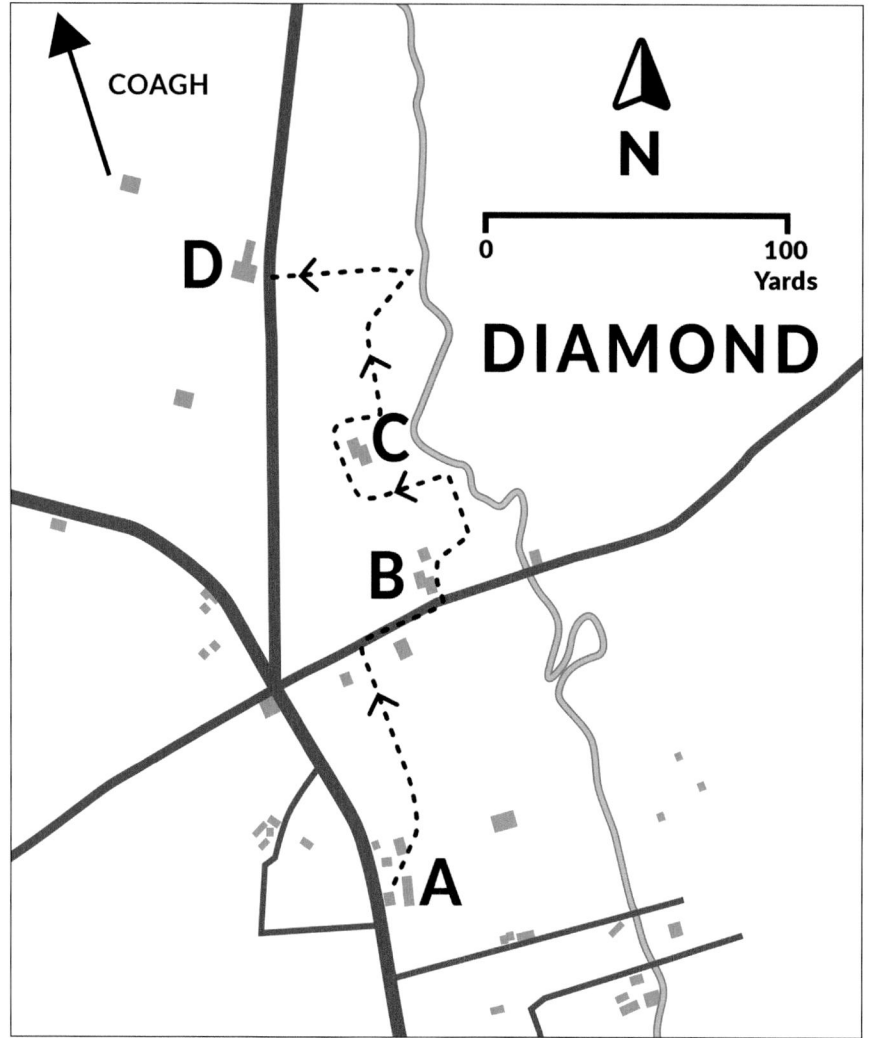

Attack on Private Glen Espie
A: Contact, B: 1st Bungalow, C: Elderly Man in Window, D: 2nd Bungalow/
Car Taken

needed to go to the toilet. I lifted my concealed lightweight issue body armour and put it on under my work clothes; it wasn't the easiest item to work in so I did not wear it all the time.

I headed to the Ardboe taking an extended route into the area. On arriving at the cottages which looked out onto the main road adjacent to the local shop and petrol pumps, I reversed the van in and kept my wing mirror in line with the front door. Watching for any suspicious activity in the mirror I did some paperwork. Nothing happened so I got out of the van and walked the short distance to the house, my heart pounding, fully expecting to be ambushed from an entry on my left or the door to be flung open and a burst of shots.

I went to the front door, stood to one side and knocked. If someone fired through the door I would not be in the direct line of fire.

The front door was opened a few inches by a male person. I advised him I was from the Housing Executive and was there to repair the burst cylinder. He said 'OK son, go ahead. You know where it's at, at the top of the stairs'. I pushed the door open and went in as the male person went through a door from the hallway on my right into the living room and closed the door. Relieved at having talked, as I thought, to the occupant, I relaxed as it appeared it's just another burst cylinder, all in a day's work. On entering the hallway I turned left and walked to the bottom of the stairs. Just as I was putting my hand onto the staircase I was aware that the curtains were drawn on the window at the bottom of the stairs and the hallway was very dark even though it was only 2.15pm.

The door to a downstairs bathroom to the right of the staircase was open and as I was taking all this in, a male of stocky build was standing in front of me; he had stepped out of the bathroom just as I came level with the open door. I became fixed on his face. He was wearing a black balaclava. I could see his eyes and mouth perfectly; he had a pistol in a two handed grip pointed at my chest and was literally only inches from my body.

The initial shock to the system literally stops you in your tracks as you stare at this frightening figure, this huge head, the pistol pointed at you just like you would on a range day. My first thoughts were 'F**k, this is it' as the gunman fired hitting me on the left side of my chest in the heart area. The sheer force of the shot was like being kicked by a horse. I was lifted off my feet propelled backwards down the hallway and I fell to the ground lying against the open front door. As I looked up at the gunman he stepped forward and levelled the pistol at my head. I remember thinking in those milliseconds my life really did pass in front of me like a cinema screen in fast forward; I thought of my wife, my children, mum and dad. All the people who really mattered in my life flashed across my brain in a fraction of a second. As the gunman levelled the pistol to my head I ducked and rolled out of the open front door. Getting to my feet I ran past my van to get away from the gunman who fired after me. I could feel rounds going past my head and had covered 10 to 15 metres when I was shot again on the left shoulder; the impact of the bullet spun me round and knocked me to the ground. When running I was trying to get to my pistol under the boiler suit holstered on my left side; now, lying on my back, my head towards the front door of No. 3, I could look back over my head and saw two terrorists running from the doorway towards me to finish me off. They looked to be running in slow motion; the effect of adrenalin on my brain meant that I was thinking so fast everything in real time looked like slow motion.

When lying on the ground I was able to draw my pistol but the injury to my left shoulder meant I could not cock it in the normal fashion; I forced it into my left hand, pushed forward with my right, and chambered a round. Bringing the gun over my head I fired at the terrorists who were about halfway to me. When I fired back the terrorists hit the deck. I rolled onto my belly and went to fire again. Nothing happened; the pistol had jammed. I couldn't clear the pistol, the gunmen were too close, so I jumped to my feet and ran round the side of the last two houses at the end of the square. Clearing a 5 foot high chain link fence at the back of the houses in one bound, I ran behind Forbes' filling station. People there saw me and kept pointing at me and the direction I was running in, I assumed to the gun team. I climbed over a wooden fence and then crossed an open field for about 150 metres. When running my breaths were coming in large gasps, my heart was pounding and my lungs were on fire; the hedge at the far side of this field seemed so far away and I was expecting to be shot again out in the open ground.

On reaching the edge of the field I tore into this large thorn hedge and forced my way through it. I was able to clear the jammed pistol and take stock of my situation. I looked back towards the filling station where I could see men moving about and pointing towards the hedgerow I was in. There was quite a large group by this time but I could not make out if the gunmen were there. This was the first I was aware that I was wounded now seeing the front of my boiler suit was covered in blood and it was coming from my mouth. My left lung had been damaged and this was where the blood was coming from. I had never been shot before, I was alone, wounded, in a Republican area and a terrorist gun team free to move about at will. The nearest safe haven was the village of Coagh some five miles away. To get there I was going to commandeer a car and either drive it or force the driver at gunpoint to drive me to the village of Coagh.

I had to move now or be cornered; too many people knew where I had gone and I was only 200 metres at most from the shooting and I decided to go to a bungalow on the north side of the Diamond. Having worked in the area and been on numerous patrols in the Ardboe I had a good knowledge of the ground. I had to cross a road and keep at least one field away from any road or houses to get to this bungalow, taking me only 300 or 400 metres from the house I was attacked in. I was aware that being in a Republican area no one was going to phone the police so I worked my way around the hedgerows, crossing the road when there was no traffic and in to the rear of the bungalow. The back door was unlocked but there was no vehicle so I went into the house which was unoccupied and in the hallway there was a telephone landline. The front door was clear glass visible to the road; I went through each room and in one of the bedrooms was a large scale map of the Ardboe area. Funny the things that go through your mind, I was wondering is this a PIRA ops room I have stumbled on.

I dialled 999 and asked for the police. I told the police that I was a part-time Lance Corporal of the UDR, I gave them my name, my army number that I was a plumber for the Housing Executive and had been shot in Killygonlan Housing Estate, was injured, needed medical assistance, back up and now hiding in a bungalow near the Diamond. The operator started putting me over the whole thing again. I was getting nowhere; the police thought it a come-on to draw them into the area and attack them. What a waste of time! Frustrated I slammed the phone down and saw that the floor was covered in my blood in full view of the glass front door. There was a copy of the Yellow Pages by the phone. I opened it up, set it over the blood on the hall floor, moved into the front bedroom, and observed from behind the blinds.

It was so quiet in the bungalow except for my heavy breathing now becoming laboured because of my injuries and blood loss; my heart seemed to be pounding out of my chest so I tried to take deep breaths and slow my heart rate down. I watched as a car with three men on board came slowly down the road past the bungalow and I prayed it would pass on by; it seemed to take an age for it to pass and I was worried that the blood in the hallway would be visible through the glass front door from the road. I really felt like a cornered rat and a .22 pistol doesn't really inspire confidence when the enemy is armed with heavier weapons than you and free to operate in their local area.

I decided to leave the bungalow and I remembered that we were told that a farmer in the area not far from here had the house shot at and I had seen the bullet strikes on the front wall one time when on patrol. I moved down the hedgerow keeping the road on my left and some 200 metres away crossed the fields making my way to the farm. Crossing what I thought was a derelict I detected movement at a window. As I pointed my pistol at the movement, an elderly man raised himself up on one arm to look out. When he saw me covered in blood and with my pistol pointed at him, his eyes just seemed to grow larger: as I moved he fell back onto his bed. I covered about half a mile and was becoming weak and weary and the pain was setting in. Pressing on, I used the hedgerows as cover now, but about three quarters of a mile from the attack in Killygonlan I had to cross a road to the bungalow I was heading for.

There was no one around and the house was locked. I took a milk crate and smashed a window in the bathroom at the side of the house and went in. Luckily, there was a phone and I dialled 999. Again the same gutless response and the operator gave no hint of how they would respond other than this could be a ploy to draw the Security Forces into the area to attack them. I was becoming tired and weary and slammed the phone down and went into a bedroom and lay down on a sheepskin rug. I was drifting off to sleep and I just wanted to rest, however the will to survive kicked in. I believed that if I went to sleep there I could die there or I could be discovered there and the IRA capture me; after all I was really in their back yard.

I moved from the bungalow out through the back to the farm yard where I found a Mini parked in an open shed. The keys were in the ignition and I got in and thankfully it started up. I reversed out and headed out the laneway to the road; a gate blocked my exit and I had to get out and open it. Back in the car I lay down low inside and drove onto the road half expecting to get both barrels from the farmer for stealing his car. I drove erratically and fast, hunched over the steering wheel. I headed to Coagh and pulled up outside a house where I knew the people living there. I rolled out onto the road in great pain; I shouted to a young lad to get help, the car rolled on down the road and crashed into a fence. The young lad was frozen to the spot; here was a man armed with a pistol, and covered in blood, lying on the side of the road. What a sight to be confronted with!

As I lay on my back looking up at the swirling clouds above and the grey sky which just a short time before had been a beautiful sunny spring day, this just reflected how I felt. The young lad went and got help and a lady arrived and took me into the house. The young lad was sent to get the doctor who lived in the village and I remember lying on the couch being examined when I heard the sound of the Saracen armoured military vehicles heading past the house to the ambush area; I had survived and I knew then that I was safe.

After the ambush attack in the Ardboe in March 1978 I was off work for six months and went through a number of operations, eight in all. I had little money coming in other than my statutory sick pay from work and we had to manage as a young family as best we could. It was suggested that I apply for a grant from the Benevolent Fund which I did and the Adjutant, Major Joe Cantley,[13] came to our home and gave me a temporary loan of £1000 which I would have to pay back and I duly did that when I received a settlement of £5000 for my injuries.

Some things lie heavily with you, such as the time I asked through the Battalion for solid heavy wood front and back doors to improve my security at home; I was turned down for that and unknown to me the soldiers in G Company whom I served with had a whip round, bought the doors and fitted them. I felt very humble that my fellow soldiers would show me such kindness and consideration for my family.

Eventually I considered myself fit to return to full-time work and part-time duties with the UDR. First I had to undergo a medical with the Army and the Medical Officer (MO) recommended that I was to be retired on medical grounds. This, he explained, would allow me to draw a full army pension; I did not see it in this way at all. I wanted to return to my duties as a part-time soldier, I felt it was my duty and made my case very forcibly with the MO who reluctantly agreed to sign me fit for operational duties. I was twenty-one years of age.

---

13 Maj Joseph (Joe) Cantley MBE 1920-2000: 8 UDR 1970-81: (then 5 UDR).

About seven years after the ambush a local RUC officer arrived at my home with the body armour and some other effects. They were going to be disposed of and he thought I would want to have them back. I still have the wallet with two £5 notes and the matchbox I was carrying. The first round that hit me in the chest went through them and the body armour stopped it.

I had little faith in the .22 issue gun as being an effective personal protection weapon and purchased my own, a revolver, the same type which I had been attacked with; it worked and had serious stopping power.

Some neighbours ignored me, put barriers up, others very discreetly came to visit and one gave me a St Christopher and made me promise I would carry it at all times. I did and I put it in my wallet and carried it for years until it eventually disintegrated about six months before the second attack.

East Tyrone continued to be a dangerous area throughout and our Battalion suffered a high level of incidents, murders of off-duty personnel, attacks on patrols, and against our bases.

Some things stick out in your mind like when I arrived home one night and my wife had bought lots of clothing from a travelling gypsy. Some months before a travelling gypsy had asked my wife to use our toilet and she said no that her husband did not allow it and he said he would put a curse on her husband. So when the gypsy arrived selling clothes she thought it better to buy from him just in case and you dare not laugh out loud, especially when she said that I had been shot once and she did not want it ever to happen again. Another time just as I was about to go on duty (you wore your uniform and travelled wearing a civilian coat over it) a work colleague who I would class as a Republican arrived at the house with a friend of his and asked if I would solder a leak in his car radiator. I was in uniform and said 'Yes of course. Come on in' and all they said was 'I see you're on duty tonight Glen', not with any malice. That's just the way it was in the countryside.

Our neighbour was arrested out near my father's farm when an on the run terrorist, Ryan, was found hiding out in his house. This was a major success but it made you wonder was our neighbour responsible for setting me up.

We had moved from Cookstown to live at the home farm where I was born on the east side of the town. I worked out that if the IRA were to attack me again I was most vulnerable leaving for work in the morning to go to Cookstown where I was employed with the Housing Executive. The laneway I lived on was about half a mile off the road and it merged with a neighbour's; I kept the hedges short giving me a view of the area and the main road. The perfect place I believed for an attack to be mounted was from our neighbour's two storey house, down on the road. A gun team could easily take over the house and mount an attack on me turning out onto the road to head west into the town. I walked through a number of ambush scenarios and in all cases I had recognised that if I survived the initial burst of gunfire, injured or not I would exit the car and roll into the drainage ditch which I maintained was deep enough to provide me with some degree of protection. I had changed and upgraded my privately owned protection weapon to a semi-automatic pistol, now with a magazine able to hold more ammunition than the revolver.

The morning of the 19th March 1987 was clear with a light skiff of snow still lying in the fields. I went through my routine checking the outer area visually then checked my vehicle for an under vehicle booby-trap; my mind was occupied with work issues as I drove along the laneway. Before leaving, the children wanted to come with me to get into school a bit earlier, but I made some excuse and headed on, on my own. Emerging onto the road without stopping, which is always the way I played it, I saw in the distance the school bus heading west to the town too. My pistol was holstered and I was changing into second gear when I saw a green car coming from my neighbour's lane onto the road in front of me on my right hand side. I thought this was my neighbour for he drove an identical car. This notion was quickly kicked into touch as the car sped into the road in front of me facing towards the east blocking me and screeched to a halt. There were three people in the car all wearing balaclava masks and I thought, as I was taking all this information in, not again. There is something very frightening about masked terrorists and the front passenger and rear passenger door behind the driver were thrown open as I stood on the brakes of my car, my hand on the door handle to get out. Two gunmen emerged from the car armed with G3 7.62mm assault rifles and opened fire with their automatic weapons at my car, just two or three car lengths away from me. My car vibrated from the burst of automatic fire hitting it. I could see the front passenger side gunman leaning between the open door and using the roof of the car to steady his aim and he was wearing a green army-style parka; below the door I could see his trousers tucked into the top of his boots.

My thoughts were 'This is it this time' three well-armed terrorists, I was totally out-gunned; my chances of survival were very slim but I was moving, I had rehearsed and trained for this ambush many times. I dived out onto the road as the rounds pounded into the car and at this moment my left wrist was shattered. I drew my pistol in my right hand and using the car as cover, keeping below the window line, I went down the side and round the back of the car and dived headlong into the drainage ditch on my left side (Linford Christie could not have done it any faster).

Peering out from the ditch my car blocked my view of the terrorist vehicle and I crawled forward along the ditch till the terrorist car came into view, and I returned fire shooting single handed firing three quick shots; I hoped that this would frighten them off.

The second gunman in the rear took cover and took no further part in the attack. The front gunman readjusted his aim onto my position in the ditch. We were about 10 or 15 metres distance apart and I tried desperately to hit and kill the gunman. The rounds being fired at my position were tearing up the ground around me, lifting sods of grass and throwing dirt in my face, rounds were going over my head and cutting the hedge and bushes to ribbons behind me. During the fire fight I could see the gunman recoil from the rounds he was firing, the driver was revving the engine at full blast and sinking lower and lower in the car till he was peering out below the steering wheel as I fired at them. The front gunman was yelling into the car, readjusting his aim. It was obvious he had done this before and he was not going to stop. I knew I could not win this fire fight and, low on ammo, I did not want to have to change mags at this distance and although I had practised changing mags with one hand they would be on top of me when they realised I was not firing. After this I fired single aimed shots at the front gunman, trying to hit and kill him; never in my life before or after have I ever wanted to kill another person so much.

The front gunman yelled into the car, fired one more burst at my position and slid into the front passenger seat, and the car moved off. I was fully expecting the rear seat gunman to rake the bottom of the ditch I was in as they moved past my position, as they had the advantage. I lay down in the bottom of the ditch my gun on my chest, I would fire the last of my rounds in the magazine as the car slowed giving the rear gunman a clear view of me. The gunman's car did not slow but accelerated away; it was only then as I turned to follow the car that I saw the school bus pulled up behind my car.

Pumped full of adrenalin, I came out on the road behind the school bus. The gunman's car stopped about 200 metres away. I dropped to one knee and fired one round at the car. I could not work out why they would do that manoeuver unless one gunman had stayed behind to finish me off and was in the hedgerow somewhere. I started a frantic search of the hedges; I was convinced this was the case.

People were out on the road, my neighbours whose house had been taken over by the gun team during the night were shouting but I took no notice; I saw my car's rear tyre was shot out. I jumped into it and accelerated away; my aim was to go to Cookstown, alert the Security Forces and get the follow up started. About a mile down the road I saw an Army mobile patrol. I stopped them, told them what had happened and to get the follow up going and trap the gun team. The patrol commander wanted to give me medical assistance but I was having none of this; I would go on to the police station in Cookstown.

There in the debrief I was bleeding from my left arm where I was wounded, my left wrist shattered and still armed with my pistol and in great pain, I felt terrible, but I had survived.

I was rushed to hospital and my family were told of the situation.

The doctors and nurses working in the Accident and Emergency Department were very skilled and would have dealt with the mayhem of terrorist atrocities in East Tyrone and Mid Ulster. Straight away I knew I was in good hands when I reached hospital. I was in pain, terrible pain from the gunshot wound and although the adrenalin was wearing off my mind was still focused on the attack, so sudden and violent, and the inner strength I found to function and keep in control.

I was no longer in control now; I let go, I was in the hands of others, a team who calmly and efficiently worked on me. Once the pain relief was administered I had little recollection of events and was relieved to see my wife and others later in the morning.

My stay in hospital meant I would have to have an armed guard, such was the potential threat from terrorists, and my Company provided part-time UDR soldiers to cover the detail. There was little to do, time dragged by in hospital and I was recovering well. I used to feel sorry for the night time guard who would more than likely have to go straight to their work the next day. Sometimes I would make them rest, hop up on my hospital bed and take over the detail myself. It gave me something to do, kept me occupied.

When eventually I went home from hospital the routine of a busy family life soon took over. I saw my neighbours whose house had been taken over by the terrorist gang during that night and from where the gang had mounted their murder attempt on my life the next morning. They were a devout Christian couple who told me they prayed and sang hymns to the gang through that night and told them that by doing the devil's work they would have to answer one day to Christ our Lord. A poem was recited about a terrorist's testimony to the dedicated young men of East Tyrone PIRA and one of the murder gang said 'You will be writing a poem about this' – and they did.

They also told me that at daybreak on the day of the attack they overheard the gun team leader discussing my routine: 'The curtains will be opened and Glen will scan the area from his house. Then he will proceed outside, check his car and go back to the house'. Obviously I had been under intense observation for some time. The day before the attack when I was driving into work I saw a known Cookstown suspect in a car close to the RUC Station, parked on a piece of ground where an attack on the police station had been mounted before. I went straight to the UDR Centre and reported this, thinking of course that the RUC Station was being targeted when in reality PIRA was confirming that my vehicle, route and timings had not changed.

I had no car; my own car was beyond repair so I borrowed my father's car and again I was put on basic sick pay from my full-time job. There was no other income and I was given a £1000 loan from the Benevolent Fund which would have to be paid back from any future compensation claim. In all honesty there was little support from the Battalion but we did not expect anything; we had volunteered, many other members of the Battalion and their families were under just as much threat and pressure or dead.

One night I was driving home, my family were with me, our children in the back and my wife beside me. It was late and we were driving on the lane-way to our house, when I looked into the back and saw my children crouched down in the foot well lying as flat as they could. I asked them what they were doing. They said they were taking cover from the gunmen if I was attacked. I stopped the car and burst into tears. I told my wife I was so, so sorry for what I had done to my family, that I had been so selfish so dogmatic always stating that no terrorist would drive me out of our home, that I would be taken out in a box first. I told my wife that I would ask at work for a transfer to another area and would sell our home.

My wife agreed and was relieved that I had taken this decision. My employers were very helpful and my request went through; now we had to sell our home. This proved difficult; we had built our home on my father's farm and it was not going to be easy to sell due to the attack on my life, there would be a very limited source of potential buyers. I completed a private sale and a UDR soldier offered me storage space for our possessions until we had another property sorted close to my new place of work.

I remained on desk duties until I was discharged from 8 UDR on medical grounds in 1989.

Glen's wife, Marion, shares her recollections:

My father had served in 5 UDR and shortly after I started going out with Glen there was a shooting in Coalisland. His father was in the Land Rover and he jumped over a wall, so that was my first encounter with the Security Forces. Glen was only 18 or 19.

We got married in 1976 and had our daughter later that year and then young Glen a year later.

The first attack on Glen was on the 22nd March 1978. We lived in Tullywiggan, between Cookstown and Tullyhogue and Glen worked for the Housing Executive. I had an old twin-tub washing machine which wouldn't work and I had a heap of nappies to wash. The fire wouldn't light and the youngsters were yapping! Then Glen came in and said he'd been called out to Ardboe. He went upstairs and took the flak jacket and a polo neck jumper belonging to me. He doesn't remember that, but I do! I never got it back because it was cut off him!

I was busy getting on with the housework when I saw a black police car coming in on two wheels. Next thing a police woman came and said my husband had been shot. We had no phone, nothing. But I knew in my head that he took the flak jacket, but nobody else knew that at that particular time.

His father worked at the Cement Works and the police car took me to collect his mother and then go and lift his dad. You must remember that Glen's younger brother and sister were only seven and ten at the time.

Then I was taken down to Magherafelt Hospital. I have absolutely no idea who looked after our children while I was at the hospital. I've gone over and over that in my head, but I can't remember. It had to be a neighbour: the baby was only seventeen months old.

I could hear Glen talking but his mother couldn't understand why he was still talking if he had been shot. She thought he was dead. The wound was a millimetre away from his heart and it had done some damage to his lungs. He was kept in Magherafelt for about a week and was guarded by the UDR and the police. His sister was a student nurse at the time in the hospital and the newspaper reporters were trying to get in to interview him. There were some other nurses who would have let them in, but she was very protective of Glen.

When he came out of hospital he wasn't taken straight home; I had to drive him from the place where he left the Housing Executive yard in Cookstown to the place of the incident. He wanted to go back, he HAD to go back and that was the only thing in his head. Quite honestly, to this day I don't know how he did it. I drove and he kept talking, nervous talking, talking it through. He had stolen a car to get away and he drove it to Coagh and crashed it there. The first person who came to him was the mother of another UDR man, so you believe in fate.

I was very lucky because Archie Martin[14] and Day[15] and Shirley lived beside us. Mrs Gillis came and sorted out the clothes and washed them and the Martins all rallied round to help me. Shirley Martin was my neighbour, but I didn't really know her. She was married to an officer and Archie, her brother-in-law, was very senior and my husband was a Lance Corporal so you respected those people. Then one day, maybe nine or ten weeks after the incident, she mentioned the Benevolent Fund to me and I asked her what did she mean? I had never heard of the Benevolent Fund. She asked if I was getting help and I said 'No'. I said that my parents were helping to support us even though they didn't have a lot of money, but my father was a good gardener and grew vegetables and so on. She said: 'If I ask Archie to talk to you will you tell him what the financial situation is?' I said: 'I've nothing to hide'. So Archie came and spoke to me and I told him I didn't have any income apart from the sick pay Glen was getting from work, but he wasn't getting any UDR money. I didn't work and we had two small children. Then Mr Monteith[16] came; I think he was the Adjutant (*he was the Admin WO C Company*). I was given money to buy a washing machine. Fred Mitchell,[17] who was shot in Coagh, was my coal man, and he threw a couple of bags of coal in and people rallied round. Major

---

14 Maj Archibald (Archie) Alexander Martin MBE UD 1924-2005: 8 UDR 1970-81: Second in Command 8 UDR 1977-81: Rates Office Manager.
15 Capt David (Day) George Alexander Martin UD 1934-2005: 8 UDR 1970-89: Accountant.
16 WO2 James (Jim) Henry Monteith 1930-: 8 UDR 1970-77: (5 UDR until 1983): MID.
17 Pte Fred Mitchell 1937-2006: 8 UDR 1971-82: Coal Merchant: Shot and seriously wounded while driving his coal lorry on 30th January 1981: He suffered brain damage, loss of speech, and severe

Turner[18] was very kind too. Then we went to a solicitor and put in a claim and we thought we were rich because we got £5,000 for all that. We didn't have very much debt because my attitude was 'If we didn't have it, we didn't have it'. My mother and father-in-law were very good to me as well as my mum and dad. Even just simple things like buying me a packet of washing powder.

Glen had always been Army minded so I knew what I was marrying, but when you're young it goes over your head and I didn't realise the reality would be so bad. We had two small children, but I didn't work and where was the money going to come from? Nobody came near us. How were we going to live? Fresh air, for months! I had to go every week and get his sick pay and I remember this Roman Catholic man he worked with, stopped me and gave me a wee religious talisman to give to Glen. Glen carried that about for years and he was very fond of that man. But the reality is that somebody he worked with had set him up, because they knew what he would do. I remember he said to me a few weeks beforehand that he'd been somewhere and he felt afterwards that it was a dry run to make sure that he would be the plumber and to see how he would react to the call out. When he went to the house in Ardboe that day, he was invited into the house. It was a set-up.

Glen's wound, the one near his lungs, wept for a long time. It was terrible for a long time. He had to get skin grafted and when that happened it was hard to watch a man cry. It wasn't the shooting, it was the after effects. He felt his career was over and he wouldn't be able to soldier again. That was really hard for him. Then there was the sweats and getting up at night, the nightmares, locking the doors, and the 9 mm under the pillow. When I think about it, people don't know how lucky they are nowadays. I have to be honest; it was very tight. Many times, we hadn't tuppence. But I looked at the McLarnons who had lost their children, but at least I still had Glen. (*McLarnon children were a brother and sister in their late teens or early twenties. The girl was engaged to be married that year. It was a Saturday afternoon and they were driving back towards Stewartstown from Cookstown when they came upon what they thought was a road accident; a car had gone off the road. They stopped to give assistance and were both killed outright when they went over to the car. It was a PIRA trap for the police.*)

Our social life was always to do with the UDR. We went to the Wives' Club once a month and that was a godsend because it was the only outlet you had. It didn't matter whether it was the Colonel's wife or whoever, there was no divide and you could just have a bit of chat and craic and you were all in the same

---

paralysis of the right side, which confined him to a wheelchair: He died from these injuries on 7th June 2006.
18 Maj (Albert) Samuel Turner MBE UD 1932-96: 8 UDR 1971-91: Second in Command 8 UDR 1985-91: Meat Inspector, Ministry of Agriculture.

situation. It was something we all really enjoyed. We went away on outings. We were on 'The Price is Right'. I remember that in the hotel we stayed in, we went upstairs to the bar. There was a dance, or something, but we didn't realise it was 'Divorced Singles' night! We really enjoyed the craic.

In 1987, we were in the process of getting planning permission to build a bungalow at Glen's home place at Drumcraw. We had saved to build it and we didn't have a mortgage and Glen was doing a lot of the work himself. At that time, I worked for a clothing company in Cookstown. The girls from Kildress and Ardboe would have talked about where they were going that weekend, for example, but we never talked about what we were going to do. Today I work in an environment where I make decisions based on policy and procedures alone. I don't take sides and that's my attitude. It wasn't the likes of an ordinary neighbour that set my husband up; it was a person belonging to the Provisional IRA.

When the second attack happened, on the 19th March 1987, Glen was still working for the Housing Executive and my mother-in-law, Granny Espie and my daughter, Sharon, usually travelled with him in the mornings. My mother-in-law went to the UDR and my daughter went to school. That particular morning, it was frosty, and Granny Espie said she didn't feel well. Something had happened at work and Glen was going in to deal with it so he told Sharon to get the bus. So Glen left and was driving down the road and the next thing 'tat, tat, tat, tat….' I thought: 'There's something not right here'. His brother Brice Junior was in his car and I saw a bus stopping, but it still didn't register. Brice came running towards the house shouting 'Shooting, shooting!' He was in such a panic he crashed the car and he actually jumped through the window. I went down to Glen's mother and I told her something had happened. She went hysterical and then there was a phone call to say it was Glen. He was shot. I must have phoned Dessie Gordon[19] but I kept thinking I should have pressed the 'panic button' at the house. For whatever reason, I always associated that button with night time. Glen was at the end of the lane so he wasn't in sight, but there was something about this bus stopping when that happened that made me suspicious. He says I'm wrong, but I still maintain that the weapons were taken away in the bus.

Then there was a suspicious device, a schoolbag or something and we couldn't get out. We were stuck at the house; it was a scene of crime and so on. He was taken away to the military wing of Musgrave Park Hospital but I had no car, because it had been shot up. That was a real hullaballoo from the UDR – it was incredible – trying to get a car and it took a long time to get a vehicle. That night we managed to get to see Glen in hospital.

---

19 Sgt Desmond (Dessie) Gordon BEM 1958-: 8 UDR 1977-90: Car Repair Business Owner.

I could maybe forgive the IRA because Glen wore a uniform, but I still wonder what would have happened if Glen's mother and our daughter had been in the car. They knew that they travelled with him and they were prepared to kill them. He knew the consequences of wearing a uniform but my daughter and my mother-in-law were innocent. I will never get over that, because the person that set them up was across the road, a neighbour, who knew who pulled the curtains, knew our routine. Mr Crozier's house was taken over. He lit the fire and he preached the Gospel to these boys. They used the same colour of grey car as the woman down the lane. By good fortune Glen's instinct and professionalism and what he was taught kicked in. Even before that, what we made our children do was awful, because there was a refuse dump nearby and if there were any strange cars in the area, the youngsters would have played around there and they took down the numbers of the cars.

We have never really talked openly to our children about this. We have put that in the closet, which is wrong, because we're putting history in the closet. I don't think Glen's nieces and nephews really know what happened and neither do my nieces and nephews. It just doesn't affect the person; it affects the family circle as well. It affected my mother because she was good friends with Glen's sister. Glen's mother died of a broken heart and those incidents did not help. Twice her son had been targeted and there were other different incidents like mortar attacks in Coalisland involving her husband.

We lived in a bungalow so we asked for security. What we got was a proposal for net curtains. Raymond Glendinning[20] held a fundraiser in the UDR centre to raise money and we got a door. That's what we got to try and stay in a family home. No cameras, bullet-proof glass, reinforcements, nothing. Other people around us were getting different things and you wondered what you had to do to get help. We were offered a house in Newmillls for a few months, but that was all.

Glen wouldn't accept that as it meant leaving the family farm and so on. Then one evening as we were going round to visit Granny and Grandpa Espie, Glen looked round and Sharon and Glen were cowering down in the back of the car and Glen turned to me and said: 'I can't do this anymore. We're going to have to do something'. It wasn't what we wanted to do, but we had two young children and what sort of life were we going to have? I worked in a shop and the boss was very good to me.

All those years ago, I was more naïve and more trusting and felt that the Benevolent Fund would know to give you help, without being asked. But when somebody gave you £5,000 in compensation and thought that was enough to

---

20 Sgt (Raymond) John Glendinning 1956-: 8 UDR 1974-92: (R Irish until 1996): Van Salesman.

keep you going! How was I to know that fund was there and there was nobody coming to tell me?

We then decided to sell the bungalow. Granny and Granda Espie were still living on the farm. But there was a problem. We couldn't sell it on the open market through the Scheme for Purchase of Evacuated Dwellings (SPED) because it could go to anybody, including Republicans. There wasn't a problem about having a Catholic on the lane – that was not the issue – but you could have had a Republican buy it. Putting the house up for sale was one of the hardest things to do, because that's part of the family heritage gone and then the farm had to be sold later. It didn't affect me as much then as it does now because that is lost and can't be replaced.

This was 1987. Glen got a job in Ballyclare and we bought a house near Doagh. I think we got money from the Benevolent Fund to help us to move. The Reverend McClintock of Kilbride Presbyterian Church, near Doagh, was a real gentleman and he did a lot to help us. Glen got his compensation for his injuries some years later and to this day, whenever you get your money, if you have got money from the Benevolent Fund, it has to be paid back. The first thing I bought was a granddaughter clock. It was made by a wee man in Ahoghill and the verse was: 'Time in thy hand'.

I think Glen went back to the UDR for a year and then had to leave on medical grounds. He couldn't use his hands properly and had lost sensation in his fingers. He had to wear a glove for a long time. He had always wanted to open his own business but because of his injuries and getting constant chest infections he couldn't do that. He then went to be a charge hand with the Housing Executive and honestly, if it hadn't been for the Housing Executive, we'd have had nothing. It tests your marriage to the very limit.

Glen took up running and the children joined Boys' Brigade and those kinds of organisations but I stayed in the house for weeks and weeks. Eventually I met a lady called Doris Crawford, who called on behalf of the church. She was my salvation. Then I decided I'd better do something with my life and I got a wee job. It was a form of depression and probably delayed reaction to everything. I'd spent all that time trying to be strong for everyone else.

We only moved back because Glen's brother was killed in a motorcycle accident. A few years ago there was a series of death threats and nobody knew who was sending them, but as Glen said: 'When the IRA shot me, they didn't tell me they were coming, so why would they send me death threats?' But it cost us £1,500 to put a fence up at the back of the house. Glen retired at 53, because the only place he would be vulnerable was when he was going to work.

I'm not like the Bloody Sunday people who are looking for revenge. My husband's case was turned down because they didn't think it was worthy of investigation to find out who shot him TWICE. It was a year after the shooting before the police interviewed me. One year. The gun that was used was one of the guns that was used in Loughgall; it had been used previously to shoot Harry Henry[21] (*civilian building contractor shot dead outside his home*). I think it was Lynagh's.[22]

Sometimes your partner is in this closed box and everything is 'Me, me, me'. I don't say that in a selfish way, but that's reality.

The UDR were going out, not to get Catholic people, but to get the Provisional IRA and to protect the community from terrorists, no matter which side they were on. This is the bit that I can't understand, and of course there were bad apples, but our lives would not be what they are today had it not been for those men and women.

Sammy Brush 13th June 1981

Sammy Brush[23] served in A (Aughnacloy) Company 8 UDR. Most of the men and women in that Company lived close to the border with the Republic of Ireland; they faced an internal threat from East Tyrone PIRA and a cross-border threat from on-the-run terrorists. In countering these threats they paid a high price. The Company was a very close knit team with a frontier and committed spirit.

His Company Commander, Major Ken Maginnis, recalls:

> I was concerned about Sammy because he was a postman: his routine took him to some high risk areas and was very predictable. One day I decided to keep an eye on him when he made deliveries. I watched him from a vantage point on a higher road. When he put the post through the letter box and turned his back to leave, the door opened. It seemed to me that at this point he was very vulnerable.

---

21 +Harry Henry 1935-87: Civilian contractor who worked for Army and RUC: Killed 21st April 1987.
22 Seamus (Jim) Lynagh 1956-1987: Tully, Co Monaghan: In 1973 badly injured in a premature explosion of a 5 lb bomb at Moy: Sentenced to 10 years' imprisonment for possession of explosives (*Dungannon Observer* 29th June 1974): Released 1978: Suspected of involvement in killing of former UDR soldier in 1980, tried in Dublin but acquitted: In 1981 charged with IRA Membership but bailed and went on the run: Sentenced to five years' imprisonment for possession of ammunition (Monaghan 1982) and released in 1986 (Magill article 30th October 1982 and Urban, *Big Boys' Rules*): (*Tyrone Courier* 21st April 1982 and Ed Moloney, *A Secret History of the IRA*): Senior figure involved in planning and execution of an extensive assault on RUC Loughgall. He was killed in this operation, 8th May 1987: A Heckler Koch 7.62 rifle recovered at the scene was used in the attack on Glen Espie 19th March 1987 (*Tyrone Courier* 13th May 1987).
23 CSgt Samuel (Sammy) John Brush MBE BEM 1942-: 8 UDR 1970-92: (R Irish until 1997): GOC's Commendation: Postman: Councillor Dungannon District Council 1981-93 and 2005-15.

I noticed he was not wearing his flak jacket so when I was next at the base I had the Company Sergeant Major march Sammy in and made it very clear that he had to wear one or I would not allow him to stay in the Company. He protested that it was difficult to do so under his shirt but in the end he agreed. I then asked to see his Personal Protection Weapon (PPW). When he produced it I saw it was a .22" Walther, the standard issue weapon; small and light but almost useless. Most people at risk carried their own, heavier PPW, so I encouraged him to buy one too.

About six weeks later Sammy was delivering to an address. When he had put the post through the door and turned his back to leave, the door opened and a shot was fired at him. It hit him in the back but he was saved by his flak jacket. He was faced by another gunman who fired two shots at him – one hit him in the flak jacket and the other went into his shoulder. Unable to use his right hand he fired back using his left and hit the gunman facing him in the spine as he tried to escape.

McGeough[24] managed to escape over the border to Monaghan and then to Dublin where the bullet was removed. He then fled to Europe.

Some years later Sammy was on duty at a polling booth in Northern Ireland when McGeough walked in. Sammy told the RUC that this man had shot him all these years ago; McGeough was arrested and served two years, the maximum under the Belfast Agreement.

Sammy tells his story:

I was reared on a farm just outside Aughnacloy. My father was a farmer on the Ballygawley road out of Aughnacloy and I went to school at Aughnacloy Primary School. A lot of the time we would have walked. It was a very long lane in to the house; it was nine tenths of a mile long.

I was actually born across the border in the townland of Derrylavick, which is just on the border at the Ravella Bridge. You turned in right at the Ravella Bridge and there was a lane went along there, more or less along the riverside.

---

24 Terence Gerard McGeough 1958-: Dungannon: PIRA: Escaped from Police Custody Monaghan 1981 (*Tyrone Courier* 8th July 1981): Arrested on Dutch/German border 1988 with two AK47s in car (*Tyrone Courier* 7th September 1988): Held in Germany four years for offences against British Army: Extradited to USA for attempting to purchase SAMs (in 1983) (Oppenheimer, *IRA: The Bombs and the Bullets*): Imprisoned and released in 1996 and deported to ROI. (*Wikipedia*): Arrested (NI) in 2007 and convicted in 2011 for attempted murder of Sammy Brush and related offences (1981) (18th February 2011 Crown Court in Northern Ireland STE8060): Sentenced to 20 years' imprisonment for attempted murder of Sammy Brush, 10 years for possession of firearms, and seven years for membership of PIRA all to run concurrently: Released after two years in 2013 (*Wikipedia* and *Belfast Telegraph* 31st January 2013).

And that's where I was born and then in 1946 (I was born in '42) they moved to Dernabane outside Aughnacloy. That's where I grew up and that's where all my memories are.

So, as I said, I went to Aughnacloy Primary School and then to Dungannon Royal. I left the Royal after I did my Senior; I got Maths and Physics – that was the two subjects I passed in – and I left school then and started to work on my uncle's farm. And between that and working at home (I had two brothers you see, and they were working on the farm as well), I eventually decided there wasn't room for me, so I got a job in Moygashel. And I worked there for, I suppose eight or nine years, till I was made redundant and then I had joined the USC in 1960 and I served in it until it was stood down on 30th April '70. And I had already applied to join the UDR and I got enlisted in it in May of that year. Whenever I was made redundant in Moygashel there wasn't a place for me to go full-time on the UDR at that particular time but they brought in this full-time/part-time and that was basically to guard the police stations.

I remember when they started that and I went to Aughnacloy Police Station and I was Guard Commander there. There was three shifts and I had one shift, but I was overall Commander. We had to build the sandbags; we had to do all the donkey work and at that time, as well, I think that was in August 1971, there was the division of 6 UDR into 8 UDR and they took over the Youth Hall at Aughnacloy and all the work that had to go into that. So between it and the Police Station, I was there until about February and then full-time in the Company from that on till 1977, when I left full-time. I was Staff Sergeant and I had been doing the Permanent Staff Instructor (PSI) and the Admin work as well, for there was no Admin WO in the Company at that particular time. I left that and got a job with the Post Office and because the wife had a shop in Ballygawley, what was in my head was that the old Postmaster in Ballygawley was reaching retirement age and I thought that perhaps the Post Office would give me the option. That's how that came about and I took the job that was made vacant when Alan Anderson was injured in Clogher whenever Eva Martin was killed (*mortar attack on 6 UDR at the Deanery in Clogher in 1974*) and he and the wife had been blown up going out the lane when he was going to his work one morning. When he retired on medical grounds, I took that vacancy and continued on part-time Sergeant in the Company in Aughnacloy. I worked at that until '81 until the shooting. Everybody knew that I was a target and an easy target, because of what had happened to other postmen.

So I was as well-prepared as you could be prepared in a case like that. I was living in Ballygawley and it was dead handy – I was walking down the street to the Post Office and getting the van and it was an easy target. I must say that the Regular unit that was in Aughnacloy at the time did quite a bit in trying to give me some cover. They even went out with me with radios to see where there were 'blind spots' or to see was it worthwhile giving me a radio. But it wasn't worthwhile, because on the routes where I was travelling there was only bits and pieces where you could get coverage. Nowadays it would be a different story, but at that time, that's the way it was.

I had stood for the Council in Dungannon and the election was in May of '81 and I got elected there (elected as Ulster Unionist Councillor for Clogher on Dungannon District Council 20th May 1981). But as I say, I was as well prepared as I could be, because Ken Maginnis had said to me maybe six months before that: 'I'm going to buy my own weapon because these things are useless and I'd advise you to buy one as well'. This was the Walther G2 combat weapon. So I did buy a Smith and Wesson, a .38 Smith and Wesson revolver, with a five-chamber, not a six-chamber, because I wanted something that was easily enough concealed but was going to be able to be used whether I had two hands or one hand. That was my point on that one. And as well as that, I carried loose rounds in each trouser pocket, five rounds in each pocket. I also wore the light body armour all the time when I was out, even though it was a torture, especially in the warm weather. That one was the first one that came out. It didn't have a removable cover, it just had to be sponged down every evening, for you would have sweated and as well as that, it was completely tight. There was no elastic so your movement was restricted. I carried the weapon in a shoulder holster and that's what stood to me when the incident did happen.

I drove onto McGarvey's street with a white envelope addressed for a Mrs Mary McGarvey, first class, Cravney Irish, Ballygawley, it's Armaloughy Road, Ballygawley anyway. There was two other houses in that lane but I had no other letters for anybody in that lane that day. It was a Saturday; it was our UDR Open Day at Killymeal and I was rushing round to get finished to bring my young son over to it and only it was a first class letter it wouldn't have been delivered that day. There was nothing that really aroused my suspicions apart from two small things, but it didn't alert me at the same time. Mickey Russell drove a Volkswagen Beetle, a green one, and his car would be there, maybe a couple of days a week, so it wasn't odd to see his car. The only thing that struck me as a bit funny was that it was a bit further down the street than it would normally be. And the other thing – when I was getting out of the van I could see movement in the house and the thing that struck me as a bit funny was that the front door was closed. Now in warm weather, if there was anybody at home, usually the front door was lying open, you know, but it was closed that day.

And then the next thing was, the gunman came out. I was just turning away from the door when he fired the first shot and it hit me here (upper left chest) and the body armour stopped that one. It was like the kick of a donkey; it spun me round but I was already turning anyway, and then the next shot missed the body armour and went right through the right lung and came out in the centre of the back. The body armour stopped it going out all right and that was the one that put this hand (the right hand) out of action. It cut the nerves going to the right hand but I didn't know that. It was just like a bit of a sting, you know. I just kept going. The vehicle was sitting with the engine running and the door open, but I ran round the back of the vehicle and the other boy – I knew there was two, because when I was trying to get this weapon out, and the hand was coming out without the weapon and I couldn't understand that for two or three attempts and I still kept going, but I could hear the firing. The Post Office jacket I was wearing had eight bullet holes, but there was only four hit me. There was two hit me in the back as well, but the body armour stopped them. They damaged the kidneys quite a bit. The shock waves from stopping these things reverberate through your whole body.

At that stage I knew I had to get the weapon out with the left hand and that was a problem. But I got it out anyway and I just turned round and I fired two shots at one of them – he must have been twenty yards away, but he went back down the street again. I had run up and out onto the lane and headed up towards these other houses. That was the direction I had gone.

I don't think they expected me to move. And when I got the weapon out and I fired the two shots, the first guy he got out of the road then; he went back down towards the house. I could hear then this wrecking and rattling in the hedge. Where I was, I thought there must have been somebody trying to get through that and I couldn't see because in the month of June, those hedges are in full growth. You couldn't see a thing. But I fired two shots at that, where the noise was and that noise stopped. And then I knew I was then in the situation where here I am, having difficulty breathing. I've fired four rounds so there's only one left and I have to get re-loaded if I can. So I managed to get the cylinder open and got the four empty cases out. And if I had only had spare rounds in the right-hand pocket I couldn't have done it, so it just shows you how it all worked out. So I got the four rounds into it again, and closed up and I knew the only way out was the way I came in and that was back to the van. I had to go back for that was the only way out for me, for if I had been gone out towards the road I'd have been tempted to go on and I wouldn't have been fit to. Whatever was there, I was going to have to face it. That was it. But there was nothing there only Mrs McGarvey standing at the door. And I got into the van, the engine was still running, and reversed out and drove to Ballygawley Police Station, about a mile and a half, and I just sat and blew the horn. But I can't remember crossing the A4 and that was a busy road at that time. And how I got across it I just can't remember.

When I was going down the Armaloughy Road, from McGarvey's, there was a fairly steep hill with a left-hand bend at the bottom and then it turned right again. It wasn't an 'S' bend, but there was a fairly sharp bend and there was a two-storey house on the side of the hill. And I thought to myself: 'I mightn't make it round this bend here', so I fired a shot out of the Post Office van to try to alert the people in the house. But they were in Portrush that day and there wasn't a soul about the place. Nobody ever heard shooting and in any other circumstances, if I had fired a shot, they would have heard it from miles away!

I was losing blood and I could taste it in my mouth. There wasn't blood in my mouth, but it was the blood going into the lung and I thought I was tasting it. That lung was punctured straight through so I was losing blood into the lung and out of it as well. I was in danger of passing out, so as I say, I just sat there. George Gilliland was one of the policemen in Ballygawley Police Station (he was later killed in an attack on the same station) and I said: 'I've been shot'. He went back in and raised the alarm, but there was only two of them on duty and the other fella, I think it was only his second or third week and he was down in Gervais's (supermarket) getting something for their lunch! And George was on his own in the police station. And he got the car out and Jim Kerr, who was another postman, came along and between George and Jim (I was fit to help them a bit) they got me out of the van and into the police car. George drove me to Dungannon to the hospital. He did a great job – he was driving, he was manning the radio, was trying to get information from me and trying to pass it on and he didn't even know where the hospital was. I says: 'Well, go up into Church Street'. At Church Street there was a barrier and there was a couple of policemen there. And one of the policemen hopped in and we finished the journey.

So whenever they got me in there then, they just cut the clothes off me and gave me a transfusion and put up another drip. The doctor says: 'I'm going to have to give you an injection now to put you out for I want to put a drain into the lung'. I says: 'Just you put the drain into the lung and never mind the injection'. He says: 'You'll not be fit to'. I says: 'You go on ahead, and I'll tell you if I'm not fit'. So boys, I didn't think the lung was that far in, but when he put this in between the ribs and into the lung, I thought it was never going to stop! I wanted to stay conscious as long as I could because I hadn't seen any of the family or I hadn't seen anybody and I says: 'I'm going to stay alert as long as I can'.

It was the Postmistress that rang up and she told my wife, but there was very few police on duty that day. It was a Saturday and the fella that was left behind, he was just learning. It wasn't any of the reserve police, because they would have known the area.

Well then, they packed me off to the Royal (Victoria Hospital, Belfast) and by the time they had finished with me in there in the theatre in Dungannon, my wife and step-daughter had arrived and they seen me whenever I was getting into the ambulance and they followed on down to the Royal. When I got to the Royal I was coming round a bit; the blood that I had been getting and all that… And they brought me into the theatre and it was Gibbons who treated me. He was there and they told me they were going to have to put me over and do surgery. I knew nothing then till about midday the next day. I was in the Intensive Care Ward and there was a nurse with me all the time for about a week. There was a physiotherapist – she was the name of Patton – she gave me some abuse! But it was all good for me, surely. There was a lot of stuff came out of them lungs – it was serious. You were coughing up and she was pummelling you. I used to say to her: 'God help the man that ever gets you, for you'll give him some hammerin'!'

I didn't claim to have hit anybody, unfortunately, because I didn't know whether I had hit anybody or not and if I had said: 'Look, I think I have hit somebody', maybe the reaction might have been different … I don't know. McGeough and another man (*Vincent McAnespie[25] was charged with the attempted murder of Sammy Brush and other offences but was acquitted*) was the two and McGeough had been hit. And McAnespie's granny lived further up that lane and his uncle lived at the other end of that lane so they had plenty of safe houses to go to. He was on home territory there. And then, you see, down at Peter Russell's,[26] where they hid the weapons, someone drove them down, out that lane. They had went out from the Golan Road to the Armaghloughy Road – that lane went right through, but we never would have went through as postmen, because there was a part where it went up along a field… there was gates and stuff like that on it.

Commenting, the interviewer said:

> Well they were in their local area. They had safe houses to go to, they didn't expect you to survive the initial hit on the doorstep, so you were a bit of a problem for them. And now they've got an injured bloke as well. They never expected you to fire back – to be in a position to fire back and they weren't capable of a follow-up. He then asked Sammy a number of questions about the incident:

Q. Were they masked?
Sammy: Oh aye, they were.

Q. Did the gunman come out of the house or round the side of the house?
Sammy: The house was a two-bay, single storey house. Unfortunately, I never had a photograph of that house because it makes more sense when you're telling people about it. But it's gone now and there's a new house in its place. There was a lean-to

---

25 Vincent McAnespie 1963-: Aughnacloy: Arrested 2007 and charged with attempted murder of Sammy Brush and related offences (1981): Found not guilty on all charges (18th February 2011 Crown Court in Northern Ireland STE8060).
26 Peter John Russell 1932-2007: Aughnacloy: Joiner: Convicted 28th May 1982 for possession of two .45 Webley revolvers and ammunition. (*Tyrone Courier* 24th March 1982 and Crown Court in Northern Ireland STE8060 18th February 2011).

shed at the lower gable of it where apparently they kept sticks and turf and stuff like that for the fire. There was a door out of the living room to that shed, out of the other gable. Now that's where the first gunman came out. He went through the shed and came up from the gable of the house. He was face on to me when I was turning and if I had turned the other way, he'd have been behind me and I wouldn't have seen him. So there was a lot of things that happened by chance that made the difference. The first gable was facing out towards the lane and the other gable facing down the yard. It was built at right angles to the lane. What amazed me (and still amazes me) was I thought: 'The only way out of here is go back; I'm going to have to face whatever's there'. And that was it. There was no panic, there was just the biggest shock whenever the first gunman appeared and the first couple of shots were fired. And after that, everything was clear.

Q. You had a plan. You were adapting, you were thinking, you were in control, you had the ability to be in combat, you had your pistol working.
Sammy: Afterwards, they warned the wife all that is going to happen to me some time or another (delayed shock), because 'at the moment he's on adrenalin'.

Q. Franklin tells it similarly and Glen Espie too, this ability to function mentally through it all, to read the situation, make a plan instantly, 'This is what I'm going to do' and get on with it. Whether it be training or mental preparation. Franklin speaks about his mental preparation 'for when it would happen'.
Sammy: When I was telling this to people, some would say 'Why on earth did you carry on as a postman whenever you knew you were in such danger?'

Q. I suppose the way we looked at it, like the boys in Pomeroy, who were living on the edge of Cappagh with their farm, did that mean they were going to have to up and leave?
Sammy: That's the point.

Q. Like the border situation, you were serving right from the start and you knew the comrades you had lost in your home Company, who were murdered in their beds and murdered on the road and shot at, and yet that was what we did.
Sammy: That was what we did, is right, and unfortunately too many of our people upped and went, in my opinion, too soon, too quickly. A lot of people moved out of areas and terrorism was seen to be working. And when it was seen to be working then they knew to keep at it.

Q. Could you have asked to be given a less dangerous route?
Sammy: Well, you see, that was what I would have called my safest route. I would have done three routes. That would have been my normal route, but then the relief man who came in any time there was anybody off, taking holidays or sick,

always came in and did that round and I had to do one of the other rounds. So I would have counted the other two rounds more dangerous.

Q. Would you have run through scenarios in your head at times when you were in those more dangerous areas?

Sammy: In places you would have thought 'I could be in a bit of danger here', but the one place that I wouldn't have thought I was in danger was the one place that it DID happen!

Q. Would you have prepped the van when you came into somebody's yard to be able to exit, or did you just stop where it was convenient to the door?

Sammy: Well, normally you knew when you went onto a street, you went onto it the same way and you reversed round or whatever it was and you didn't vary that because you couldn't really vary it. The only other thing that I might have done, if I had letters for some of the other houses further up the lane, I would just have stopped, got out of the van and walked down to the door, instead of driving in, but because I didn't have to go any further I turned and drove in.

Q. Had there been any triggers prior to this in the days beforehand that you noticed?

Sammy: That letter was deliberately sent and it was actually a notice about the Benburb Sunday, but it hadn't been sent from the Benburb Priory.

Q. Would the people in the house have been in on this?

Sammy: I think they were. That would be my feeling. And Mickey Russell, maybe he was in on it as well, because he had parked the car further down the street than he normally did. The only innocent one that was there was Willie Hall, a neighbour. He would have been there maybe two or three days a week. Mrs McGarvey would have made him dinner. He lived further away up the Cravenny Road. But he lived on his own and many's the time I would have seen him on the road, walking, and maybe I'd give Willie a lift in the Post Office van, you know.

Sammy continues:

They took his (Willie's) coat and wrapped the injured man in it. Willie thought he would have got out to warn me. He says: 'I'll have to get out to make my water. So the boy just stuck his gun in my back and says: "Come on with me down the bottom of the garden" and that was that'. So he was marched out at gunpoint and marched back in again! They had arrived at six o'clock in the morning, or so. They were there long enough, anyway.

I was off work for about eleven months. The doctor for the Post Office cleared me fit to return to duty and the Post Office wouldn't offer me any alternative work, apart from a job in Southampton or one in Edinburgh. Even Harold

McCusker (*James Harold McCusker 1940-1990 Ulster Unionist politician*) had a meeting with them, but the union (which you had to be in), they were absolutely no use whatsoever. Their attitude was, I think, that you could be a danger to your work colleagues. So there was absolutely nothing there for me. The only thing the Post Office did for me was they paid me for six months' full pay and they were cutting it then to half pay and my solicitor said to them 'Could you not pay this man his full pay and then you'll get it back whatever time he gets compensation?' So they agreed to that and then they had to be paid back. The only thing the Battalion would offer me was full-time/part-time. They wouldn't offer me full-time unless I gave up the Council. I said: 'Well, why should I give up the Council?' I was full-time/part-time for sixteen years until I was fifty-five in 1997. After that I worked as a civvie storeman in Armagh and then I got a transfer to Clogher in and around 2000. When Clogher closed I moved to Omagh.

So I left the Post Office. There was nothing else I could do, but it still sticks in my gullet the way that they handled it. I had only been four years with them and so I didn't qualify for a pension either. The doctor said: 'If I put you in for a pension on your medical, anything you get from the Post Office will be deducted from your compensation. But I don't see why the Post Office should pay for this – it's the Northern Ireland Office should pay for this'. And he was right on that score. But at the same time the Post Office should have been able to offer me alternative employment somewhere in the negotiations. The union was hopeless and you had to be in the union. Do you remember, there was a postman shot in Belfast, a Catholic fella, at a sorting office, I think it was since the Good Friday Agreement and the union brought the postmen out for a day on strike. And I remember Talk Back ringing me up to ask how did I feel about it? 'Well', I says, 'I'm glad to see that the union's doing something now, because they did nothing for me'.

When asked, 'Now with the police investigation going on while you were recuperating, did they recover the weapons?' Sammy replied: No, a suspect had the weapons hidden in Peter Russell's house. Peter Russell wasn't at home that day. None of them were at home, but he knew where the key was, so he went into the house and hid the weapons. And Mrs McCann had been told on the Sunday beforehand to be at home on the Saturday, for she might be required to do a run and she didn't know anything about this, but whenever he hid the weapons, he was out on the road and Mrs McCann brought him into Aughnacloy and dropped him off at his sister's house. The sister was married to McCabe and they lived nearly opposite the chapel in Aughnacloy. She dropped him off there and she didn't know that anything had happened at this stage. But whenever the McCanns heard what had happened Joe reported where these weapons were hidden. The police went out and searched and didn't get them. He had hid them in flower pots or something. I don't know what sort of a search it was. It was bad work. Then Peter Russell went to McCann's and he says to Joe: 'Give me a hand. We'll have to get these bloody weapons out of here'. So they took them and they hid them in the toilet at the quarry (Hadden's quarry at Tullyvar). The quarry wasn't going at that stage and eventually that became the dump. Joe McCann again reported where these weapons now were, so this time they went and they got them (two .45" revolvers). Unfortunately neither of the McCanns was able to give evidence in court: Joe was dying and he died before the trial was over.

But from the outset, from those two people were arrested on the day of the count at Omagh, the day that McGeough stood for the Assembly, and then after he was eliminated, he was arrested outside the count. And he spoke to me that day, in the count in Omagh. I was talking to Arlene Foster *(Arlene Foster 1970-: DUP: Member of Northern Ireland Assembly for Fermanagh and South Tyrone since 2003: First Minister of Northern Ireland 2016-2017 and from 2020)* and he came along and he says: 'How are ye, Sammy?' And Arlene Foster says to me: 'Did he speak to you?' I says: 'He did, surely'. I ignored him. And then the next thing was, he went outside and he was arrested. I got the shock of my life for I had been asking why this man was allowed to stand for the Assembly and I didn't think anybody was listening to me but, obviously, somebody was and then McAnespie was lifted. From the outset, they maintained 'We've got McGeough, we'll get a conviction there, but we're not sure about McAnespie'. So they concentrated on McGeough. Now the only reason McGeough was convicted was the fact that he was hit and injured. And he wouldn't go to the witness box. They thought he would have.

He went to Monaghan and got medical help, the bullet was taken out of him in Dublin. The Garda made sure that never came as witness evidence. They said it was the same material as the rest of the rounds in my weapon, but they couldn't say it was fired by my weapon. But if I had shot him in any other circumstances, they could have told for sure!

Asked if there was some satisfaction when there was a court case eventually, Sammy replied:

He (McGeough) had been all over the place; he had been in Sweden and all that and then he came back after serving time in both Germany and America. He came back to Dublin and went to Trinity College and got his degree and then he was teaching in Dublin. Then whenever the uncle died, the farm the uncle had in Brantry was left to a cousin or somebody in New Zealand. But whatever happened, Gerry got it eventually, and then he started to come over there and lived there quietly.

Health-wise, I would still have pains from those injuries. And after a period with physio and so on, you get better, but then in later years, they come back again. That hand never was right. The sensation came back to those two middle fingers but they are more sensitive than the other fingers on that hand. There was one time where if I had just touched them, you'd have thought you were sticking needles in me. Even touching the hairs on the back of the hand. Many's the time I burned those fingers and got blisters but you couldn't feel a thing. At the start I used to have to hold a pen a different way because I couldn't grip. Now I've adapted to use the left hand for a lot more, even holding a cup. Most of the time, it's my left hand now.

At the time of the incident, my son was ten, just big enough to know. The daughters were older than that, so they would have coped better than my son.

Sammy concludes:

Our God and soldiers we alike adore, even at the point of danger, not before. After deliverance, both alike requited. Our God's forgotten and our soldiers slighted.

Raymond Richardson 26th March 1980, 8th May 1983 and 30th September 1985

I[27] was born up at Whitetown here; the wee back road goes up there, to the left, just opposite Roughan Lough (*about two miles north-west of Coalisland*). It was a small farm at that time. There was my mother and father and two brothers, three brothers altogether.

I done bits and pieces on the farm but I was a joiner. I served my time as a joiner and started a small building business on my own. I started off first of all just making stuff for people and then I started building houses and went on like that. I suppose that was around 1965, '66 that I actually started out on my own. I was getting on rightly. I always remember, I joined the USC and then moved over into the UDR.

I enlisted in the UDR in March 1970 and served with G Company 8 UDR based in Cookstown. In early 1972 I was leading a patrol near Coalisland operating vehicle check points; at approximately 2330hrs I withdrew the patrol to a safe area to have some refreshments. A short time afterwards we received a radio message instructing us to go to Battalion Headquarters at Dungannon where our brief was that a shooting had taken place in the area that we had been patrolling near Coalisland; our patrol was tasked into the Coalisland area to support the Regular unit and the RUC. Later in the night we learned that a suspect terrorist had been shot dead by a covert patrol of the Regular unit based

---

27 Capt Robert (Raymond) Richardson MBE UD 1937-: 8 UDR 1970-92: (R Irish until 1993): Building Contractor.

in Dungannon. In the days following this incident it was common gossip that it was me who had done the shooting and that they would get me for it: although every effort was made in the media to deny that the UDR was involved in the shooting it was still mentioned in a pub two weeks later. One can imagine how I felt since I was operating my building business in the general area.

Later in 1972 I was on duty in G Company HQ as duty officer when I received information regarding the hijacking of a van about six miles to our east. On receiving this I recalled a mobile patrol to back up our foot patrol already covering the centre of Cookstown. A short time after I had taken this action the mobile patrol reported having apprehended the wanted van together with the driver and one other and was in chase of another car which they believed to contain a bomb. The vehicle was located a short distance from the town centre, the driver and his passenger had escaped. During the court appearance of the two prisoners which our patrol had detained, and a further two were arrested and charged with the attempted bombing, I was subjected several times to abuse such as being spat at and other remarks by the terrorists' supporters. Finally on the last day of the trial which ended in January 1973 a number of female supporters attempted to attack me saying I would pay for this; all of this took place in the court room in the presence of the judge.

The *Mid Ulster Mail* throws a little light on this, reporting on 20th January 1973:

COOKSTOWN BLAST CHARGES

The Northern Ireland Winter Assizes in Belfast was told on Wednesday how a stolen red mini-van led to the arrest of two men who, along with another, faced charges of causing explosions in Cookstown last March and April.

The men – Gerald Martin Donnelly[28] (22), electrician, Drumaney, Coagh; Laurence Joseph McNally[29] (20) labourer, Annaghmore Cottages, Coagh; and

---

28 Gerald Martin Donnelly c1951-: Coagh: Labourer: Sentenced (1973) to seven years' imprisonment for causing the explosion, five years for possessing firearms for unlawful purpose, seven years for conspiring with persons unknown to cause an explosion in Cookstown on April 24th: He also received a two year sentence for the theft of a motor car on April 22nd, six months for taking and driving a motor vehicle on April 24th and three years for carrying firearms with criminal intent: All sentences to run concurrently (*Mid Ulster Mail* 20th and 27th January 1973).

29 Lawrence Joseph McNally c1953-91: Coagh: Labourer: Sentenced (1973) to seven years' imprisonment for causing the explosion, five years for possessing firearms for unlawful purpose, seven years for conspiring with persons unknown to cause an explosion in Cookstown on April 24th: He also received a two year sentence for the theft of a motor car on April 22nd, six months for taking and driving a motor vehicle on April 24th and three years for carrying firearms with criminal intent. All sentences to run concurrently (*Mid Ulster Mail* 20th and 27th January 1973): Killed Coagh 3rd June 1991 (Magee, *Tyrone's Struggle*).

Patrick Joseph Quinn[30] (20), fisherman, with the same address as McNally – also faced charges relating to the possession of firearms and the theft of a car and the taking and driving away of the mini.

Mr Ronald Appleton QC, outlining the case for the Crown, described two explosions in the Burn Road area of the town in March and April last year. He said that on March 3rd a bomb caused £20,000 damage to the Rural District Council Offices and on April 24th a second explosion in the area damaged 47 buildings. Mr Appleton said that two of the accused, Donnelly and McNally, were apprehended by a UDR patrol in the centre of Cookstown a few hours before the April 24th blast, after a report that the vehicle, a red mini-van with a roof rack, had been stolen earlier in the day.

Before opening the prosecution case, Mr Appleton asked Mr Justice Kelly if UDR and civilian witnesses could be identified by letters of the alphabet. The judge agreed to the request.

A sergeant in G Company 8 UDR, stationed in Cookstown, who was described as Sergeant 'G', told the court that on the night of April 24th he was operating a road checkpoint south of Cookstown. He was later instructed to carry out a patrol of the town centre during which he spotted a red mini-van. He instructed the driver of his Land Rover to pull over and stop the van. Sergeant 'G' said that he brought one man out of the van and instructed him to put his hands over his head. The second man, in the rear of the vehicle, was instructed to do likewise. The two men were searched and handed over to the RUC.

At this stage Donnelly asked the witness: 'What did your men find on us?'

Sergeant 'G': 'They found nothing.'

A police witness said that he cautioned the two men and asked them to account for being in possession of the stolen car. 'Neither made a reply', he said. The defendants challenged statements they were alleged to have made in the absence of the jury, but Mr Justice Kelly ruled they could be admitted.

Donnelly, in a statement alleged to have been made at the police holding centre in Armagh, said that at the time of the March explosion at the Rural Council Offices, he was a member of the Official IRA, but left the movement one week before the April explosion to join the Provisionals. The statement alleged that Donnelly was accompanied by McNally and Quinn when they set off to plant a bomb at the Council Offices. Donnelly said that the original target was the Bureau (The Dole) Office and the Council Offices were an alternative.

---

30 Patrick Joseph Quinn c1953-: Coagh: Fisherman: Sentenced (1973) to five years' imprisonment for causing the explosion, and three years for possessing firearms for unlawful purpose: Both sentences to run concurrently (*Mid Ulster Mail* 20th and 27th January 1973).

He allegedly said that they planted the bomb at the Council Offices instead of at the Bureau Offices because there was a function at a nearby parochial hall. The statement alleged that Donnelly and McNally were armed with revolvers and provided cover for Quinn while he set the bomb in the hallway of the offices.

Raymond Richardson continues:

There was a period when all appeared quiet, at the end of February 1980. In March, at least three suspicious incidents happened that put me on my guard. On 26th March 1980 there was a shot as I turned in at the gate of the house. I was living up in the Brackaville Road. The first shot was fired; actually I believe they fired the shot accidentally. It was about twenty to twelve or so at night. I was just coming out of Cookstown. I always had a habit of, I'd drive up fairly sharp to the house and I stood hard on the brakes and drove in. And just as I turned in, the shot went off. I more or less abandoned the car – I got out of the car and drew my gun and fired a shot. I fired it at where they were. Almost immediately 8/9 further shots were discharged. They fired in the opposite direction! I fired one more shot but could not identify a target. I'd always had the idea that if I was shot at comin' in through the gate, they would come from the wee lane up at the side of the house. My wife, Betty, was present in the house when this occurred and activated the alarm system.

Then in 1983, I broke my leg in the UDR centre and I was walking on a crutch. I hadn't brought the van home for ages; some of the other boys was driving her. But I started to go out a wee bit, round the jobs and I took the van to pick up materials and I drove her in the gate. On the Friday night I took the van home (the car was in the garage) and I just parked her along at the side of the bedroom window. On the Sunday morning, I got up and I let the dog out as normal but this morning the dog done an exceptional bit of barking, just round the front of the house. I didn't really think very much of it, but I went for my breakfast anyway and put my uniform on, for I was going over to Cookstown to do Duty Officer for the Company was going down to Magilligan. I got prepared to go. The gates was closed so I opened the gates and come back again to the van and took the usual look through it. I always had the idea that they wouldn't put anything under the wheel arch. I didn't think they would do that. I thought if they were going to do anything at all, they would know I'd check the van and they'd tie it on the exhaust pipe or somewhere like that. I actually got down on my belly.

I was very nearly going to get in and says I, 'There's four wheel arches' and there! – was this thing, the size of a loaf. It was held on with magnets. It had dropped down a wee bit. I didn't see it coming back in again from opening the gates. And when I seen this thing, first of all, I had to awaken my wife and aged mother-in-law who was asleep in the bedroom only a few feet from the bomb.

Raymond Richardson's House and Van

I had to take the car out of the garage past the van and take her away out of there. We got her up anyway, and took her out the back door, onto the lane. There was a lane up the side of the house. I rang the UDR and the police first of all and got her out. Betty she took her up to her own house, just out of the way altogether. The old woman was suffering from dementia and it was not easy to explain the danger to her.

The Bomb Disposal crowd were told about half eight in the morning – they arrived at eleven o'clock. They had the wee robot and they looked all round the van. They reckoned it should have gone off. The van was OK.

It was a wee yellow Ford. Armagh Council owned her. I bought her off Dan Davidson. She was yellow with a black roof, so she was very distinctive. I drove her for maybe another six months but didn't bring it home again. Sammy Wright gave me a wee garage; he lived up at the top of the lane. But then, I was having to drive up there and walk down that lane again. Then that was about the time he bought Mitchell's filling station and he gave me a wee house down there to put it in.

I had a workshop down, just above the pub (Brackaville crossroads) and then the pub was blew up and it wrecked the workshop. We used it for a good while and then moved over to where I was building a house, and I was getting fed up – we had the roof (of the workshop) covered in polythene and every time there was a wild night, next thing it was raining in again. There was a hayshed just behind the petrol pump; if you went out at Gilmore's crossroads and turned right, and there was a petrol pump. It wasn't used.…. In at the back of that. He had an old hayshed. Ah now, it wasn't in great shape! I asked the owner would he let it to me. He said: 'I'll do better than that. I'll let you have it, free.' So I got it fixed up and I don't remember any bother, but you were looking straight over at Powerscreen.

They put up cameras and all. I could see what was going on from inside the workshop. A couple of times, somebody plastered it with grease so it couldn't be used. It was kind of just carry on.

One record said:

A booby-trap IED was placed in the front wheel arch of Captain Raymond Richardson's van which was parked by his house on Brackaville Road, Coalisland overnight. He noticed the device as he prepared to leave for UDR duty in Cookstown at 0850hrs. The device was neutralised by ATO at 1315hrs. It consisted of 2.5 kgs commercial explosive (Frangex) and mercury tilt switch and had been attached to the vehicle by 12 × one inch magnets taped to a plastic ruler.

Under Vehicle IED

Then on 30th September 1985, Raymond continues:

> I had just gone out of the house. They rang from Cookstown, looking for the key of the safe; it must have been half ten or nearly eleven that they rung me. The bar was looking for change or something. And I was just going to go down to the bar and the Ops Room shouted: 'Raymond, you're wanted on the phone'. So I went to the phone and Betty was ... very emotional. She had a half story ... She said there had been an awful 'Bang!' and the glass was all broken. I reported this to our operations room and left for home.
>
> On arriving home the house was already cordoned off and the sentries could not tell me what had happened except that a bomb had exploded. On going into the house I found my wife and her mother being attended by a Woman Police Constable (WPC). My wife told me she was not sure what had happened but there had been a very loud bang and on opening the door from the lounge to hall she found the hall filling with smoke and dust then the window glass started to fall. She was in a very distressed state and a neighbour took her and her mother to their home and got the doctor; after that she went to her sister's.
>
> They had set a bomb on the windowsill. If there had been anyone in the bedroom ... Either of the two incidents could have killed her. This incident could have killed her if she had been in bed. She WAS in bed the time I found the bomb under the van.
>
> Betty went to her sister's. There was no glass. I went down to Kennedy's Engineering Works. There was two windows to be replaced altogether. The only time we lodged a claim for personal damages was that one, but with bungling solicitors and medical people, after three years they came to the conclusion that there was nothing wrong with us, but the Northern Ireland Office offered us a thousand pounds because they said it was 'a nasty experience'.
>
> There was a boy, a psychiatrist, he was complained about up in Enniskillen – a real head case. He worked down at the Mater hospital – Betty and me both had to go – that was about the third psychiatrist's report. Some of them was good. The solicitor says: 'You've got a good case'. The Northern Ireland Office sent us to this boy. For a start, he didn't know we were coming. He said: 'I'll see yez anyway'. Even at reception they knew nothing about it. I don't know what happened. He came down and he says: 'I'll see yez anyway'. He had no notes, he had no nothin' and he wasn't a damn bit interested. And he says to me one time: 'What did you do when this happened?' I says: 'What could I do?' He says: 'Did ye shite yourself?' He was ridiculous! I still rue that I didn't write to him or to the Home Office. Then Betty says: 'I'm going through no more of this carry on. We'll take the thousand pounds each'.

Betty added:

> When the bomb was placed on the windowsill I was lying on the settee when it went off and I thought to myself: 'God, what's that?' and I looked up and the curtains started to move and the glass fell out of the window. And then I opened the hall door and the hall was full of smoke and the glass was all out of the front door. But I just put them things out of my head.
>
> Three or four times it happened and I was in the house – me and my mother just…and like Mammy she had dementia but she knew something was going on. I had to give up my work to look after my mother when that happened. We were afraid she would open the door to somebody and not realise. We had to take the keys out of the door and she was small and she couldn't have reached up to turn the lock.

Raymond continues:

> We repaired our home and then moved to our present house in January 1986.
>
> I was constantly receiving warnings of high threats sometimes at 3 or 4 o'clock am; then one Saturday morning in April 1991 on rising I found another note posted in our letter box warning of a very high threat in the Newmills area. As this was by now normal I passed little attention. On Sunday afternoon my wife and I went for a drive and on returning another note was awaiting me, asking me to contact Battalion Headquarters on the telephone. I did and they asked me to come in.
>
> I was told that the threat was now identified as against me personally either at home or one of the houses I was constructing. I was asked if I would consider leaving my home together with my wife also the building site so that they could keep watch; I was not very happy about this but agreed as long as my workers' wages was paid. We moved out of our home and my wife stayed with a friend and I moved into Battalion Headquarters. This lasted until Friday when we were allowed to return as we were going for a short Easter break, and this was only allowed under a heavy military presence. We returned the following Friday but after one week the threat resumed and we had to move out for another four days.
>
> Except for the usual warnings nothing happened until March 1993 when I received a telephone call from the RUC asking if they could come and talk to me. I told them that I would rather go to the police station and on doing so was told that the threat was again very high to me personally and that it would be better for my safety if I moved out of the area, and that the only safe place would be across in England. After a long conversation I arranged to let them know my decision by next morning; having had the experience of compensation I decided not to move.

I retired from the Regiment in May 1993, my family and I having paid a high price. In January 2003 I suffered a heart attack and in August 2005 I had to undergo surgery; when recovering I had flash backs from past experiences. On being discharged from hospital I find that I am also almost incapable of any work and even driving for any length is difficult.

Brian Hamilton 23rd August 1989

Brian Hamilton[31] recalls:

I didn't join until late 1971. It was only when this fella ran after me for about six months; I'd no notion at all, and this guy, Roy Moffett,[32] who was killed in 1974, he did contracting work, farming contracting, and then a fella from the other side of Stewartstown, Eric Kells,[33] said 'Oh come on Brian, if you join, I'll join', so that's what happened. And that was about the end of 1971 and I signed on 3rd January 1972. I was 19 at that time.

This is the family farm. We've been here from about 1924. My grandfather was here, and father was here. I have an older brother, who lives close by and does bodywork, and I have a younger sister. She used to work at the Mid Ulster Mail for many, many years.

I was living at home with my parents and we were just building up, I suppose. It was a small farm at that stage. We had 26 acres at home here, and then we had an out farm down at Killywoolaghan, Ardboe. It actually ran into Lough Neagh and it would have been owned by my grandfather's two brothers, who farmed it. It was 28 acres, but it's all moss type ground, but they would have farmed down there. I don't remember them. But my father rented it out because it's seven miles from here and at the time he thought it was too far away, so when I left school I thought 'OK, it will give me something to do', so we got a scheme through the Government to clean it up and we started to keep stock down there as well.

At the same time, we had neighbours here, a brother and sister, and they owned about 65 acres and my father would have done most of their tractor work. The two of them never married, so when they eventually retired my father was offered the whole farm. He had thought it was too much and we discussed it; that was way back in 1967. So it was £400 an acre, and we thought

---

31 WO2 Robert (Brian) Hamilton BEM UD and Two Bars 1948-: 8 UDR 1971-92: (R Irish until 1999): Farmer.
32 +Cpl Thomas Ferguson (Roy) Moffett 1939-74: 8 UDR 1970-74: Agricultural Contractor: Killed 3rd March 1974.
33 Pte Eric Kells 1945-: 8 UDR 1971-72: Auto Engineer.

'Well, we'll buy half of it', so we bought 30 acres at £12,000 and then we got a grant and we built a milking parlour. We were one of the first to have a milking parlour in this part of the world. We built it ourselves and saved a bit of money as well.

I had been in the Boys' Brigade for many years until I was 18 or 19 I suppose. When I joined the UDR I thought it would only last a short time and I thought it wasn't going to affect that much, and I could cope with it all right. And because I was here on the farm, I suppose you spent most of your time, because it was all new to me and we were out of money, and you had to repay it.

My parents were worried, I'm sure. My father was in the B Specials and I'm sure they were a bit concerned, but I'm one of these people who wouldn't say anything about these things to anyone anyway.

It was into '72 before I was signed on. I was supposed to go to a different platoon and I ended up in Coalisland Platoon, with Kenny Marsh,[34] in 4 Platoon, G Company.

The first night I was to go out on patrol there were so many in Cookstown, the place was coming down with men in the big hall. Albert Cooper[35] and the fellas were out and they were ambushed outside Annaghmore. Albert drove out to Artie's crossroads (east of Coalisland). They were driving the old Commer van and he drove out of the ambush area and saved the rest of their lives. That probably unsettled me a wee bit, knowing that this was reality. I suppose prior to that there was a bomb in Stewartstown here. There was man killed at the Imperial Bar and there was two or three injured and that was as close as I was prior to that.

Travelling to and from the base I took no particular precautions – like everything, you just took it in your stride. I travelled from here in uniform. At the start there weren't so many incidents and you just took it for granted that 'I'm OK here'.

The incident where Roy Moffett was killed, I was driving the other Land Rover. We were up at Gortin range, that was March 1974, a Sunday. When we were going up to the range there were eight of us, four in each Land Rover. We had the short wheel-base Land Rover. I was driving it going up to Gortin. I was at the front. Coming back there was the C42 radio – it (a Land Rover) wouldn't start up at Gortin and anyway someone said: 'Brian, you go ahead' and then this explosion happened at Donaghmore, just near Teebane there, just this side of Teebane actually. Half the explosive didn't explode so they were blown out. And we rushed back and Roy, he died …. he was very badly

---

34 Maj Kenneth (Kenny) Lynn Marsh MBE 1924-2011: 8 UDR 1970-79: Engineer.
35 +WO2 Albert David Cooper 1948-90: 8 UDR 1970-90: MID (posthumous): Businessman: Killed 2nd November 1990.

injured, broken neck …. he lived for a short time; he was transferred to hospital. The next morning I was going about my business; I didn't tell my parents anything and then a neighbour came round, I was milking cows; we had just a wee byre beside the house, here (it's all changed from that now) and he came and enquired about me. They said I'd had my leg blown off and my father came out. And I heard this and I said, 'For goodness' sake!'

And the others, there was Austin Anderson,[36] Bert Stewart[37] was driving it. He is the only one that's living, he lives down at Coagh. In the Land Rover that I was driving there was Tommy Benson[38] and Albert McCollum.[39]

There were several other incidents. There was one night we were coming out of Coalisland and they shot at us from the old railway bridge. Another incident was when we were doing a three vehicle patrol from Brackaville. They had been doing an OP for two or three nights and then they came back down through into Coalisland and they were fired at from the chapel grounds, Brackaville chapel. A bullet missed me by inches.

There was the incident where Trevor Harkness[40] was killed, in 1985, in Pomeroy. I was the patrol commander that night; there were two six-man foot patrols. We were dropped off on the Carrickmore road out of Pomeroy. The same night as the nine policemen were murdered in the mortar attack on Newry police station. We heard it on somebody's radio. Anyway he was killed and Gary Patterson[41] was injured, that's Tommy Benson's stepson (*see Chapter 7 for more on this incident*).

So the date of this so-called incident, the Thursday 23rd of August 1989. That morning, it was a nice day, sun shining, and we had bought a farm off an uncle the year prior to that, a 40-acre farm. I had booked a fellow to come and do round bale silage on one of the fields. He was supposed to come after lunch time. I was cutting the grass out the front here, and the police arrived in and said 'Just be careful. There's a general threat, but nothing against you. Be on your guard', sort of thing. That was fine, I had a 9 mm pistol at that stage. I went on ahead anyway and cut the grass and a car came down past the house at this stage of the morning, but I never passed any more remarks about it. A suspected terrorist was sitting at the passenger side.

Then whenever I was done, after lunch time, I was waiting till this guy came. I decided to bring the cows in early to milk them in case this guy would come because I was going to stack the bales. I was milking the cows … it was a

---

36 CSgt William (Austin) Anderson 1927-1999: 8 UDR 1970-87: MID (Twice): Farmer.
37 Cpl William Robert (Bert) David Stewart 1950-: 8 UDR 1972-80: Plumber.
38 WO2 Thomas (Tommy) Reginald Benson BEM 1933-2000: 8 UDR 1970-92.
39 Pte (Albert) George McCollum 1945-1994: 8 UDR 1972-78: Engineer.
40 +Pte Trevor Winston Harkness 1949-1985: 8 UDR 1970-85: Farmer: Killed 28th February 1985.
41 CSgt Gary Patterson 1965-: 8 UDR 1983-92: (R Irish until 2007): MID: Milkman.

very windy day too, so tin would rattle and I'd be looking out every so often, looking to see about this fellow coming to do the silage. I was nearly finished and I looked through the window and I seen my sister coming up round, scared looking, and thought something had happened to the parents. So I went out and said 'What's happened? What's happened?' 'Did you not see them?' she said. I said 'What are you talking about? See who or what?' And then she mentioned these boys.

A car had been hijacked between Stewartstown and Brackaville. Two brothers and a sister lived on their own just at the side of the road, never married, and they hi-jacked the car, same kind of car as the neighbour drove, a Peugeot, same colour as well, I suppose thinking that I wouldn't catch this on. Luckily enough if it hadn't been for my sister I probably wouldn't be here today. She lives in Cookstown and she was visiting at the house, looked out of the window and these boys went past, hooded with rifles, and then … if you go out of the back door here, there used to be a higher wall than there is now. You couldn't really see behind but there was a gap and she could see two guys going over towards the milking parlour. She shouted at them and at the same time my father rang the police.

There were two doors into the milking parlour, one from the outside and the other, a smaller door, on the inside, which was purpose-done that way. And you would normally open a door right to left but I had this door opening the other way. I don't even know how far they got in or didn't get in and she shouted and scared them. Apparently they went back to where the three hostages were and that's it.

So the police came out; they were very quick coming out and the helicopter was round about as well. They were just here in a very short time as well. Just thinking in terms what would have I done if I had seen them, a few years prior to that I had a bullet-proof window put in the upper part of the milking parlour. So if I had looked out and seen them, would I have shot at them? With instinct, you probably would have. But I don't know, I didn't see them so …

So then the police were here and I think it happened around 5, half 5 in the afternoon and then the fella arrived to do the round-bale silage and I thought, if he had arrived five minutes earlier, he would have blocked their way going out! So then the fella asked me did I want him to come back tomorrow: but I said, 'For goodness' sake!' So I went up anyway and stacked the bales.

I think the Brigade Commander was due to visit that night in Cookstown and nothing would do Ronnie Nesbitt[42] but he would bring him out here to the 'war zone'. They couldn't understand how I could be doing this! What was

---

42 Maj Ronald (Ronnie) Irwin Nesbitt UD 1947-: (10 UDR 1971-85): 8 UDR 1971-92: (R Irish until 1996): MID: Businessman/Driving Instructor.

I to do? Sit in the house, twiddling my thumb? They're gone! They're away, and I am still here.

My father had a Canadian cousin staying with us. They happened to be away visiting that whole day. She and her husband would come over every other year and I had planned to take them to Donegal the next day and so I took my two parents and the two of them away for the day and it was the best thing ever! Got away from it all. We'd have maybe talked a wee bit about it, but not that much. My sister tried to keep as much as possible from them. No shots were fired so there was obviously no big investigation.

I did not notice any 'spotting' prior to the incident. I would have had good neighbours. The only one would be at the top of the hill. If the neighbours had seen something suspicious, they would have said something to you, you know, like a car sitting somewhere or whatever … But when you're on, you're on. I suppose whenever Roy Moffett was killed, at the time I said to myself I'll stay on here, not to get revenge as such, that's the wrong word but maybe to avenge? Then I got into the Battalion shooting team and of course that got you away. My biggest problem was getting the farm covered. You couldn't get anyone to volunteer to do it.

The fatigue never really bothered me at that time. I suppose I was pretty fit, but the neighbours would have said: 'I don't know how you stick it, Brian?' You just go on, I suppose, but the rest of your life was destroyed. You had no social life. Going to church or to the Masonic or whatever, you didn't want to leave your car in Stewartstown in case there was an under car booby-trap. So you just didn't bother doing it. But even the neighbours too – we used to work with the neighbours across the way here, in the silage cutting, and they'd be thinking 'Maybe they'll put a bomb in the wrong place or whatever'. And I got that sort of impression before we pulled … working together. It wasn't so much not working together, but it's just we got contractors in to do it ourselves. But the neighbours are all good around here. But once you go beyond half a mile up the road there … If you look up on the hill there, there was a boy would have been a spotter for them.

Regimentally, they said we'll put all these lights on and get the boys to come and put cameras and stuff on. And I said 'That's all right, if you want to do that, that's fine' but they put them round outhouses and all and the whole thing lit up at night. I don't want to sound ungrateful but it sort of drew attention.

But I've seen me leaving gates open up the road for coming home at night. If there was a heavy threat on, you'd stay at the base but you had to come home at some stage. I would have driven into the field and walked down the back roads in to the house here. And some of the fellas were good, that were based in Cookstown, they would have escorted me. At the time we still had the land down in Ardboe, and I suppose I was told not to go down there. The Colonel brought me out a couple of times and warned me, change your vehicle, don't go anywhere for two or three days. But you changed your routes and stuff like that as well. It was a mile in to where we had the place down there and a mile out again. So when we bought the farm from my uncle in 1990, we sold the place in Ardboe. Even the Catholic neighbours said that they were glad I was moving out. They didn't say it to me direct but they said it to other people.

And I didn't want to put anyone else under threat. Would I do it again? I probably would, you know. If you didn't know what the outcome was going to be, you probably would, but not if you knew you'd end up doing nearly thirty years!

4

Greenfinches

Greenfinches, the women soldiers of the UDR, were very important in every battalion, but in 8 UDR they were even more so because of the relatively small male population available for recruitment. Most of the signals, intelligence and administrative jobs were carried out by women; they deployed with the men on many occasions and shared their dangers.

Private Carol Watson 1983

The majority of women soldiers in the Battalion had a husband, father or other relation also serving which compounded the stress both on and off duty. Because of the nature of their roles Greenfinches were involved in incidents, albeit indirectly.

Roberta Abraham

I[1] grew up on a farm outside Dungannon. My family were very well known and well liked in the surrounding areas. Most of our neighbours were Catholic but that didn't matter. Coalisland, a large Republican village, was only four miles away.

One of my earliest childhood memories of the UDR (although at the time I didn't know it was to do with the UDR) was in the early 70s, when I was around eight or nine years old. I remember my mother sitting me down and telling me that I was not to play in the forest that surrounded our home for the foreseeable future. She did not give me a reason why. I found out years later that SAS soldiers were watching the farm from the forest as intelligence had been gathered on a hit on my brother who was a member of the UDR. Thankfully, the hit never happened for whatever reasons. I think it was a few months later that flares and distress signals were installed in the house. I was under strict instructions never to touch them unless directed by the grown-ups. I do remember that I was never left alone in the house for a good few years.

I began to realise that the UDR was going to play a big part in our lives as my brother and two of my sisters had joined as part-time soldiers while holding down civilian jobs. I remember being bribed by my big sister to attend hockey practice with the promise that we would call in to the camp on the way home for a beer (my sister had the beer, not me) and a game or two of pool. I suppose that was when I started thinking of joining up but I was only 15 so I had to wait.

I first applied to join the UDR in 1981 but my application was rejected and I was advised to apply again the following year. This I did but I then had a chance to work in Israel on a kibbutz. I jumped at the chance and it was while I was in Israel that I heard that I had been accepted into the UDR. Luckily for me the vacancy was kept open and on 3rd January 1983 I was sworn into the UDR by the Assistant Adjutant of 8 UDR, Captain Joan Doyle.[2]

I had only planned to stay part-time, working nights in one of the part-time companies, when the opportunity came to work on a full-time/part-time basis. As I had no other employment at the time, I was very happy to accept. I did not revert to full-time status until August 1986, and I am very proud to say that between the UDR, The Royal Irish, and the bespoke Aftercare Service, I served a total of 30 years, reaching the rank of Colour Sergeant.

---

1 CSgt Roberta Abraham 1963-: 8 UDR 1983-92: (R Irish until 2007 and then After Care Service until 2012).
2 Capt Joan Doyle 1955-: 8 UDR 1979-83: PE Teacher when part-time.

Serving in the UDR had its ups and downs. We had restrictions placed on us as to where we could go, who we could be friends with, and travelling down South was a big no no. There was an added complication of remembering where you worked – and your family had to know as well.

My sister and I went to the same hairdresser, who was a Catholic. I had told him I worked in the hospital (in those days, the first thing anybody asked you was: 'Where do you work?'). My sister was in with him about three months later and he asked if I was still at the hospital working. My sister said no before realising what had happened and then she had to make up a new job for me, ring me to tell me what it was so I could get my story right the next time I went to have my hair done. To save any bother, I changed hairdressers.

There was also the threat of being targeted by the IRA while you went about your daily business. It was mainly the part-timers who were targeted at their civilian work or at their homes but that didn't mean you could be less alert. Cars needed to be checked every time they were left unattended in case the IRA had planted an UVIED, and that included your whole family having to check. Routes and timings were varied while travelling to work but there were always one or two routes you could not avoid taking and you had to be extra vigilant at these times. My mother and father had years of worry especially to have four children in the UDR, three of them part-time. I heard many years later that they never got to sleep until all of us had come home safely, and that included when we were out socialising because that was when a lot of part-time UDR soldiers were attacked.

I was fortunate enough not to be directly involved in any incidents while serving in the UDR. One of my friends was not so fortunate. We were both working in the Signals Platoon which involved night shifts. My friend was always worried about being in the camp at night, especially as the IRA had launched a few mortar attacks on other bases. I think it was a Monday night, and I was sitting at home when the news came on. Killymeal House had been hit by mortars. My first thought was of my friend. There was no other news at the time, so I drove into town and went as close as I could to the camp to try and find out what happened. Needless to say, I didn't find out much but I did know no-one had been injured, at least physically. My friend left the UDR shortly after.

One Saturday morning in August, I received a phone call asking if I could come in and cover a shift in the Ops Room. I had just arrived and got settled in when a contact came over the police radio. The permanent sangar at the bottom of Church Street (Dungannon) had been attacked and the policeman manning it had been injured. The gunmen were fleeing the scene. The watchkeeper and I jumped into action. We had been briefed on what to do in a contact situation and it was our job to control the follow up actions of the Army. The QRF were deployed, the Ops Officer, Ops Warrant Officer and Commanding Officer were called in and any available patrol was deployed. It was my job to listen to both our radio and the police radio so I could advise what was happening. The police were in pursuit of the gunmen, and we were able to co-ordinate what was happening and where best to send our call signs (*patrols/QRFs*) in the hope of catching the gunmen. Unfortunately, the gunmen crashed into a garden and escaped on foot; fortunately, the policeman survived.

The role Greenfinches played in the UDR was vital. Not only did we man the Ops Room but we also deployed on patrols when required. I have been involved in many patrols including Eagle (helicopter) VCPs, searches and the normal foot patrols. The patrols would have taken place all around our TAOR and I have searched females in Cappagh and was scribe for VCPs in Coalisland. On one particular patrol near Coalisland we stopped a vehicle during a routine stop and I went over to get the driver's details and it turned out to be someone I knew from Coalisland but hadn't seen in a couple of years. I remember him looking at me in surprise and then a smirk coming onto his face. I didn't let on I knew him and got all his details and he was allowed to proceed on his way. I reported the incident to the Intelligence Cell and was told that while he was not involved in the IRA as far as we knew, he was a Republican and that I should be extra careful over the next few weeks.

While being a member of the UDR meant you needed to be vigilant at all times, it was not all bad. We still needed to train in order to be professional in our role and I can remember competitions were the norm to help us achieve this. One competition was the Anderson Liddle Cup, an annual competition held at Ballykinler for the men. However, the powers to be decided that the females should be allowed to enter the competition and all the UDR Battalions were to enter a team. The competition consisted of various scenarios which involved contacts, search awareness and fitness. We would also be marked for our presentation.

We trained for weeks before the competition including weekends. I don't think I have ever been so fit. On the day of the competition we had creases in our uniforms as sharp as knives. We could do no more. Once we were inspected, we were then paired off and given a stand to go to. Myself and my friend were picked for the signals scenario and thankfully it seemed to go all right. The team then had to complete a circuit around Ballykinler which involved orienteering to find the various stands and once at a stand, to solve the problem that was presented to us. We had 45 minutes to complete the circuit.

All our hard work paid off. We were the only team to complete the circuit within the time and we had scored practically maximum points at every stand. We had won. Needless to say we were ecstatic and so was the Commanding Officer at the time. When we arrived back at Killymeal House he invited us all up to his house for drinks and then he opened up the George Shaw[3] bar for us.

---

3 +Maj George Shaw 1929-87: 8 UDR 1972-87: MID (posthumous): Killed 26th January 1987.

The other aspect of being a member of the UDR was to try and gain recognition across the water with the rest of the Army. To them we were a bunch of TA soldiers and they didn't really know anything about us. One way to put our name on the map so to speak was through sport. As I was quite sporty, I was soon snapped up to play hockey, squash and tennis for the Battalion. I am glad to say that our sporting teams did rather well in England.

I can remember two competitions I was involved with that made people start to realise who and what we were. One was a seven-a-side hockey tournament in Aldershot. The tournament was played over three days and included 44 teams from all battalions. There was also a team of Army players taking part. The highlight of the tournament was playing the Army team and holding them to a draw. At the end we came 18th out of 44 and won our group. I can always remember the cheer that went up as we collected our prize.

The other competition was a squash competition held at Winchester. Myself and two others made up the team and we had been playing squash on a regular basis prior to this. It was both a team and an individual competition and we were doing quite well. I had reached the semi-finals of the individual competition and my opponent was a tall, left-handed player who was quite intimidating on the court. It did not start well. I had no confidence in myself, and my opponent was soon 2-0 up (it was the best of five games). During the break my team mates came up to give me some encouragement and advised me to 'go for every ball'. With this advice in my head I went into the third game a different person. I went for every shot and soon it was my opponent who was floundering. Word must have spread around the complex because when I looked up at the gallery during the 4th game it was packed with people. I could see my team mates silently cheering me on, one of my old bosses giving me the thumbs up. I couldn't believe that these people were here to see our match. It made me more determined to win and after a long hard slog I eventually came out the winner. I was over the moon, people were cheering and clapping and my opponent gracious in defeat. Unfortunately, my opponent in the final was just too strong but I was so happy to be runner up.

I believe that the competitions we took part in over the years helped people realise that the UDR were soldiers who took pride in who they were and what they did.

A few last words about the After Care Service where I ended my service:

When the R Irish/UDR was disbanded one of the conditions that Peter Robinson (First Minister) insisted on was a bespoke Aftercare Service. This was an extension of the Welfare Department. It consisted of four field offices: Portadown, Enniskillen, Coleraine and Belfast which was where the Aftercare Headquarters was also based.

Each team consisted of a Team Leader who carried the rank of Sergeant, two field members who were Corporals and an administrator who was a civilian.

Headquarters consisted of all civilian staff, about 10 in total. The Aftercare Service would help eligible veterans and their families with medical help including counselling, physiotherapy and respite breaks, benevolence, and sign-posting especially for debt advice.

I was one of the Team Members in Portadown and while we held a rank, we were not part of the military as such. We had no uniform and completed no annual training.

Aggie Simpson

When the first civil unrest started in the Province I[4] was in my first year at Aughnacloy Secondary School. In 1972 I left school at 16 and got a job as an egg packer at Reids of Carnteel but left after about nine months later to become a veterinary receptionist for Stephenson and Kyle in Aughnacloy.

When the UDR was formed my brother joined as a part-time soldier and he suggested to me that I also should join when I was old enough. I was also encouraged to do so by my former headmaster Cormac McCabe[5] who was a part-time Captain in charge of the Aughnacloy Company.

I got all the paperwork sorted and was waiting to join up but unfortunately I never got to serve under Captain McCabe as he was abducted from the Four Seasons Hotel in Monaghan on 19th January '74; he was tortured and shot, and his body was dumped over the border near Clogher.

On 11th February 1974, five days after my eighteenth birthday, I was enlisted into 8 UDR and became a Greenfinch in L Company in Aughnacloy. I went the first night with my brother and was shown into the Ops Room; my first thoughts were that everyone was a lot older than me. There were three other Greenfinches in the Company, all wives of part-time soldiers and I was shown the ropes.

I settled in quickly and found it easy to plot location, code and decode locations. As well as radio operator I accompanied foot and mobile patrols on the ground, logging information at VCPs and searching females. I remember during the winter how bitterly cold it was on these patrols.

I did regular training at Killymeal including first aid and drill. Greenfinches were not armed (*UDR Greenfinches were never armed*) but we were trained to fire and make safe weapons when at annual camps and at local range days.

---

4   CSgt Aggie Simpson 1956-: 8 UDR 1974-84.
5   +Capt Cormac Mervyn James McCabe 1932-74: 8 UDR 1971-74: MID (posthumous): Teacher/School Principal: Killed 19th January 1974.

When I finished my duty in the early hours of the morning I had to drive home and although we were told to vary our times and routes you had to eventually turn into your laneway. Our house was fitted with a rocket alarm because we were not that far from the border with the Irish Republic.

After a couple of years I took up a full-time post at Killymeal House and transferred to HQ Company. I joined the Intelligence Cell which had another Greenfinch Sergeant. We kept a P card system on known and suspected terrorists and gathered information from wherever we could, from patrols on the ground and VCPs; newspapers for photographs and death notices were good for identifying family connections. Our off-duty soldiers were encouraged to report suspicious activity to the Intelligence Cell or company bases and even though there were no mobile phones in those early days, this stream of information was for the most part in real time so patrols could be directed to follow up leads where appropriate. I remember after Private Gibson[6] was gunned down and killed while cycling to his work near Dungannon from his home in Coalisland, an off-duty soldier, on hearing of the murder, reported that when driving through Coalisland earlier that afternoon, he had seen men at a bridge acting suspiciously. A follow up by the Army and RUC found discarded masks and boiler suits hidden under the bridge which had been used by the terrorists who murdered Private Gibson (one terrorist was subsequently convicted).

Ivan Davison[7] was that soldier:

I was driving along the back roads from the east side of Coalisland heading to Cookstown. It was a Sunday afternoon; the roads were quiet and I was in no rush. My full time job was a professional bus driver with Ulsterbus. I knew this area well and of course had patrolled along these roads for many years.

On approaching a junction near Moor Bridge, close to Coalisland town, I saw a car approaching from the side road at a T junction just ahead of me. I slowed down indicating for the driver to proceed; it was just a courteous gesture, something we as bus drivers would often do on these rural roads. The car hung back, did not proceed which I thought was odd and as I drew level with the vehicle the people in the car were head down, no acknowledgement of me, again a bit odd. I slowed down, passing the junction. I was watching in my rear view mirror as another car arrived and the cars went on to the bridge, men got out and proceeded to throw bags under the bridge. I continued my journey and within a few minutes I was stopped by a UDR patrol at Tullywiggan

---

6 +Pte George Samuel (Sam) Gibson 1927-79: 8 UDR 1970-79: Security Guard: Killed 29th April 1979.
7 Pte (Ivan) Alexander Davison 1956-: 8 UDR 1977-86: Bus Driver.

Bridge. These soldiers were all members of the Company at Cookstown that I served in. Dessie Gordon[8] was the stop man on the VCP; he asked where I was coming from and proceeded to tell me Sam Gibson had been shot dead just a short time ago, when cycling to his work in Dungannon from the town of Coalisland where he lived. I knew Sam very well; we had served together in the UDR for quite a few years and he was the most conscientious, modest and honest man you could have ever wished to know. I then told Dessie about the activity I had seen at the Moor Bridge, the two cars, men throwing bags under the bridge. It was definitely suspicious and not that far from where Sam had been gunned down and killed. Dessie radioed the information on to our HQ at Killymeal House near Dungannon and I went straight to the UDR base.

I was out on patrol that afternoon when the Company Commander arrived and took me to Killymeal, our Battalion HQ in Dungannon, I was debriefed by the Intelligence Cell about every detail I had saw at the Moor Bridge earlier, shown car colour paint cards as we tried to identify the colours and makes of these two vehicles, which we managed to do. A follow up acting on the information I had given resulted in the recovery of boiler suits, gloves, masks and footwear used by the gunmen who had murdered Sam that afternoon. The RUC arrested a young man Corr[9] from Coalisland, a neighbour of Sam Gibson and he confessed to his involvement in the murder, membership of the PIRA and moving the gun team for the murder. The Corr family and the Gibsons had been neighbours for years. Mrs Corr had attended Sam's wake, her son was convicted and given a jail term of seventeen years for his part in Sam's murder.

Aggie Simpson continues:

It was important to build up as much information on a suspect as possible from DOB (Dates of Birth), vehicles they used, who they associated with and who they were related to. We were later joined by an ex Regular Army soldier who had done his 22 years' service and had been a chief clerk. He was invaluable to us as he passed on his knowledge and trained us in the running of a military office, and around this time a Warrant Officer from the Scots Guards was attached to us on a two year posting.

I had reached the rank of Corporal when I was told I was being transferred to the Ops Room, I was gutted by this but threw myself into the day to day

---

8 Sgt Desmond (Dessie) Gordon BEM 1958-: 8 UDR 1977-90: Car Repair Business Owner.
9 Oliver Alphonsus Corr c1961-: Coalisland: Apprentice Welder: Sentenced (1980) to 17 years' imprisonment for conspiring to murder members of the Security Forces, membership of the IRA, and other charges: 'Corr also admitted acting as driver for two PIRA men who shot dead Mr Sam Gibson a part-time member of the UDR on 29th April 1979': Given a concurrent 15 year sentence for possession of the guns used in the attack (*Tyrone Courier* 15th October 1980).

running of the Ops Room. By now the Battalion was growing and was becoming very professional. More younger men and women were joining and we had a very good full-time Platoon. As well as being in charge of the Ops Room I trained the new radio operators and during this time I was promoted to the rank of Sergeant.

From the start of the Troubles, Dungannon town centre commercial property was attacked on numerous occasions with car bombs and incendiary devices and the Battalion suffered casualties with murders and attempted murders of our off-duty personnel, attacks against patrols and military and police bases. I recall an incident when one of our civil servants, based at Killymeal, when driving through Dungannon along the Circular Road accompanied by her mother, an IRA gang shot at a Regular Army foot patrol close by, hitting their car and her mother was killed. It was just not safe to socialise in the local towns off duty. Within the camp we had a mess where we could relax, have a game of pool or darts or a drink without the fear of having to watch your back; we were very much one big family. Throughout my service in East Tyrone with 8 UDR, the threat from Republican terrorists remained at the highest level.

At the end of 1978 both the Operations Room and Intelligence Cell moved to Castle Hill in Dungannon and were combined with the Regular Army unit based there, with our Battalion leading on intelligence assessments in support of day to day military operations in East Tyrone. The collation system we used was mostly by manual record keeping and visual displays. My main task within the Intelligence Cell was to set up the Search Cell. I researched and plotted on overlays all past incidents, shootings, murders, culverts, derelicts, hides, weapons found, home locations of suspects, off-duty targets and all this information was invaluable in the planning of search operations for our Battalion, the RUC, and new Regiments on roulement (*short tours*) in East Tyrone.

One night when returning home from duty in the early hours I noticed a car parked just before the entrance to the housing estate where I lived. I thought this was unusual so I decided to drive past so I could note the VRN, make and colour. I reported it the next day and suddenly Special Branch were very interested as the car was owned by a known PIRA suspect. Within the next couple of weeks the occupant of the house, Seamus Morgan,[10] was arrested and questioned and later released. PIRA assassinated him in March 1982.

---

10 Seamus (James Gerard) Morgan c1958-82: Dungannon: Van Driver and Photographer: Body found in Forkhill March 1982 (believed to have been killed in Dundalk on 5th March 1982): On a list of alleged informers killed by PIRA taken from Government files released to the Public Record Office (*Guardian* 30th December 2019): PIRA telephoned two radio stations saying they had executed one of their members for allegedly passing information to the Security Forces (*Tyrone Courier* 10th March 1982).

By now I was a Colour Sergeant and had returned to the Intelligence Cell as office manager and we had about 16 full and part-time people in the cell. We had cells at each of our Company locations manned by part-time staff who provided operational briefings for patrols and debriefs. I liaised with the various RUC branches, Brigade, and Tasking and Coordination Group (TCG), providing Operations with the best possible information and direction for military patrols and assessments of the terrorist threat. It was about this time there was an anniversary parade for the hunger striker Martin Hurson[11] who died in 1981 and the IO (Intelligence Officer) asked me to accompany him to see who was moving about in the Galbally area where Martin Hurson was from. We set off in an unmarked car in civilian clothes, taking a tape recorder so I could record the make and colour and VRN of vehicles and headed to Galbally. We recorded loads of registrations and I spotted Peter Sherry,[12] a known activist from Dungannon in with the main command group from the Cappagh area and this was our first indicator of his position of importance now in PIRA. Though we thought we could just drive past unfortunately this was not the case. Local Republican activists were controlling the area; suddenly we were flagged down and told to pull in and park. Panic and fear hit then and I thought this is how it was all going to end, but the IO said we would go back and park at the hall as it would be easier to get out when the parade finished. Thankfully they said OK and we reversed back and waited a few minutes and headed off, but within minutes we were stopped again and asked where we were going; again the quick thinking of the IO who said we were on our way to visit family in Carrickmore and we were told to be on our way. It was only when we returned to Castle Hill that I realised the IO was as scared as I was. However

---

11 Edward Martin Hurson c1954-1981: Cappagh/Pomeroy: Fitter: Sentenced to 20 years' imprisonment on 29 charges relating to explosions 1972-1976 (including landmines at Cappagh 1975, Galbally 1975 and Reclain 1976), conspiracy to murder and possession of firearms: Following appeal a retrial was ordered: In September 1979 given concurrent sentences of 15 years for causing an explosion in 1975 and five years for membership of the IRA: Hunger striker died 13th July 1981 (*Tyrone Courier* 30th November 1977 and 19th September 1979, and *Irish Republican News* 14th July 1981).

12 Peter John Sherry c1955-2018: PIRA: Dungannon: Sentenced to seven years' imprisonment March 1975 for refusing to recognise the Court and using an imitation gun to force the drivers of a lorry and a car to hand over their vehicles; they were later found burnt out. (*Dungannon Observer* 29th March 1975): Charged with a variety of terrorist type offences in 1979 and 1980 but found not guilty when super grass Patrick McGurk refused to give evidence (*Tyrone Courier* 11th February 1982 and 26th October 1983): Sentenced to life imprisonment on 12th June 1986 for conspiring to carry out bomb attacks in London and elsewhere in the south of England during 1985 (*Independent* 11th September 1994 and *Tyrone Courier* 25th June 1986) and the bombing of the Conservative Party Conference in Brighton in 1984 (*Guardian* 10th June 1986).

next day we set about finding out ownership of the registrations and collated the information.

I had built up an excellent working relationship with the various branches of the RUC and we provided detailed information for the RUC collators about associations with suspects, gained from VCP activity and off-duty reports. Our search cell was very active and had some good results from directing rummage and planned searches for terrorist munitions in East Tyrone. One off-duty report referred to an active hide near Coalisland and this was reported to Special Branch who assessed the potential to develop this from their resources. This again was real time information and I was tasked to accompany a small team headed up by resources from TCG.

We met at Castle Hill camp, it was night time, the area in question was put out of bounds to all patrols and a person briefed us that he would have his men secure the area. Once that was done we would move in an unmarked car to a drop off point and I would accompany the people in the vehicle who would have full operational control. We waited till the early hours and deployed to the area. An hour or so later we returned to Castle Hill camp where the search team who had deployed to the area of the hide brought in three weapons. SOCO who I knew, was there, we chatted, it was all very professional; this was just a normal day's work for this unit. The weapons were test fired for their ballistic history in a pipe range in the camp and the leader thanked everyone for their patience. Needless to say no one was to discuss this outside of SB and then I was stood down and went home.

Around this period of the early eighties a major success was achieved by the RUC when an active member of PIRA from Dungannon was turned and he was prepared to give evidence in court about PIRA members, their activities and their role in terrorist atrocities in East Tyrone. He was referred to as a super grass (he was one of the McGurk[13] family, a known member of PIRA). During his wait for a court case to be called his mother passed away and her funeral was held in Dungannon. The local gossip went wild with everyone wondering if McGurk would turn up for the funeral of his mother. On the morning of Mrs McGurk's funeral the super grass arrived at Killymeal, escorted by the RUC and he was brought to a quiet area of the camp where we waited and I remember he was treated with the reverence you would pass to anyone who has just lost their mother. He took a little whiskey I recall, not unusual at an Irish wake in those days and I suppose this small gathering was. A patrol reported the cortège was en route to the burial ground and McGurk was brought over

---

13 Patrick McGurk c1948-: PIRA: Dungannon: Fitter: Sentenced to six years' imprisonment for carrying a firearm with intent to commit the indictable offence of false imprisonment and other related offences (*Tyrone Courier* 11th October 1972).

to the helipad and it took him to the graveyard to see from the air the final resting place of his mother. After the interment in the graveyard he was flown over her home and back to base. He was very appreciative for this, thanked us and went on his way.

I retired from the Regiment in the late 1980s when I married and I moved to Scotland to be with my husband. I had met him when we were on an adventure training exercise based at Folda House which was administered by the Household Division to which our Battalion was affiliated. We visit family in Aughnacloy and I still remain in touch with my extended UDR family. I was saddened when I saw the destruction by fire of Killymeal House where I spent much of my service life.

5

Our Towns Devastated

Attacks on Property – Commercial Bombings

Successful PIRA attacks on commercial property sapped everyone's morale. In East Tyrone Dungannon was the principal target. There were two types of device. Blast incendiaries consisted of a small amount of commercial or military explosive attached to a can of petrol with a short time fuse. They were usually placed outside the property. The cassette incendiary had a small charge, operated on a long, often acid fuse, and was placed inside the property in clothing or other item likely to burn well. They were designed to go off after the premises had closed allowing a fire to take root. The aim of both types of device was to cause maximum damage.

In addition there was the danger of car bombs which could do tremendous damage to property and also inflict mass casualties. Town centres were especially vulnerable until vehicle access to them was controlled or forbidden. On most occasions PIRA gave a warning of car bombs and blast incendiaries but sometimes communication failed and then casualties occurred.

Warnings were also given on occasions to lure the Security Forces onto a secondary device or to gain information for a future attack such as the location of an ICP or cordon.

Countering these threats depended on the alertness of the public and the owners of commercial premises. Once a device was initiated a major fire took hold. This and the possibility of further devices took a long time, often all night, for the police and soldiers to deal with, sealing off the area, evacuating everybody, and clearance of the device. All the time there was a risk of booby-traps and shooting attacks on the cordon. Everyone became very tired and wanted to get back to their homes, or in the case of part-time soldiers to their jobs, but there were no quick solutions.

The effect on a town and everyone in it was debilitating. Shops and commercial premises of all types were lost and often took many years to replace. With them went jobs and so a loss of income for them and for the town.

It was not even necessary for the terrorists to plant a device; the Security Forces could be stretched just as easily by hoaxes (dummy devices) and scares (no device just a telephone warning), neither of which involved any significant risk for the terrorists. Commercial bombing also gave the terrorists the opportunity to collect payment of protection monies from the owners of premises; and it was no coincidence that certain building firms were prepared to step in very quickly after an attack.

Multiple, coordinated attacks stretched resources to the limit. Just dealing with a large number of attacks was difficult but there was also the uncertainty of not knowing what more was to come; reserves had to be kept ready in case PIRA attacked elsewhere. On 25th September 1983 seven bomb and blast incendiary attacks and one hoax were mounted against premises in and around Dungannon over a two hour period between 10 pm and 1 am next day. Four premises were destroyed.

Between 1970 and 1992 there were 631 IED attacks against commercial properties in East Tyrone of which 464 fully initiated; 253 of these were incendiaries and 73 were vehicle bombs. The remaining 138 were bag IEDs, consisting of commercial and home-made explosive packed into bags, suitcases and innocuous carriers such as shopping trolleys and prams. The most extensively bombed town was Dungannon. In the town 240 IEDs were planted: 110 incendiary (79 fully initiated), 101 bag (70 fully initiated) and 29 vehicle IEDs (22 fully initiated).

Car Bomb Scotch Street Dungannon 18th June 1974 © Victor Patterson

Car Bomb Scotch Street Dungannon 18th June 1974 © Richard Scott

Blast Incendiary Derryvale, Coalisland 14th May 1980

A D Company patrol heard the sound of breaking glass at Derryvale factory. During investigation, the patrol found a device which later exploded causing minor damage. The patrol arrested two men who were trying to escape from the scene and both were later charged with causing an explosion and PIRA membership.

Joe Kerr[1] was the patrol commander:

> Prior to the Derryvale Incident I was a member of a foot patrol commanded by Jackie McMenemy.[2] We served together in J Company, a part-time Company based in Dungannon. We were on foot patrol, late one evening on the edge of Dungannon town, near the Ballygawley road and the Lisnahull junction, when I spotted a flashing light in the darkness from high ground

---

1 Cpl Joseph (Joe) Henry Kerr 1942-: 8 UDR 1971-92: (R Irish until 1997): MID and GOC's Commendation: Factory Operative.
2 WO2 John (Jackie) Samuel McMenemy BEM 1935-2020: 8 UDR 1971-92: (R Irish until 1993).

on the north side of our position. I told Jackie what I had seen and to be careful. There was something odd about that and we went firm in the area for several minutes. Nothing more was seen so we continued on our route and probably had only gone 50 metres when the Ulsterbus Depot went up in flames. Blast incendiaries had been put into the buses causing massive damage to the fleet, destroying many buses. The Fire Brigade was tasked. We gave cover to the brigade who tried to save some of the buses; few survived intact. A massive blow to the public and school transport system, this was an easy target attacked many times until eventually the depot was relocated to a more secure area of Dungannon. The flashing light was obviously used to warn the perpetrators of our presence in the area. The people of Dungannon were disgusted with this type of attack as it impacted greatly on everyone's lives in some way or other.

A local person from this area of Dungannon came to see me shortly after the burning of the buses and gave me the names of five local young people who were involved in the attack. He made me promise that his name would never be divulged; I passed the information to the Commanding Officer and although pressed hard by the police to divulge the name, I had made a promise and I stuck to it. The police arrested and charged some of this group. I remember one was sent to the young offenders' detention centre because of his age and he did not serve a long sentence. On his release, the same person came back to see me saying that he was very afraid of this lad and he could not help me anymore. These were very dangerous people who controlled the area he lived in.

Leading on from this, we were on a foot patrol in the Coalisland area late in the evening in May 1980. I was the patrol commander, we were moving to the outskirts of the town on the north side, heading into an area called Derryvale. There were a number of small businesses around the Derryvale area. Some had been attacked by PIRA in the past and they were vulnerable, easy targets. It was a very windy night and as my patrol made its way down a hill into Derryvale, again I noticed a light flashing from high ground near some houses on our left. I stopped the patrol, warned them to be careful and proceeded on our route. I had two men deployed at the front when we heard glass breaking somewhere ahead of us.

The strong wind was blowing towards us, into our faces. We moved forward and then we heard people coming running up to a wall towards us, close to a factory which produced wooden furniture as its main business. We nabbed the two men at the wall and held them while one of our soldiers went forward to the factory to check around. He saw broken glass and a large blast incendiary device sitting on the window sill of the broken window on the inside of the building. They must have had their back to us as we patrolled towards the factory and the wind alerted us to the sound of breaking glass. If the flashing light was a warning to the bombers, they obviously had not seen it this time.

The patrol arrested the suspect bombers, brought them to me and I radioed in that we needed the police and the Fire Brigade to be tasked immediately. I split the two suspects up so they could not communicate with each other and the RUC were with us very quickly from the Coalisland station and I handed them over to the police. We discussed the light I had seen flashing near the occupied houses on the hill overlooking the road. We went up with the police to the area where I saw the light and they called at the houses and spoke to the occupants. They didn't enter the houses, just made sure the occupants were OK, not under any duress. The blast incendiary exploded but the Fire Brigade now on site with us was able to deal with the blaze very quickly and minimal damage was caused to the furniture factory. We gave cover to the various agencies until stood down. The police dealt with the two arrested men,[3] we made statements and I never did find out what happened to the bombing team. Things were just so busy in East Tyrone that there was hardly a week went by without a serious terrorist incident.

Bomb in Thomas Street, Dungannon 4th June 1973

Private Tom Stewart lived in Thomas Street. His father, Senator Billy, owned the chemist shop (Stewart and Chapman) in the square. Tom was going to bed when he saw out of the window a terrorist putting a bomb outside the offices of the Electricity Board.

Tom Stewart[4] tells his story:

> I joined the UDR when I was twenty-one, on 28th June 1972 and did two years, until 1974. George Shaw[5] and I joined the same night and we signed on at Killymeal. We were issued with the 'green' uniform and a 7.62 SLR. I got a really horrible rifle. It must have been one of the original ones, with the steel butt and wooden stock. When you went to the range the normal gas setting was 7. Well, mine worked at 4, whatever was wrong with it, and it used to knock me back about a foot every time I fired it!

---

3   Brendan McPhillips c1959-: Brackaville: Unemployed.
    Paul William John Corr c1960-: Brackaville: Welder.
    Both jointly charged with possession of two bombs with intent to endanger life or cause serious damage to property on 14th May 1980 (and other offences): McPhillips was also charged with membership of the IRA (*Tyrone Courier*, 21st May 1980).
4   Pte Thomas (Tom) Stewart MM 1951-: 8 UDR 1972-74: Local Government/Public Health Inspector.
5   +Maj George Shaw 1929-87: 8 UDR 1972-87: MID (posthumous): Killed 26th January 1987.

I'd just completed my training and qualified as a Public Health Inspector and I joined because I thought it was the right thing to do. We were a family very much focused on service and I felt it was my civic duty. In my job I was doing a duty to the public and joining up was an enhancement of that.

Before I qualified, my first job was doing a survey of bin collections. I sat on a bin lorry for a couple of months and got to know all the fellas. It was hard, hard work; the men would maybe have cycled to Dungannon for an eight o'clock start. It always left me feeling that the low-paid were so badly looked after. Those men could have been lying in their bed getting 'the dole', but they cycled to their work and cycled home again because they couldn't afford a car. They never complained and they were real gentlemen. If they saw a woman coming along, struggling with a bin, they'd have shouted over to her: 'Leave that there, missus!' and take it for her.

Just after I qualified, I was sent to Omagh as a Public Health Inspector. I loved working in Omagh and had no ambition to come back to Dungannon but when there was a reorganisation of local government in 1973, there was a staffing issue and the easiest solution was to move me to Dungannon a week before the reorganisation took place! And that's where I spent the remainder of my career. Initially, I worked mainly as a District Inspector. Environmental Health is a massive ambit; we did unfit housing, food hygiene, food standards, health and safety, public health complaints, the role was unending. I also did one or two days a week in the abattoir and eventually I worked there full-time. It was hard physical work but it was a very happy environment and I enjoyed it. I did post mortems and had a managerial role as well. When the abattoir was sold by the Council, I went back to the office job which I didn't particularly like.

When I joined the UDR, I was posted to K Company. We did a lot of foot patrols around the town and a lot of guard duty. Unfortunately, we didn't get out on mobile patrols too often. It was fairly well paid in those days, £2.79 a night, but I think I only got paid for half the duties I did! Somebody said to me one night: 'You only do that for the money'. I tore up the cheque for the month's wages in front of him. Being in the UDR left you feeling vulnerable at work. We were on call at work so when you got a call to go to a premises, you weren't sure what was in store.

On 4th June 1973, I remember because it was my mother's birthday, we'd been out on patrol the previous night I think, and I was absolutely shattered. It was a lovely June evening and I was going to bed about half past ten. In our house in Thomas Street, I had an attic bedroom with a rather peculiar dormer window, glass down either side of it, at the front and at the peaks. I was standing at the window, looking out and I saw these two, a man and woman, coming up from Union Place. There was just something about them; they were furtive. They walked across the road to a gated entry at the end of a terrace of houses, beside the Electricity Board offices. The gates were set back slightly into the terrace and usually kept closed, as they were that night. They stepped back in there and were looking about them but didn't say anything. He set something on the ground.

There was a UDR Land Rover patrol which came along and he grabbed her and started kissing her and fondling her in the gateway. It was a J Company patrol and of course they were jeering and cat-calling from the back of the Land Rover, the usual thing. When the patrol went past, the two of them looked out again and I then knew there was something going on. I went and grabbed the old Enfield .38 issue revolver (we were only allowed to carry it to and from duty, and I had never fired it). Apparently these guns were used by the Tank Corps during the Second World War. We used to have debates about whether you should shoot it or throw it and decided that throwing it might be more accurate! The man bent down and just as I was about to challenge him, the sparks started coming out, so I was two or three seconds too late. The realisation hit me then: 'I'm going to die' and my hands were shaking, shaking terribly. I said to myself: 'God give me strength to do what I have to do'. And my hands stopped shaking.

My father was sleeping downstairs because he'd had a stroke and wasn't very mobile, my next door neighbour was a leg amputee and he went to bed early and, just next to where they primed the bomb, there was a baby of only a few weeks old. You process all this very quickly; there's the instinct to look after your family but also a degree of anger: 'How dare you come here and do this to us!' At least three people were going to die so I knew I had to keep doing this and the only way to have any success was to make him defuse the bomb. I challenged him: 'Army! Hands up!' and they did put their hands up.

I had been stamping on the floor to alert anyone downstairs and my mother phoned the police. They arrived and shouted at the man to move. 'I can't', he said, 'there's a boyo up there has a rifle on me'. Then the fuse went out. It was a Cordtex fuse, the kind you'd see on a Western, with the sparks flying out of it.

There had previously been a bomb in the same place and it had blown my brother out of bed; glass went everywhere. My sister was away at the time and a triangle of glass went through the head of her bed. She'd have been killed.

They gave themselves up and were hauled off to the police station. The ATO was called and that was about it. The bomb contained nine half-pound sticks of gelignite and ten pounds of home-made explosive and there was going to be no warning.

I had to go to give evidence in the High Court in Belfast as Witness 'A', but it was in open court and I was visible to everyone. The police brought me to Belfast and we parked at Crumlin Road jail and walked through the tunnel. Afterwards, l was dropped off at Thomas Street and told: 'Look after yourself, lad'. It was at that stage where, if there was only one witness, they got shot. There was a lot of pressure. It was later that I got a letter to say that I'd been awarded a Military Medal. The Queen presented me with the medal at Buckingham Palace in 1975. She was totally briefed and spoke to me, although she probably couldn't understand my Tyrone accent. I brought my mum and an uncle who lived in London.

I was offered a reward, but I wouldn't touch it. I was just doing my duty. They also offered to make me an acting Lance Corporal, but again I refused. I worked with men of forty, fifty years of age, who had the wisdom of Methuselah, but little education. I've always had the greatest respect for those people and I wasn't going to be the wee irk with a grammar school education who was giving orders to people who would be a hundred times better at it than I ever would.

The woman was Eileen McCrea, daughter of 'The Duke' McCrea from the Donaghmore Road, near the Sprickly Well. The bomber was Ciaran O'Donnell,[6] Plunket O'Donnell's son. In court O'Donnell said McCrea knew nothing about the bomb and she got off. The defence lawyer said that 'her affections for this man had been cynically abused'. The bomb was in the lining of his duffle coat and he had carried it over his shoulder. After the previous bombing, a damaged jacket was found lying in the rubble. On the day of the trial 'the Duke' McCrea opened the door of my father's shop and shouted at my father: 'She got off' and my father replied: 'She's lucky to be alive'.

I remember going in to get a firearms certificate for a pistol the next day and the constable said to me: 'We don't do this for everyone, you know. You're so lucky'. I said: 'You don't get two bombers handed to you on a plate every day!' I got a firearms certificate for a Star .22 pistol, which was just marginally better than the Enfield!

My father had a chemist's shop in Church Street, Dungannon close to St Anne's Church. He was not a man of many words. They had their windows broken a few times by blasts, but not to the same extent as damage to businesses in the Square or Scotch Street. They were relatively lucky. There was never any direct attack on them. I suppose those that were doing the bombing realised that the church was an attack too far, although it did a lot of damage in the church which is only now being found. It lifted the roof and dropped it and it means very expensive repairs to St Anne's. However the businesses in Scotch Street were decimated.

---

6 Eileen McCrea c1955-: Dungannon: Waitress.
Ciaran Francis O'Donnell c1954-: Dungannon: Joiner.
Both were charged with planting a bomb outside the Electricity Board in Dungannon on 4th June 1973 with intent to endanger life or cause injury to property: O'Donnell was subsequently convicted and sentenced to seven years' imprisonment: McCrea was acquitted. (*Dungannon Observer* 9th June 1973, *Tyrone Courier* 18th July and 19th December 1973): O'Donnell PIRA HMP Magilligan (*Dungannon Observer* 20th December 1975).

It was part and parcel of our work as Public Health Inspectors; we regularly had to go in and clear food shops. I remember going to a grocer's shop in Main Street, Fivemiletown and there was a door into a store in the main part of the shop which was jammed shut by the force of an explosion. There wasn't a mark on the door. But when the door was opened there were tea caddies that had been pierced with lumps of glass. That was typical. You'd get glass, ground glass, everywhere and anywhere. It was a major decision for someone aged twenty-two or twenty-three to clear a shop of goods worth thousands of pounds. But it was just part of a day's work in those days.

6

Searches and Rummages

The terrorist supply chain was long and often interdicted, so the PIRA quartermaster had to hide his weapons and explosives where they would not be found. At the same time he wanted to ensure that if they were found they could not be attributed to him. Long term hides tended to be buried where they could be overlooked, to ensure they were not found and staked out, and also have some form of marker so that they could be visited by day or by night.

Finding these hides without specific intelligence was difficult. Careful analysis of the available information could indicate likely areas to be searched. It was then a matter of thinking like the terrorist faced with the problem of siting his hide. Even then a great deal of time and effort in all weathers was spent meticulously searching an area, often without success.

A search was mounted when there was information to base it on, and it was usually carried out by a trained search team with the appropriate equipment. Rummaging was a normal patrol task.

When a hide was found the ideal was to do so in such a way that it could be staked out and the terrorist caught next time it was used (referred to as Op Clean). This was rarely possible. Clearance of such a hide took a long time because of the risk of booby-traps.

The terrorist had to move his weapons, ammunition and explosives and tended to do so in small quantities by vehicle using cut outs. Dead letter boxes had to be recognisable but there were hundreds of sign posts and other markers on the highways. Patience, inquisitiveness and many other talents were required to make a find. Some men had the nose or the eye. Success came as a result of many unproductive hours of rummaging.

Always there was the threat while rummaging of a booby-trap or a remotely controlled device. So this task required the utmost caution. A device would not necessarily be where the transit hide was but could well be aimed to catch a clearance operation.

Granville 26th May 1974

Jimmy Scarlett[1] recalls some early successes:

> I was a mechanic by trade and worked in a number of garages in the Dungannon area. I joined the UDR in '71 as a part-time soldier. There was three of us joined and I was driving the MGB GT at the time and we came down the road from Omagh with all the kit in the back. It was still 6 UDR and we used to have to go and do guard in Omagh. And then 8 was formed and we went over to Killymeal then. At that time there was no fence round it and no guard room and you slept in lorries. Then they did up a stable in the courtyard as a guard room and put a picket fence round the place and you just did prowling and guard duties. When K Company was formed in Dungannon, we worked out of the base at Killymeal House. We did patrols about three evenings a week. I now worked as a Civil Service mechanic in the MT in Killymeal during the day and part-time in the UDR at night and at weekends. I was in 41A of 12 Platoon.
>
> In the early 1970s the IRA carried out a number of attacks on police stations and one of their favourite weapons was the RPG-7 rocket launcher. Pomeroy police station was attacked a few times and they used RPG-7 rockets. The night the IRA attacked them in 1972, the rocket mustn't have went off because it was found stuck in the sandbags in the top sangar. Mervyn Boyd was in the sangar when it happened. The security wire was up by then. If the weapon didn't travel a certain distance, it didn't arm the head. There was a wee wire linking the head and the tail and going through the wire the tail got caught and broke the arming wire to the warhead.
>
> By 1972 we had just moved to live in Granville (*one mile south-west of Dungannon*) on the edge of a Republican stronghold. I used to go out walking regularly and I'd go up the hill behind my house and just keep an eye to see what cars were going past. I was curious to know what was going on around me and we were trained to be watchful, even when off duty, and to pick up on anything that didn't look or sound right. You got to know everybody's car and what time they were coming home for instance, and you got to know that if some car shouldn't be there, it wasn't right, y'know.
>
> Now there was always one car that came at a certain time to a derelict farm behind my house and it would take about twenty minutes to do whatever it was doing and then left. I picked up on this.... So one Sunday, we were out doing a normal patrol. I was a Lance Corporal and a Section Commander and I decided to take my section to check out a few derelicts in the same area where I'd noticed this suspicious activity. It was the second one we searched. The

---

1 Cpl James (Jimmy) Scarlett 1949-: 8 UDR 1971-85: Vehicle Mechanic.

house isn't there any more. It was derelict and full of hay and there was cattle, calves and that in it as well. There was an old half loft and the first thing we found was a cleaning kit for the RPG. It was in a big long canvas bag and there was all the cleaning kit in it and the sights. So we knew we were onto something. We looked all around the house and then we found the pipe bombs, hidden under hay. We kept on looking, which I suppose we shouldn't have done as the bombs were there, but we knew the rocket launcher had to be there somewhere too. The rocket launcher wasn't in the house however.

It was wearing up to night time and coming near the end of the search so we decided to move the Land Rovers out onto the road. At that point, out of the corner of my eye I could see somebody walking across the fields close to where we had found the pipe bombs. It was nearly dark by then and I called for someone to put a flare up. I was expecting a hand flare instead of the big Schermuly flare. But by the time they got the flare up whoever it was had long gone and the flare blew the wrong way as well.

Well then I knew something had happened so I went over towards the derelict but I could see nobody. I got the men back in to do a rummage at the place where I'd seen the man and we found the rocket launcher, buried into the hedge in a barrel. It was in transit and it was ready to lift. I would say that whoever I saw was coming to lift it. I'd say that fella probably didn't see us and it's only when we started to put the Land Rovers out on the road that he knew there was something wrong and he got out of the way. It's just a pity we didn't catch him but at least we got the rocket launcher and that's the main thing.

Later, the forensic people said that this RPG-7 rocket launcher was the same one that was used in the Pomeroy attack when Mervyn Boyd was in the sangar.

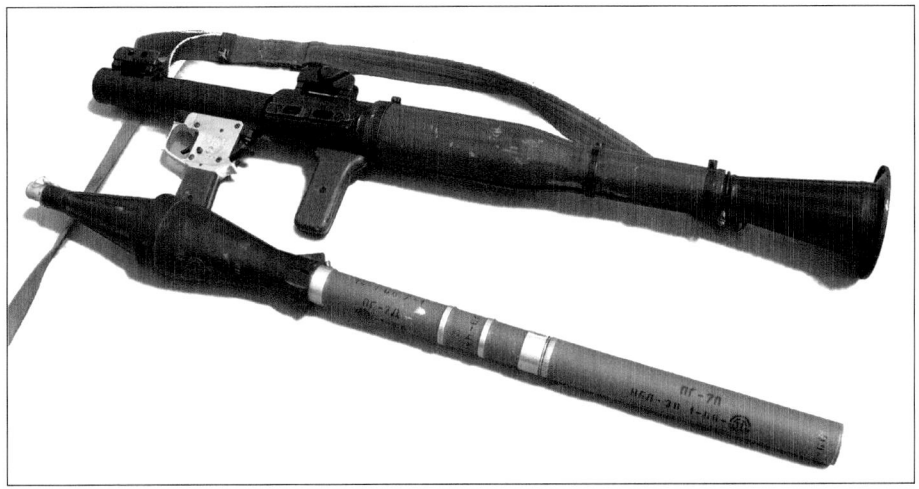

RPG-7
Shoulder-launched, anti-tank rocket-propelled grenade launcher.
Soviet Union manufacture; maximum effective range 300 metres

Our section 41A, all part-time soldiers, had some amazing successes, through hard work and diligence. One incident that I remember was when we recovered two guns at Aghnagar one night. We were on patrol in a Shorland and a Land Rover. At that time, if you met a car on a wee road, the first Land Rover pulled in and let the car go past and the second one stopped the vehicle further along the road. I was in the Shorland and saw the Land Rover up ahead letting this car go past, but before he came to us, the driver of the car took a road to the right and we went up after him. There were two weapons thrown out of the car and we drove over them just to get the men in the car, but the Land Rover came up behind us and lifted two rifles off the road.

We caught the vehicle and arrested them but then we had to take the Land Rover and go and get the dog handler. That was two people away in the Land Rover for there was nobody in Killymeal to bring the dog out. So that left only four or five people guarding several suspects. One of them I had worked with in a garage in Dungannon, Patsy Gildernew.[2] Then the police came and Geordie Thompson was one of the policemen and of course he knew me and called my name out in front of the suspects!

We had no powers of arrest at that time. There was only three policemen and they would take nothing to do with it, so we brought the suspects into Dungannon to the police station and I had to hand them over to the Military Police. I had to have my picture taken holding one fella and handing him over to the Military Police and they arrested him and handed him over to the RUC. Legally that's the way it had to be done. The rifles were .303s. Gildernew was convicted and got some months in jail.

Another success by 41A was the time a local farmer who lived near Granville got information from a Roman Catholic neighbour that there were guns hidden in a derelict farmhouse. He passed on the information to one of the men in my section and the information was passed to the police. There was a follow-up search and they found two AK47s in transit. The fella that gave the information got an awful hidin' from his neighbour. He was nearly killed. He was a powerful good man, but the neighbour, he was a bad fella.

I was medically discharged in 1990 after I lost the sight of an eye in an industrial accident at Killymeal.

Killucan (by Dunamore), West of Cookstown 25th September 1983

A C Company patrol found the following during a planned search: 37 bags ANFO × 25 kgs each, totalling 825 kgs; 6 × bags fertiliser × 50 kgs, totalling 300 kgs; and 21

---

2 Patrick (Patsy) Gildernew c1951-: Brantry: Labourer: Charged with possession of a .303 rifle and ammunition on 21st February 1974 (*Tyrone Courier* 27th February 1974).

× booster bags × 5 lbs each, totalling 105 lbs. It is estimated that the explosives had been there for a considerable time; due to this and weather conditions, the HME was in bad condition and had started to congeal. On 23rd May 1983, a CWIED estimated at 400-600 lbs was detonated in a culvert; the HME used in this incident was also a bad mix and had started to congeal, which was probably due to deterioration while the HME was in storage. The device was on the Limehill Road, north of Pomeroy and the target an RUC patrol. The lead car was some distance in front and the car attacked was behind; it was unmarked and had only been operating from Pomeroy for ten days. The device only partially exploded but it still caused a 15 foot crater into which the police car fell; two constables had minor injuries.

RUC Vehicle in Crater

The Commanding Officer 8 UDR at that time wrote:

> Every week I held a meeting with the Company Commanders to review progress and give them operational tasks for the forthcoming week. This ensured every soldier felt he or she was contributing to the overall effort. Searches were amongst the most difficult to task because they were usually based on detailed analysis by the Intelligence Cell and/or a process of elimination of all the likely places for weapons and explosives to be hidden. Sometimes the RUC would ask for an area to be searched but if they had any hard intelligence a covert operation

would be mounted, and we were kept well out of the way. Furthermore, searches done by us had to be cleared with the RUC; if the search was successful there was inevitable suspicion that we had some intelligence which we had not shared with the RUC. Trust was all-important.

I gave C Company the task of searching the sandpit at Killucan because it had been identified by the Battalion Intelligence Cell as a likely place for a PIRA long term hide, and it had not been searched in detail for a long time. When the explosives were found I am sure some of the soldiers thought I had known they were there whereas the find was as the result of a lot of meticulous hard work by the Intelligence Cell and then by the men of C Company – and some luck!

Lieutenant Tom McKinney[3] commanded the operation that day:

On Friday 23rd September, I was informed by our Company Commander, Major Turner,[4] my platoon patrol task for Sunday 25th was to carry out of a search at Lough Doo, near Dunamore, accompanied by our Search Dog Handler, Sergeant White.[5]

I was asked to check with the Intelligence Cell, in Dungannon, to find out if there was any up-to-date information on our search, which had been initiated following information of munitions in the area. The main intelligence I gained from the briefing was that the munitions were close to water, or in the area of the lough. I spoke to a member of my platoon, who lived quite close to the area, and he said that there was a house in that area, and in his opinion, the man living there was the Quartermaster for PIRA in that area. On the Sunday morning, which was very foggy, we all reported for duty and were briefed. We were duly dropped off at Lough Doo, and we organised the search teams to search their specific areas.

Sergeant White informed me that the dog had been out on searches all week and was not really interested in carrying out any searches that morning. I told him to get the dog working along a track, where I told him to hide something. When the dog found it, the dog was over excited, because there was obviously something more on this occasion. Sergeant White looked more closely at the area where he had hidden it, and realised that the ground was disturbed, and covered by an old tarpaulin, in turn covered by gravel. At this point he put his

---

3 Capt Thomas (Tom) McKinney MBE 1940-: (Inniskillings/R Irish Rangers 1958-1982 to WO1 (RSM 1 R Irish Rangers then 6 UDR)): 8 UDR 1983-92: (R Irish until 1997): GOC's Commendation (for his actions on 14th November 1988).
4 Maj (Albert) Samuel Turner MBE UD 1932-1996: 8 UDR 1971-91: Second in Command 8 UDR 1985-91: Meat Inspector, Ministry of Agriculture.
5 CSgt Robert (Chalkie) William White 1957-: 8 UDR 1978-92: (R Irish until 1997): MID.

hand under the tarpaulin, lifted it up, and found a pallet, which he discovered had at least 10 bags of a suspicious substance. This was later confirmed by ATO as ANFO. I immediately told him to check the surrounding area, for a secondary device, but the dog did not find anything further.

We were asked to assist ATO to get rid of the ANFO, which we did by emptying the bags into Lough Doo. The helicopter duly arrived to extract us, and we boarded, when the loadmaster passed his headphones to me for the pilot to speak to me. I was pleased with this, thinking he would congratulate us on our morning's work, but he wanted to pass on the bad news of the mass escape from the Maze Prison that morning. I told him of our find, and we were flown into Cookstown base.

Dessie Gordon[6] provides some background on the area and was there that day:

I joined in May '77. In fact, when I was getting my uniform that was the time that Captain Shiells[7] was shot when they were preparing to go to camp. I served the entire time part-time in Cookstown. I started off in G and H and then we transferred everybody into C Company. I served in 2 Platoon in G Company, then moved to 9 Platoon in the new C Company and after a few years, in '84, I was moved to 8 Platoon as Platoon Sergeant. I was there until I left in September 1990. We were on patrol nearly every other night because we worked a system between 8 and 10, or 7 and 9 Platoons, so when I was in 9, I worked in conjunction with 7 Platoon. Then at weekends, you could be out with 8 or 10 and I think what drove us to be out so often, apart from everything else, you were afraid of the other boys finding something and you not there! You wanted to be part of the action, no matter what.

In civilian life, I was working in RA Patrick's Ford garage and then I got an offer of a job with Auto Supplies in Ann Street in Dungannon, as a sales rep. On Mondays, I was in the Donaghmore/Cookstown area, on Tuesdays I was in Moneymore, then up towards Stewartstown and finishing around Tamnamore. On Wednesday, it was up towards Ballygawley and Finlay's quarries, to the Finlay plant, then to Aghnagar and I called with MK Plant in Cappagh. From there, it was up to Finlay's quarry at Galbally crossroads and then back towards home. Thursday was the day for tidying up jobs around Cookstown and Friday was similar, but the big danger was just going to the office. Also, before I left the office every day, I had to ring all these customers to tell them I was coming and to bring them any parts they needed. So you were just setting yourself up

---

6 Sgt Desmond (Dessie) Gordon BEM 1958-: 8 UDR 1977-90: Car Repair Business Owner.
7 +Capt Walter Eric Shiells 1927-1977: (previously RN): 8 UDR 1972-77: Businessman: Killed 29th April 1977.

every morning. Of course, you were doing part-time duties every other night and meeting the men from Cappagh that you were delivering auto parts to during the day!

The worst was the day I called with M&K Plant and the fella who normally placed the orders said: 'Give me ten or fifteen minutes. Go and wait in the wee Portacabin round the back'. There were two girls sitting in there, typing. You can guess how long that ten minutes felt and I kept watching the window, expecting to see a couple of boyos running past with balaclavas. It was absolutely mad.

Anyway it was coming up to Easter of 1979 and RA Patrick sent the car salesman to call with me one evening and asked me to come back to the garage. I left Auto Supplies on the Good Friday and on the Sunday, we were out on a patrol on the Carrickmore Road out of Pomeroy, just down past Lagan Transport, and there was so much going on – a girls' accordion band actually paraded through the checkpoint at one stage – and a bus arrived. We stepped onto this bus and lo and behold, two of the boys out of Auto Supplies were sitting on the back seat of the bus, going to the Easter (Republican) Commemoration Parade in Carrickmore. After returning to RA Patrick, I remember a period of a few weeks when three local suspects were parked at Quinn's Bottling Supplies nearly every morning watching me travelling into work.

I worked with RA Patrick for a while and then started working independently and, over time, I got involved with repairing motors for the police. Apart from wanting to work for myself, it also lowered the threat of driving in and out of the same place every day at the same time. When I was out on patrol, my wife always went to stay with one of her two sisters, so I would have come home here at night on my own or else go to whatever house she was staying in, to take the children to school the next day. On other occasions, I stayed in the base and came out here in daylight. You just tried to vary the routine.

A couple of Sundays before this find, we were out on a foot patrol coming from Lough Doo, from the main Omagh road just above Teebane. We went up the main road, swung that hard left corner and were approaching a small incline in the road, when two cars came down, with at least four men in each car. It was a straight road, so there was nothing we could do, but you could see them braking hard and they swung off suddenly in at a two-storey house which was still under construction. It had just been moved into. We ran up the road, knowing there was something funny about this, and by the time we got up to the yard everybody was inside and the cars were empty. So we radioed for the police and they came up (we had made a sort of semi-cordon round the place), and they went in and had words with the people inside and seemed happy enough about it.

Then about a week before this incident, we were out at Donnelly's crossroads on the Gortacladdy road, heading for Pomeroy and there was a cement lane on the right, leading up to a house. Just about that point as we were walking along, we heard what we thought was one half of a radio transmission. We stayed down and listened and every now and then we could hear this across the fields. So we sent for Nightsun and a Gazelle came from Omagh. Just before it arrived, a car came up the road, we stopped it and it was a suspect from Pomeroy. We made him pull in off the road onto the cement lane and then when the chopper came and flew over us, we switched on the hazard lights of the car so the pilot knew exactly where we were and I told him we were going west of that location. He did a sweep across the fields as we crossed the fields on foot, crossed a couple of hedges and came up to a house. I radioed for clearance to enter the house, we went to the door and the man answered. He was a porter in the South Tyrone Hospital and he lived with his very elderly mother. I asked if we could come and have a look round. A couple of us went in and the old woman was lying on the sofa, all dressed in black, but we didn't feel there was anything suspicious and left. The police came and took a drive round and at the next junction there was one house with an exceptional number of cars outside it. They took registration numbers and so on. Nightsun went back to base and we patrolled on.

Then the following Sunday it was 7 Platoon's turn to be out and we were again up around Lough Doo at around three in the afternoon, doing a search for two long weapons. I remember being on the road, between the mouth of the sandpit and the house where the two cars had turned in. They are just a stone's throw apart. Someone came back and said: 'The dog's indicating down there'. They were all excited that the dog was indicating something definite. Next thing, they said they had found some bags. After that, I think we were kept on the road and didn't put up a cordon at that stage. We were cock-a-hoop about this big find and then the Commanding Officer and the police arrived and we were taken back to base. We were due to be lifted at four, but the lift was delayed. As we walked into the base, we were hit with the news of the Maze escape. It was a real anti-climax and our thousand-pounder never made the news!

This was September '83 and there had been a landmine on that Pomeroy-Carrickmore road in May or June of that year. It only partially exploded because it was starting to disintegrate through age. Landmines were rife at that stage.

Robert (Chalkie) White was the dog handler:

I came home from the Regular Army in '78 and joined 8 UDR in Dungannon. The Quartermaster of 8 UDR was my old Troop Sergeant Major in Germany and he got me into the MT. I stayed in MT for a few months and then volunteered for the Ops Platoon. After a while there, Ned Kirk,[8] who was the dog

---

8   CSgt William Edward (Ned) Kirk 1954-: 8 UDR 1976-92: (R Irish until 2006).

handler, wanted to finish, so I volunteered for the Dog Handler's Course and did that in Melton Mowbray in 1980. It was a good course; I came back and had my passing out at Ballykelly with the testing officer there. I then became operational.

I was working out of Dungannon all the time, but you could have been anywhere in the Province, tasked to wherever you were needed. I was officially attached to Headquarter Company but I worked primarily with B Company. It wasn't conventional. Nothing was conventional, I learned during my time in the UDR!

If there was any kind of incident involving Regular Army, police, it didn't matter, I was involved. If there were robberies or a hi-jacking, any sort of EOD clearance of cars or routes, anything involving Royal Engineers, I was at it. Every time you went out on a search, you had the potential to find something. Even if you were told there was something in a particular spot, it didn't necessarily mean that it was there. You could have been there to put them off or force them to move stuff from somewhere close at hand in case you got too close. There was always a reason for a search. Part of the pleasure of the job was that there was no boredom factor and I was on the go all the time but there were times when my wife didn't see me for three or four days.

My first dog was Ben, 4B35, Lance Corporal. I had him for two years before he was retired from service with bad arthritis and went to live with one of his former handlers. Then I got Shep. They were as different as chalk and cheese. Ben was an old mine-detection dog and would have searched a hundred metres down the road, crossed over and come back and then done the centre of the road, all by himself. You just stood back and watched him. Then I got that lunatic white Labrador, Shep, 0A16, and he just took off as soon as you put the harness on. There was no controlling him; he was just full of energy and you just had to let him run himself out and then start doing the job properly. But he had a fantastic nose and he would have picked up an empty case at fifty yards. The first find I had with him was a handgun, down by the canal in Coalisland, underneath an old Portacabin. One of the men crawled in under the Portacabin and pulled out a Luger pistol.

There were several small finds after that, hides of ammunition and things like that. When Cookstown was sealed off, there was an ex-Reserve policeman who found a wire as he was walking across the fields. He cut the wire and 'walked it in' and found a bomb underneath the road up at the Unipork bacon factory. Because of the diversion round the town, the police cars had to go along that road to go to the police station, so the bomb was intended for the police. In a case like that, you knew roughly where it was, but you had to clear the surrounding area and all that there.

Along the border, weapons could be brought in and taken back again after an incident. But in East Tyrone, being central, they had to store stuff, so you had a better chance of capturing it. Some of the hides that we found over the years and the way they hid them were fantastic. There was one in Coalisland where the hide was in a stream bed. They had dammed the stream, dug in the hide, which was a plastic barrel with a lid, put some muck over the top of it and then let the water flow over again, and the dogs couldn't pick it up.

We started a rumour in Coalisland that the metal detectors wouldn't pick up lead. So for a few months afterwards we found box hides covered in lead and of course the metal detectors picked it up a treat. It was a man up by Meenagh Park in Coalisland that made the hides that were lead-lined.

Up at Lough Doo, I think it was a Thursday when the search started and it was B Company. We found a couple of places that could have been hides. The holes were there, but the hide had been removed and then we found a box hide down by the old sandpit. We searched on Thursday, Friday and Saturday with B Company. Then on the Sunday (it was a gorgeous day, and they always tried to give the part-timers a search every so often on a Sunday), I was tasked to go out with C Company. Tom McKinney was the Platoon Commander and this time we were doing the areas off from where the previous search had centred. We stopped for tea and, as was usual with C Company, the van pulled up with the trays of sandwiches and the flask of tea in the back and we were sitting having a picnic at the corner of the sandpit. I had given one of the guys a piece of explosive that I carried with me, to go and hide it in this sandpit and then let the dog find it. The dog needs to find things to keep motivated.

I finished my sandwiches, got up and put the harness back on the dog. The dog went down the sandpit and then, all of a sudden, shot off to a telegraph pole on the left-hand side of the pit. He showed interest round this mound and I called him off and I said to the guy: 'You put the explosive over there'. He said: 'I wasn't even over there'. I thought this was a bit odd and so I moved the dog further along the sandpit and let him off and again he shot straight back up to the corner. I called the dog back, got somebody to hold on to him, and went across to this mound of earth by the telegraph pole. It just looked like a pile of sand, but I stood on it and scraped it away with my foot and there was a couple of wooden pallets underneath. I pulled them out of the way and there was a dead rabbit in there. I was sure that's what the dog had been after. But underneath the pallets there were some fertiliser bags. I took out my knife and cut through the bag and as soon as I did, I got a whiff of ANFO and ANNIE and I knew then what it was.

I stood up and looked at it for a while till I got into my head what I was seeing and then went across and told McKinney that I thought I'd found a pile of explosives. So we moved everybody back, got on the radio, tasked ATO and so on.

Then ATO turned up and started doing his thing with the wheelbarrow and so on. He pulled things out of the way, got the suit on and went down into the sandpit to have a look and came back up to say that it wasn't wired up; it looked like a store. He took the suit off and he and the Number Two went down with spades and began pulling some of the sand and the pallets out of the way. After a while he came back up and threw me a spade and said: 'You f***ing found it, you go and help dig it out!' We kept digging and it just kept getting bigger and bigger. We ended up with twenty-one bags of ANFO and a load of booster bags of ANNIE, all buried in, pallets on top and soil on top of that.

Find of 1 Ton HME

They think that it was intended to go down under the Omagh road at Teebane, but something had rumbled them and they had just left it there and it was believed they were actually mixing the stuff in a cement mixer in the sandpit.

That was a good day. We got back to camp and next day the Commanding Officer sent for me and gave me a 'Well done'. The cookhouse was summoned to get a bone for the dog so everybody was happy.

We had a lot of finds around Dunamore. Years afterwards, and just about a mile away from the sand quarry, B Company was out in an old sandpit and one of them came across a plastic bag. They opened it and it was explosives. It was foggy, and they flew ATO in by helicopter but he couldn't fly out. When he finished clearing, ATO was in my car with the explosives in the boot, and the WIS team, with the Number 2 and all the kit in the back of his car and that's how we went back to Armagh. That was the same night that they found the booby-trap in Cookstown base in a sweetie tin. The Regulars had the good sense not to open it. We were having a drink in the bar in Armagh when ATO got the request to go to Cookstown. Someone said: 'But we've only just left Cookstown!' but we had to go back. (*Both of these incidents were on 22nd December 1992*)

Ardboe March 1980

Ops Platoon Cookstown found 1 × Ruger and 1 × M1 Carbine on Ardboe Airfield.

WO2 Victor McNickle[9] organised the search operation that day. He explains the background and what happened:

> By the late 1970s early 1980s every battalion had established a search cell attached to the Intelligence Cell.
>
> We had search teams specifically trained in this role both for the rural and urban scenarios drawn from full-time and part-time companies and supported by Greenfinches. Their role was to clear routes, support ATO clearance operations, search for terrorist munitions and search for component parts used to make timers, HME and detonators. The RUC followed this practice; initially all search teams were trained by the military either in Northern Ireland or England. Attached to our Battalion was a search dog and handler and we could draw on other neighbouring battalions and the RUC for additional teams and dogs.
>
> The next level up in the search world was a RESA (Royal Engineers Search Adviser). He and his teams would become involved in high risk clearance operations.
>
> I was trained as a Search Adviser for 8 UDR and therefore when a planned search or follow up to an incident was declared I would plan the operation, book the relevant agencies and search teams needed to complete the operation, take advice from a RESA where necessary, and enact the legal paperwork required for lawful entry by the teams to search private property and individuals.
>
> A considerable amount of time and energy had gone into studying how a terrorist cell would conceal munitions both in urban and rural areas, their intelligence records gathered on SF patrols and bases, and the targets they intended to kill. The planned search was deemed to be an offensive operation. Its aims were to deprive the terrorists of their resources, to gain evidence, to obtain prosecutions, and to protect potential targets.

---

9   WO2 Victor McNickle BEM 1943-: 8 UDR 1971-92: (R Irish until 1999).

There were three types of terrorist hide:

The Long Term Hide: under the control of a quartermaster, specifically constructed, waterproof and likely to be anything from a purpose built bunker to a buried barrel.

The Transit Hide: most likely to be used by the active terrorist cell, well concealed. Could be barrels or creamery cans buried, outbuildings, unoccupied houses, vehicles, and usually convenient for a trusted ASU member to oversee. Very likely to be live when a terrorist attack was planned.

Short Term Hide (often called a Transit Hide): likely to be used by the ASU immediately after a terrorist attack. They needed to dispose of weapons and clothing quickly on their planned getaway route. Hedgerows, derelict buildings, gateways to fields, waste ground, streams and bridges were all potential hide areas.

Our Battalion Search Cell tried to work out where the transit and short term hides were located, and planned searches accordingly. These plans were then fed to Operations and tasks allocated to the Companies. The search picture was developing all the time as new information became available to the Intelligence Cell from people, incidents and finds.

Aggie[10] was our main collator. She had assisted a RESA to set up the Battalion Search Cell and her research after several terrorist incidents east of Cookstown highlighted a specific area where four people of interest lived. Two likely escape routes went through this area and a number of off-duty targets were living close to the area, and there was a terrorist threat targeting off-duty members and patrols too.

The Ops Officer directed a planned rural search was to be mounted and I was tasked to plan the operation and was allocated the Ops Platoon. I had RIC (Air – Reconnaissance Intelligence Centre) produce air photographs and we set about looking at what ground was overseen by suspects and what routes went through the area. We used the Winthrop theory, developed by a Captain Winthrop, in looking for markers and rummage areas for transit hides.

This effort and research produced a search plan, the fields to be searched were allocated to teams, and the method of insertion and extraction was by helicopter. Security was by a roving foot patrol, so soldiers could concentrate on searching. A search dog and basic search equipment were allocated. On the ground, I selected a command point to oversee the search and I was continually visiting the teams as was my responsibility. The day was nearly over, nothing found, when I was called for to go over to a hedgerow where 'Pal' was. He was trying to tell me something and I couldn't make sense of him. At times he was an infuriating soldier but fair play to him, he had found something hidden

---

10 CSgt Aggie Simpson 1956-: 8 UDR 1974-84.

in a rabbit hole. Well I and everyone was elated. It turned out to be two rifles hidden in a transit hide. Our search would deprive the terrorist of weapons, and evidence was gathered.

The Battalion had found terrorist munitions on occasions in the past but we were moving into a new level of offensive operations which was to prove to be extremely effective against all terrorist groupings in East Tyrone.

'Pal', Private Simpson,[11] was the soldier who made the find and tells of his success:

> During the late seventies, the Battalion had formed a full-time Ops platoon. These soldiers were much younger than myself and had trained in Ballykinler. I lived near Dungannon, was single, and really had no immediate family to look about. In the 1970s work had become scarce and I was then serving as a part-time soldier when the opportunity came to go full-time as a member of the guard force in Killymeal. At times I would be sent to work with the Ops Platoon. VCPs in Land Rover patrols during times of high threat was mostly the patrols I was on.
>
> East Tyrone, where the Battalion was based, was a dangerous area, murderous, and we had some very, very sad times. It affected everyone. Terrorism from the Republican movement bit into the very fabric of society.
>
> There were changes happening. It was obvious even to me as a Private soldier and I was told very little in those days and rumours of a full-time company were being talked about. In truth I wasn't everyone's first choice, I took a drink and was single and only had to look after myself, and probably was seen as selfish. Everyone called me 'Pal' and I had a slight speech impediment too, which when I was stressed made it difficult for me to get the right words out.
>
> Victor McNickle organised a search of some rural farmland and roads in the Cookstown area and told me to go to the Ops Platoon and join in with Stanley Gordon when they arrived at Killymeal. I didn't really fathom the briefing that our Search Cell and Intelligence Cell had become interested in this area, but Victor got Aggie to give us a briefing. I was given some search equipment, a wooden pole and a shovel.
>
> We were deploying by helicopter; it was a nice sunny day and the NCOs seemed to know their areas and when we were all joined up on the ground Victor started the search. We worked in pairs, slashing the hedgerows, prodding the ground. It's hard work. Victor was continually going round the teams, so we were on alert and Stanley was looking after security. He was a real character, a brilliant soldier who kept us all amused with his wit.

---

11 Pte Norman (Pal) Simpson 1945-: 8 UDR 1973-92.

It was an uneventful day; we had been on the go from 0600hrs and the helicopter was due back around 1700hrs and Stanley was organising the landing zone. Some teams who had completed their area were starting to check equipment. I was still searching along a hedgerow when I saw yet another rabbit burrow and went back down on my knees and stretched my arm into the burrow as far as I could, when I touched something with my fingertips. It was hard to get a grip but after a couple of attempts I managed to pull the item out and at the mouth of the burrow I saw it was a butt, of a gun.

I was shouting for Victor. I think he thought I had lost something and I couldn't get the right words out to tell him what I had found so had to point at it with my foot. Stanley came over ribbed me about waiting till home time to find something and now he would have to stay! Well we all stayed and the helicopter would pick us up when we finished. The ATO arrived and the hide was cleared; two rifles in very good condition recovered, an M1 and a Ruger. A real success and I felt very good about myself. The old soldiers still had it in them!

M1 and Ruger Rifles

It probably was the find that set my life as a full-time soldier in a different direction. I was posted to B Company as the storeman. I didn't think that being quite a bit older, they would want me. All I can say is that it was privilege to work with them, unbelievable the workload and the success B Company had against terrorism in East Tyrone. They worked long hours, and tasks changed so quickly that eventually I moved a bed into the stores. I never went home for weeks sometimes. It was great craic and although I was the butt of many jokes, this was my family. Every time I would go to resupply them on a search, all you would ever hear was: 'Go and get Pal, he has big long arms. He will find it'.

They were very protective of me; tasks would change and the patrols would need a resupply of batteries or food or equipment. People got injured, jumping a fence maybe or just take ill on patrol or something happened at their home. If they were in control of the area I could meet them at a VCP, or a team would set out markers I would recognise on the side of the road; I would stop a 100 metres on or if they deemed it too dangerous, I would be in a civilian van and we would meet on the periphery at safe houses that B Company had befriended throughout these so-called Republican areas.

I always made sure I had loaves of bread from the cookhouse in the van with our favourite brown sauce, the Houses of Parliament type. When we would meet up late at night after a patrol was extended for whatever reason, it was a welcome bit of food – fresh bread and brown sauce. They never complained; plenty of bitching and banter right enough, and they always made sure there would be a few cans of beer left by my bed, just to say thank you.

I retired when the UDR was disbanded in 1992.

Cappagh 8th August 1984

A 30 lb anti-personnel bomb was found at Aghnagar near Cappagh by 16 Platoon B Company. B Company consisted of about 120 full-time officers and men. Most rotated between guard and operations. 16 Platoon did not do guard duties so was able to conduct longer operations. On this day Corporal David Hogg[12] was commanding a patrol of three four-man teams. He recalls:

> I joined 11 UDR in '76 and it wasn't exciting to say the least. I was in Ballykinler and I actually ran into Dill Pritchard[13] in about 1981, and he was serving in 8 UDR and he was telling me about the craic down in Dungannon. He says: 'Come on down'. My father had transferred, so I transferred as well and it was probably the best move I've ever made. I arrived down, the hunger strikes were just about ending and the work was serious. You didn't get home very often, but the work was good. It was tough, but enjoyable, because you were doing something. Hurson would have been the local hunger striker. There was a lot of pressure on East Tyrone at that stage, and they had re-formed and were working in their cell structure quite successfully. Cappagh PIRA was well advanced at that stage and Coalisland was a hot spot. I went to 4 Platoon in Dungannon, Killymeal, to start. Albert (Dougan)[14] was there, Jimmy Watson[15] was there and 'Ruffy' Reid.[16]
>
> All good characters, but there were some head bangers too! I was living in Lurgan; I never moved from there. I used to go down that motorway at night

---

12 CSgt Thomas David (Boss) Hogg 1956-: 8 UDR 1976-92: (R Irish until 1998): GOC's Commendation.
13 Sgt Brian James (Dill) Pritchard 1960-: 8 UDR 1980-92: (R Irish until 2002): GOC's Commendation.
14 Lt Albert Dougan 1957-: (Parachute Regiment 1974-78): 8 UDR 1978-84.
15 Lt James (Jimmy) Watson 1957-: 8 UDR 1975-84.
16 CSgt Robert (Ruffy) David Johnstone Reid 1957-83: 8 UDR 1975-83.

and I used to laugh the whole way home, at some of the things we got up to. I used to get into bed and the wife would ask: 'What are you laughing at?' And I couldn't tell her!

I played the pipes. I was in the 8 UDR band but I hadn't much time for practising the pipes when I was in B Company. I was out of the band completely, and they were going to sack the band because there wasn't enough numbers, so I said I would go back to the band. That was a good move too. I did the full 23 years and then I stayed on full-time/part-time for a couple of years and then I went to the TA. So you're talking about 38-39 years.

You had no problem doing a job in B Company, because if you weren't doing what you were supposed to do, or up to spec, a Private soldier would come along and tell you 'That's not on here'. The comradeship was very, very good and they did cover each other's backs. You could rely on people.

The day the bomb was discovered, I was an NCO and my normal role was as a Team Commander. However, on this particular day, I was tasked as Patrol Commander, leading a 3-team multiple deployed to the area by helicopter. East Tyrone PIRA were very active and obviously we classed this as a high-risk area to be patrolling in and we were aware that bombs were one of the tactics that could be employed against us. Our intelligence brief for the area was to monitor known terrorists by observation of their areas of work or home and by carrying out vehicle checkpoint duties on the roads. That allowed us to see who was moving around by vehicle.

The other two teams were giving us cover from the high ground off the road and my duty was to operate a checkpoint with my team. It's a rural area so traffic is quite light in the middle of the day. We were moving via fields and roads en route to a target house in order to monitor what was going on. We were relatively close to a known terrorist's house, which we'd been keeping a close eye on for the past few months with intense patrolling. Intense patrolling brought risks and heightened your patrol skills. You were very aware that your patrol was a target. But there had been nothing in the intelligence brief to show that there was a bomb being created.

It was part of my duty as patrol commander on the road to instruct the lads to search as they patrolled forward. This was rummage searching. We were searching visually with no search equipment. I was in visual and verbal control of my team and in radio contact with the other two teams. The front two men were moving forward when the roadside bomb was located by one of the soldiers.

The bomb had been dug into a high bank in the hedgerow. It was well camouflaged; you couldn't see it easily. The soldier made me aware that there was something. He used hand signals to indicate that something had been found. Now we knew that we're in a situation here.

Private Allister Harkness[17] was that soldier:

> I joined the Ulster Defence Regiment on my eighteenth birthday in 1984 and served for two months in C Company 8 UDR before attending my full-time recruits' training cadre at Ballykinler; and on successfully completing my recruit training I was posted to B Company, a full-time company based in Dungannon at Killymeal House, the Headquarters for 8 UDR.
>
> I was born and grew up in the village of Coagh about 12 miles east of Cookstown. The village bordered the Nationalist area of the Ardboe, a known Republican stronghold. A number of PIRA attacks had been carried out in the area both on military and police patrols, against the local RUC station and off-duty members of the Security Forces. The threat from the PIRA remained at the highest level during my service in 8 UDR and after I left.
>
> From about eight years of age I had worked on a local farm at the weekends and school holidays, then as a young teenager I worked with a kitchen manufacturing firm based in Coagh. I knew what I wanted, and was capable of, a different life to this, so took the opportunity to join the UDR and this was to change my life forever in more ways than I could ever have foreseen, and not all of it was positive. I made mistakes as a teenager and young man and made some poor life choices which I can look back on now 30 years on. However I have never regretted that decision to serve in the UDR and B Company. 16 Platoon who I was attached to was without doubt the finest and most committed and professional group of soldiers you could ever have wished to have known. Everyone looked out for each other, the bond within the Company was something to behold and it took me a while to adjust to this as I had always relied on my judgement, my own decisions, which I had only myself to answer for, good or bad.
>
> I was the only soldier from 8 UDR on the recruits' course that I attended in Ballykinler. East Tyrone was a difficult area to recruit in for the UDR and it was apparent that the Staff and other recruits certainly recognised that the Battalion I was going to serve in patrolled within a very active terrorist area. Recruit training is a very disciplined environment and when you pass out you can be proud of what you have achieved, and you have a self-belief that you know it all. I knew some of the members of B Company who were from my village in Coagh and was very keen to prove I was no pushover, could look after myself, and was very keen to get out on patrol and do what I had been trained for. Of course the soldiers in 16 Platoon had served together for a number of years, had a very relaxed, nearly casual attitude about them. Everyone seemed to have a nickname. 'Yogi' was one of our Platoon Commanders, a brilliant

---

17 Pte Allister (Ali Bear) James Harkness 1966-: 8 UDR 1984-91.

soldier to serve under. There was plenty of monkeying around, lots of bitching about the food and what we would be doing and the kit, who would have to carry what, helicopters cancelling pick-ups at the last minute and leaving us miles to walk back to base or a safe area to go to for pick up by civilian vans, patrols extended or re-tasked at the last minute and there was no way in those days of letting your girlfriend know you would not be seeing her that evening. Everything revolved around our work; home and our social life took a distant second place.

Although at first glance things seemed casual, you had to remember these soldiers dealt daily with a very dangerous terrorist threat and had first-hand experience of dealing with major incidents. At the flick of a switch, the Platoon became a precision instrument. Never have I ever seen such a well-honed unit that could read a situation on the ground like these soldiers did. We targeted the terrorists; we knew intimately everything about their routine. It just took a sighting or change of attitude by the terrorist at a vehicle checkpoint or a disturbed piece of ground to trigger our immediate and responsive action. It did take time to learn to be an effective member of the Platoon and you were started off as the scribe at checkpoints, thereby learning and meeting the terrorists and vehicles they used, and right beside the team commander at all times. You were immediately spotted by these terrorists as a new boy. I was surprised that they were on first name terms with our commanders. Of course this was veiled threats; they had made it their business to find out about our unit and they were ruthless killers who enjoyed this one-upmanship. Soon they would have my name too and my unit had me well briefed on how to deal with this exposure on the ground when it happened and how we believed the terrorist could gather this information. You knew you were accepted and trusted when you got the job as a cover man. Now you may well be hidden in a hedgerow some distance from the main group and your team were relying on you for their safety.

At basic training you were taught when taking up a cordon position or cover position to carry out a three metre check of the ground immediately around your position, checking for booby-traps or indicators such as disturbed ground, and then a five metre sweep. This was continually drummed into us on operations and was second nature in our patrol skills.

So much for his background, he now describes the incident and events afterwards:

Our Platoon deployed to an area south of Cappagh village, a known, active PIRA area and we were the only likely target, so we knew full well the risk. We were tasked to monitor a known PIRA member in the early morning, noting his routine at his home, and then to proceed to carry out snap vehicle check points en route to another task. I was front lead on the road team with our flanks left and right forward of us covered by our other two teams a couple of hundred metres away, as we proceeded along the ground. These were country roads, very light traffic, so we were in no rush and we were geared for rummage searches when in a PIRA area or in the vicinity of a known associate of PIRA.

As cover man for a snap VCP I was well prepared to take up that position on hearing or being warned of a vehicle approaching and of course well-rehearsed in our patrol skills to always visually check my position. I had a very small shovel that I would use sometimes to get into a good cover position or make a discreet break-out point through heavy hawthorn roadside hedges when watching an area, for the patrol to use in case of emergency. Having worked on a farm, this was an easy task. I was using the shovel, not digging, but slashing at the undergrowth above me, when I hit metal. My follow up visual check revealed a metal five gallon size drum partially dug in and a wire attached, loosely coiled. I didn't need any more information; this was to be my first real terrorist situation. I indicated by hand signals to my commander that we were in danger and he took control. We withdrew and followed our practised drills about safe distances from a device, to protect the civilian population and ourselves. I remained at the ICP location until ATO arrived to brief him exactly on the location and what I had seen.

It is quite a shock to see what a 30lb HME device filled with six inch nails and metal cuttings can do, after ATO disarmed it and once forensic finished, he blew it up on site. It would have killed me and probably the other three members of the team too. Boss, my team commander, and I did not have the easiest of relationships when I joined the Platoon; for the years we served together I have the upmost respect and friendship with him which will last a lifetime.

Some years later, we were operating a checkpoint near Pomeroy when I stopped an elderly man driving his car. He was bleeding from his nose and mouth, in quite a state and had just been beaten up by his neighbour, and he was on his way to hospital. He refused our help and we got him on his way. The next vehicle into the checkpoint was a man McAvoy, totally agitated. I got him out of the car when he lunged at me to strike me and I hit him. I never tried to cover my actions up. I told it as it was. I was taken to court and found guilty. This led to my leaving the UDR. I had no option and, on the day I left, the Adjutant asked if I would do some work in her kitchen. I often wondered did she have some sympathy for me and gave me a job so as I could earn some money and get back on my feet in civilian life again.

Life moved on and I was back working in the kitchen factory in Coagh where I lived, married now with two children and an old beat up car leaking oil, but it was all I could afford, when a policeman called at the house. It was a Thursday and I thought it was something to do with this old car and I was wondering what I was going to do if he put it off the road. He knew me and said that I was to go immediately to Dungannon RUC station where someone would see me.

I have never told anyone this, not even my wife although she has an inkling of something obviously. Just recently with all the enquiries against the Security Forces coming up frequently on the media, my wife asked if there was anything she should be concerned about because of my service and I was able to put her mind at ease when I told that there was absolutely nothing.

I went to Dungannon, hoping this old car could make the journey. At the station they were waiting for me and I was ushered in, no stopping at the checkpoint. A police officer met me and said that they would be very grateful if I would help them. I was to go back home, a police officer would stay with me, and I was to have my wife (who worked in Cookstown) and our children go to her mother's, where there would be additional covert protection.

On Monday morning someone drove my car and a three man PIRA ASU murder gang that were clearly waiting along the route I would have taken, were shot dead in the vicinity of the village of Coagh. I never had one inkling that I was being targeted for assassination by PIRA. I never noticed or spotted anything unusual and I owe my life to the Security Forces to whom I am very grateful.

To have served in the UDR in East Tyrone was a commitment that only a few would make and it is a commitment for the rest of your life.

David 'Boss' Hogg continues:

The first thing I did was to draw the patrol back and then debrief the soldier to try to make sense of the situation. The soldier was able to give a good description of what appeared to be a roadside bomb with possibly a command wire leading off to a firing point. It was a five gallon drum size. Then I radioed to Battalion Headquarters that we had a suspect device. The cover teams working on the higher ground hadn't noticed anybody moving or running away so there was nothing to suggest that there was a live firing point or anybody waiting to detonate it. So the most likely scenario was that this was a major operation planned by East Tyrone PIRA.

We would have been under observation from the minute we deployed from the helicopter.

One scenario would have been that the firing point team waiting to detonate this bomb would have known they were at risk of being discovered so they would have abandoned the operation and gone to a safe house or whatever. Another scenario would be that they would know our tactics of deploying a cordon and how we would operate to clear such a device.

So we had declared this incident to Battalion to deal with, but on the ground we had to deal with the fact that they will know that we're going to cordon off the area and we had to assess the risk of being blown sky high as we were setting up the cordon. We weren't in a position to do any follow-up because we hadn't seen anyone in the area so we didn't know where to go. The lads had done very well but we now had just about enough manpower to hold the situation. It was dangerous but we couldn't walk away from it. The Provos could double guess what we were going to do next so there's a lot of pressure. We were committed to a cordon so we needed more resources. Each soldier would do a three metre check and then a five metre check of the area immediately around him and continue with this until reserves arrived.

And it's a waiting game and you could be there for hours and it was cold. East Tyrone PIRA would have known that a vehicle party would eventually arrive and so they would be vulnerable to a landmine attack as they were coming in. So it was keeping everyone safe till the ATO arrived. There was nobody dancing up and down with excitement. This was the business we did and we had to deal with it. You have to be mentally on top of the men. So we were mentally geared up for what could have been a 24 hour static operation but fortunately after a few hours the resources were made available to come and deal with it.

The Regular Army was deployed to thicken up the cordon and there had to be detailed briefing of everyone who arrived. That's a huge amount of work for the NCO to deal with on the ground. ATO arrived and the soldier who found the device had to go and explain what he saw, in detail. For the next few hours the search teams cleared the area. ATO went in and defused the bomb and the command wire would have been removed and luckily instead of taking 24 hours, the thing was cleared up in about 6 hours. The forensic evidence would have been collected and retained for analysis and things like fingerprints on the drum.

ATO decided that the easiest way to dispose of the bomb was to blow it up on the site once the forensic evidence had been taken. It's only when the explosion happens that it brings it home to you and you realise that if it had gone off every man would have been killed.

Then everybody is in a good mood and you're going home with a success story instead of possibly four men lying dead. At the debrief, one of the Regular Army teams told us that a man had come up to them at a cordon point and said: 'Sorry boys. It wasn't meant for youse. It was them other bastards we were after' (meaning the UDR).

Then our OC said: 'Is that worth a bottle of vodka?' and I said; 'No, it's worth two!'

Derrytresk, Coalisland 18th December 1984

1000 lbs of explosives was found in an outhouse at Derrytresk, Coalisland by Private Kenny Ferguson[18] 16 Platoon. Tom Finlay was the Patrol Commander: he had been

---

18 WO2 Kenneth (Kenny) Ferguson 1962-: 8 UDR 1979-92: (R Irish until 2002): MID QCVS.

tasked by Battalion to carry out a route check of a main arterial route into Coalisland. Intelligence had just reported suspicious activity. Tom Finlay[19] sets the scene with his background:

> I transferred across from 1 Royal Irish (it was the 1st Battalion Royal Irish Rangers then). I arrived in Cookstown on 1st April 1979. My memory of that day was that it was the burial of a part-time soldier in 8 UDR, by the name of Gibson; he had been murdered by East Tyrone PIRA as he was going to work along the Coalisland-Dungannon road. That was my first introduction, really, to the UDR. The reason I came to the UDR was the battalion I was with was going to Berlin and the wife wouldn't go. I still wanted to wear a uniform, I still wanted to soldier. Carol came from Cookstown, we settled back in Cookstown, and I transferred across to 8 UDR.
>
> Stanley Gordon[20] was my section commander; he was in charge in Cookstown at that time. I came across as a Private soldier. I was a Lance Corporal in the Regulars, but where you're transferring to a unit as a permanent posting, you step down one (rank). If you get posted anywhere, you keep your rank, but if you're transferring, you step down, generally speaking. At least that's the way it was then. My operational experience with the Irish Rangers was with the United Nations. We did a tour in '77 in Cyprus and that was it. They didn't serve in Northern Ireland till the 90s.
>
> The camaraderie in the UDR I felt was a lot better. They were a lot closer, simply, I think, because of the situation they found themselves in. I found some changes; there was more characters!
>
> Our patrolling effort was directed against known PIRA members. My idea was to let them know that you knew them. You knew who they were and what they were and got to know their pattern of life. If they're not where you expect them to be, ask yourself some questions as to why aren't they there. Their background, their wives, their children and really get to know as much as possible about them. They had smallholdings. They were hobby farmers and reasonably well-off, financially.
>
> You'd get to know their pattern of life. If they're not about, why aren't they about, and you would have said so. You'd get briefed on names. Of course you went out looking for them, you'd get to know vehicle registrations… more than that, get to know their vehicles. Vehicle registration for me was the confirmation that you'd got the right vehicle. This was both on and off-duty. If you were off-duty and came across them, you'd put it down as a sighting and who they

---

19 WO1 (RSM) Thomas (Tom) Finlay BEM 1954-: (R Irish Rangers 1972-79): 8 UDR 1979-92: (R Irish until 2007).
20 CSgt Stanley Gordon BEM 1957-2002: 8 UDR 1976-92: (R Irish until 1999).

were with. And hopefully there'd be a patrol nearby or a mobile, or whatever, especially if you didn't know who he was with.

The UDR were keen to engage terrorists, to make sure that they knew people were watching their every move, and the objective was to make life as uncomfortable as possible for these people.

Shootings were more likely to be used on 'soft targets', off-duty soldiers, while it was known that roadside bombs, booby-traps, culvert mines and 'come on' situations were the more likely tactics to ambush patrols. To counteract these tactics, the emphasis shifted away from Land Rover patrols and moved towards greater use of helicopters and civilianised vans for patrol deployment.

Once the routine movements of the terrorist cell had been established, patrolling then moved into a different mode. For example, once it had been established that Suspect A had gone off to work, his premises or outlying fields could be searched for the location of hides or the position of potential firing points. Good observation would reveal a piece of grass that had been recently trampled at a particular point, suggesting that this might be the next firing point. Earth or bracken showing signs of having been recently disturbed might lead to an active hide. A patrol could then come back in the early hours to follow up or confirm the intelligence.

Deployment was usually in three teams of four; this suited helicopter and van loadings. A team could be deployed to observe from high ground, with another team doing a VCP or clearing routes and this gave a lot of flexibility and control.

Soldiers realised the risks they ran by setting patterns, which the terrorist cells would exploit in their turn. For example, setting up a VCP at the same point over several weeks was inviting an attack. A foot patrol could compromise weeks or even months of careful intelligence gathering by poor tactics. For example cutting a fence as a quick way to cross into a field was telling the terrorist you'd been there. Lying in the grass for several hours whilst observing a possible firing point, for example, leaves the grass flattened. When the terrorist comes along and sees this, he will immediately realise that his planned operation has been compromised. So it required the patrol groups to think like the terrorist, to use accumulated intelligence on a suspect in order to anticipate his activities and to plan their own activities accordingly.

For a terrorist to carry out a successful operation he needs someone to make the explosives; someone to plan the location where the bomb will be placed; someone to move it into the location, and someone to detonate it. The task of B Company was to intercept the operation at any of these stages. A good example was when they found the roadside bomb at Aghnagar. In the vicinity of a known terrorist's house, in spite of our diligence, PIRA still got one over on us. They made the explosives; they knew our pattern and they planted the bomb under our noses. What made the difference between success and failure was good patrol tactics on our part. In spite of months of intelligence gathering, we had no idea that there was a bomb being planned. However, having failed at every other level of intervention, our tactical awareness worked, the basic training in patrol skills in routinely searching the area saved us from disaster.

On 18th December 1984, I was the multiple commander for a three team patrol to carry out a route check of the Derrytresk Road. The start point was going to be at Tamnamore, a small village to the south of Coalisland, and then to work our way back into Coalisland. Essentially we were looking for culverts and hedgerows and potential firing points which would overlook culverts. I deployed Boss Hogg's team to the right flank, Kenny Ferguson to the left flank and my own team to the centre. These operations are quite slow and meticulous. We're not interested in stopping cars, because you don't have time and they have to be well coordinated, so we let the pace of the road team dictate the pace of the operation. The teams would be maybe several hundred yards apart but always had visual contact.

Boss Hogg[21] continues:

I saw a white car forward on my left flank and realised it was probably watching the patrols. I was sufficiently concerned to report this to Kenny. This meant Kenny's team deviating further out to go and check out this car. The white vehicle would have seen this brick of four heading out in their direction, so the white car left the scene and headed north, away from the patrol.

Kenny Ferguson then takes up the story:

On receiving information about the white car up ahead, I moved forward into the area with my team to check out the vehicle, when I saw it leaving the area. This was suspicious in my mind, and it led me to go up to the area where the car had been. On the route back down to the road, there was a derelict house which I had a general look at. Normally you wouldn't go into a derelict without having a proper search team, but you could look in through the windows. When I was checking out the old milking parlour attached to the derelict, I saw the creamery cans with the fuse wire coming out through the lids and knew straight away what it was.

At almost the same time, I saw a blue car coming out of a laneway directly opposite the derelict and onto the road and turning north. I signalled to it to

---

21 CSgt Thomas David (Boss) Hogg 1956-: 8 UDR 1976-92: (R Irish until 1998): GOC's Commendation.

stop because I had identified the men in the car as two suspected terrorists, Peter Sherry[22] and Sean O'Hagan,[23] both from Dungannon. The car failed to stop and my initial thoughts were to shoot but the vehicle hadn't threatened me, so I decided against that action. However, I had noticed a helicopter operating over Coalisland area and although not tasked to our patrol, I knew they'd be listening out on our frequency. I didn't have its call sign but I knew they all operated with an Alpha Whisky prefix, and as we worked with these guys all the time, there was a good chance they'd recognise my voice. I called on the radio: 'Alpha Whisky call sign, operating over Coalisland, a blue car has just left my position on the Derrytresk Road near Coalisland, heading north towards you. Can you locate?'

Alpha Whisky came back immediately: 'I have your patrol in sight. I can see the blue car'. This information was also being relayed back to Battalion Headquarters in Killymeal, who by now were aware that we had a bomb and we had a vehicle escaping the scene with two suspected terrorists from Dungannon. The Battalion would have to take it from there because there was nothing more I could do at that point about the escaping blue car. As it was, the other three team multiple of our platoon was in Killymeal preparing to deploy on another, separate task, and Ned Kirk[24] was the Commander. The helicopter relayed the route of the vehicle towards Dungannon and Ned deployed his Land Rovers straight onto the Dungannon-Coalisland road to intercept the blue car with the helicopter giving him real-time information. He then apprehended the vehicle and arrested Peter Sherry and Sean O'Hagan.

Tom Finlay continues:

As the multiple commander it was my responsibility at this point to cordon the area where the explosives were and I had to focus on the safety of my men

---

22 Peter Sherry 1955-2018: Dungannon: Sentenced to seven years' imprisonment March 1975 for refusing to recognise the Court and using an imitation gun to force the drivers of a lorry and a car to hand over their vehicles; they were later found burnt out. (*Dungannon Observer* 29th March 1975): Charged with a variety of terrorist type offences in 1979 and 1980 but found not guilty when super grass Patrick McGurk refused to give evidence (*Tyrone Courier* 11th February 1982 and 26th October 1983): Sentenced to life imprisonment on 12th June 1986 for conspiring to carry out bomb attacks in London and elsewhere in the south of England during 1985 (*Independent* 11th September 1994 and *Tyrone Courier* 25th June 1986) and the bombing of the Conservative Party Conference in Brighton in 1984 (*Guardian* 10th June 1986).
23 Sean O'Hagan c1953-: Dungannon: Sentenced to 23 years' imprisonment for conspiracy to murder and other related offences. (*Courier & News* 16th January 1991): (Long Kesh H8B: Prisoner A2149): Released 30th September 1998. (PRONI): On arrest in 1988 replaced as OC E Tyrone Brigade. (Brendan O'Brien, *The Long War*).
24 CSgt William Edward (Ned) Kirk 1954-: 8 UDR 1976-92: (R Irish until 2006).

and the public as this was a really dangerous situation. Kenny needed me to get to him to confirm what he had seen in the milking parlour. Everything had happened so fast; Kenny wasn't really sure what he had seen. I confirmed through the window that there was a large bomb and made my plan of action – secure the area, preserve the evidence, brief the commanders to make sure that every team commander checked the cordon positions for potential booby-traps. We had already cleared the route from the south so there was a safe route for ATO and his team to come to us.

Kenny Ferguson again:

> So we had the road sealed and at the northern cordon point, a white car approached. Boss said: 'That's the white car I saw acting suspiciously'. There were two men in it; James Campbell[25] was one of them. We arrested the two guys, we preserved evidence by bagging their hands, separating them, and we waited till the RUC arrived to take them in.
>
> At the same time, we were still dealing with a major incident. We had to deploy soldiers to local houses nearby to warn them that there's a bomb at the old derelict and to ask them to either leave or to stay in their houses and not to go out onto the road. As well, the various follow-up agencies like ATO, search dogs and search teams were arriving and it was my job to brief each of them as they arrived.
>
> The actual clearance operation would be directed by ATO, with us providing the security.
>
> Again, we were in for the long haul. We couldn't leave until the clearance operation was finished and it was the middle of winter. You have to think of how you feed people for example, because you could be stuck there for 24 hours.
>
> As well, there were six workmen building a new house just next to the derelict, so we had to get them out safely.
>
> Then in the middle of all this, we discovered that what we thought was a derelict house was in fact occupied by an old 90-year-old man who was blind and disabled! This created a whole new set of problems. The old man was obviously unaware that there was a 1,000 lb bomb in the lean-to beside his house and I made the decision that we would have to go back into the property to recover this old man and arrange for family members to come and take care of

---

25 James Campbell c1959-: Coalisland: Charged (1984) with possession of a revolver with ammunition and 1,000 lbs explosives: Latter charge withdrawn (1985): First charge withdrawn due to insufficient evidence (1986). (*Tyrone Courier* 19th March 1986): Sentenced (1990) to 14 years' imprisonment for possession of a large quantity of arms and ammunition in 1989 (*Mid Ulster Mail* 28th December 1990).

him, in spite of the danger of the bomb exploding prematurely. He was frail and the stress of all these strangers coming in could have caused him to take a heart attack.

Tom Finlay again:

> The follow-up was in progress within a few hours. The police had visited the scene and removed the two men who were in the white vehicle and as luck would have it, the Battalion made the decision to extract us and to use our part-time D Company members to work with ATO throughout the night. So we got a rest and took over again in the early hours of the Friday morning. By lunchtime the next day, ATO had completed his clearance operation and now we had 1,000 lb of explosives to dispose of!

Find of 1,000 lbs of Explosives

This major operation by East Tyrone PIRA had been thwarted and the devastation and destruction a 1,000 lb bomb would have caused is just unimaginable. (*It consisted of 450 kgs Home Made Explosive (HME) packed into eight milk churns with booster charge and detonating cord in each. Also recovered were six boosters in a fertiliser bag, 1½ fertiliser bags ANFO, one Timer and Power Unit (TPU), one length of detonating cord, 3.5 m seismic detonating cord, one electric detonator, one firing pack, 500 m twin flex Command Wire (CW), four batteries, six pairs rubber gloves, two pairs of overalls, 50 empty fertiliser sacks and two mattresses).*

Kenny Ferguson finishes the story:

> The disposal of the explosives was to be done in the fields outside the derelict. There were six separate bombs to be blown up. The first one blew the gable wall out of the old man's house, the second one smashed all the windows in the new house that was being built and no further damage was done by the rest. When you see those things going off you realise the sheer power of what you're up against. It was nearly Christmas and when we went back in to Killymeal on the Friday afternoon, the soldiers were having their Christmas party. You can guess why none of us were used on the follow-up searches on the Saturday!
>
> Information gathered from suspects led to the recovery of a hand-gun from a derelict house overlooked by James Campbell's house. It was found by a Regular Army search team and a police search team recovered an Armalite rifle from the same area. It dealt a major blow to East Tyrone PIRA and local people were up in arms and horrified that the Provos had used a 90 year-old disabled man's house to store a wired-up bomb and next to a road.
>
> I joined in '79, in D Company part-time, because there was no full-time space then. It was the old Ops Platoon and they had their quantity and then a short time after I joined D Company, I went on a full-time course and then finally I got taken on in about July. Basically, I followed my father and my three brothers into the UDR (the whole family was in it at one stage) and just worked my way up through the ranks. I ended up doing full-time for 22 years and another year full-time/part-time.

7

Forever Vigilant

Landmines and Booby-traps

All bombs were called Improvised Explosive Devices (IEDs) by the Security Forces because they were home-made. Landmines were fired by the terrorists from a distance so referred to as Remotely Controlled IEDs (RCIEDs). Booby-traps were initiated by the victim.

The terrorists did not often employ booby-traps in East Tyrone except in attacks on off-duty soldiers, although the threat was always there. They could not afford to leave the device in position for long in case it was set off by an innocent victim. So it had to be laid where there was certainty that the Security Forces would come. This was either as a secondary device, for example to catch the follow-up to a shooting, or where the Security Forces had set a clear pattern of movement, for example though a gate, or combined with a lure, a 'come-on', to get them to a certain point such as a derelict building. That there were not more booby-traps used is perhaps a tribute to the training and procedures at every level.

The landmine was usually placed in a culvert under the road or under a small bridge. The main charge was several hundred pounds of home-made explosives (ammonium nitrate and fuel oil) with a small booster of commercial or military explosive. Where possible it was placed in an upright oil drum or a number of milk churns to keep the water out and to shape the explosion upwards. Milk churns fitted horizontally into the smaller culverts. The charge was fired remotely using a command wire (often several hundred metres long) laid along a fence or hedgerow; later it was fired using radio or other communication device. The firing point was on a small hill, a drumlin, of which there are many in East Tyrone overlooking the usually straight roads coming down from the Sperrins. Behind the drumlin was a carefully planned escape route. Four terrorists were needed to keep lookout left and right, to fire the device, and to keep watch to the rear. The biggest challenge was to assess the speed of the passing vehicle correctly and to time the firing accordingly.

The terrorists tried to plan their attack based on some regular pattern of Security Forces activity; they in their turn tried not to set patterns. The longer the terrorists sat on a device the greater the risk to them, so, if no target appeared, they resorted to a 'come-on' to draw the Security Forces onto the device. Considerable caution was therefore necessary.

8 UDR spent much time collecting information on all the culverts and bridges in East Tyrone. Some could be eliminated because they did not have all the characteristics that the terrorist required, and some because they were overlooked by people unlikely to support PIRA. The remainder were kept under observation in some way and checked frequently. Consequently many devices were discovered before they could be fired and there were few military casualties in this type of attack once the threat had been mastered.

Checking routes and likely places for devices was very demanding. It was necessary to advance in a V formation so that the wings would detect the command wire before the device could be fired. The ground was inevitably soft, even boggy, fences and hedges had to be crossed, and the rate of movement slow. It was very tiring work.

Remote attacks on foot patrols were much more difficult to deal with, especially as the speed of movement made it much easier for the terrorists to time the initiation correctly. In these cases the device was laid at the side of a road and often dug into a bank; farm yard confetti was placed in front of the charge to cause maximum casualties. The answer was to have two or more patrols operating together but in rural areas this was not easy to coordinate in such a way that the risk was eliminated completely.

Jay Nethercott recalls the early threat of this type of attack:

> It was autumn in the 1970s and our part-time company where I served as a Private, based in Killymeal House on the edge of Dungannon, was scheduled for a mid-week live firing night exercise at an outdoor gallery range about 20 miles away. This was obligatory to attend in order to meet our operational training directive and remain current.
>
> The Company Sergeant Major was in charge of the detail and we drew out our weapons, operational ammunition, flares and ammunition to be fired: it was night time when we were ready to depart at 2000hrs.
>
> We would travel in a loose convoy of Land Rovers and Shorlands. NCOs would allocate soldiers to vehicles as we were operating as a company and not in our usual operational sections. I was in the rear of a Land Rover; there were six of us in the vehicle and we set off for the range. At the briefing we were told that there was a threat of booby-traps at ranges and on the route into the range which we knew was in an isolated rural area so we would stop short, clear the route in and check the range before the live firing exercise began. Our route to the range was mostly along the M1 motorway to the east of Dungannon and when we arrived at the link road to the range, as briefed, we dismounted and started our clearance of the route in.
>
> It seemed to take an age for things to move and I was at the rear with a small group and a Shorland. This group weren't taking the clearance very seriously being right at the back and when things moved off, jumped onto the rear of the Shorland rather than walk. The Company Sergeant Major appeared from the

darkness, saw the men and went ballistic about this shambolic unprofessional attitude and put us all on a charge. I started to protest that I was doing what I should but he lit into me said I should know better so I had the sense to shut up at this stage; what a start to the night and I hadn't done anything wrong as I saw it nor had I ever been on a charge before, so that annoyed me. Clearance of outdoor gallery ranges was a serious operation and I took that lesson to heart. It proved to stand me well some years later when in charge of a range detail we discovered a pressure plate booby-trap bomb in a firing pit at an outdoor range near Cookstown.

I enjoyed shooting. It was something I had been doing since I was 11 and I was in the Battalion shooting team which meant I knew quite a few soldiers in the other companies in Aughnacloy and Cookstown; otherwise I would seldom if ever have met them and they were all great people.

Our night range exercise complete and I was pleased with my score; we tidied up, checked our stores and we were ready to return to base. Our route back to Killymeal after we left the M1 in order to vary things would change from convoy to two vehicle mobile patrols; the group I was with would travel around the south side of Dungannon back to base.

We travelled along Lisnahull; our route would be crossing the Donaghmore road and then onto the Quarry Lane. This was a threat area; patrols had been ambushed and I had been caught up in a shooting here in the past so we were vigilant and late in the night there was no traffic or people about; I was in the back of the rear vehicle when we crossed the Donaghmore road.

I never heard the explosion. The rear of the Land Rover lifted up; there was a massive red orange yellow blue flame coming out of the road behind and you could feel your lungs and chest being squeezed, then silence. We were stopped. Instantly one of the NCOs was running back to the site of the explosion which had been under a bridge on the Donaghmore road. He was an inspiring, strong leader who you would have followed anywhere in these situations and he was in control, spotting a getaway vehicle on the Donaghmore road powering up. He fired at it and we engaged it; in seconds it was gone.

No one was badly injured; luckily the blast had not opened the road but the threat of a secondary device or shooting attack was all too real in this area so we were given our orders to establish a cordon, stop anyone entering the scene, divert traffic and provide cover from the high ground.

The Regular Army based in Dungannon and the police arrived at the incident very quickly. Everyone fell into the well-rehearsed drills for this type of clearance and follow up operation which was all too well practised in East Tyrone due to the high level of terrorist activity.

I was on a cordon point when the Company Sergeant Major who had arrived earlier and was coordinating with the Regular Army commander, sent for me. My first thoughts were what have I done wrong, now expecting to get a another rollicking, but he just looked at me when I reported to him and said that there were two street lights lighting up the area of the scene which ATO would be working in and to shoot them out, then go back to my cordon duties. I moved position so I would not be shooting into houses on the higher ground and, one shot at each light, task done.

You spend hours when on these types of cordon operations; they take time to conclude. Eventually we were stood down, went back to base, cleaned our rifles and declared ammo expended. No one asked for statements thankfully and, tired, there was no banter or joking this time, just thankful. The Company Sergeant Major sent for the group I had been put on a charge with earlier and I thought does he never stop. He looked at us said he hoped we had learned our lesson and understood now why he had given the orders to clear our range and in light of the good work we had done tonight he would not now put us on a charge. He came over to me and said 'Well done' for shooting out the lights at the incident, for when he was discussing the clearance with the Regular Army commander and the street lights the ATO wanted removed, the Regular Army commander was not too sure he had anyone that would do it. The CSM said one of his boys would do it, one shot each, then said if I had made a hash of it he would have had it in for me embarrassing him!

Jay continues:

The terrorist used the landmine attack very effectively in Tyrone. Police, Regular Army units, the UDR and civilians all paid a heavy price in terms of death and injury to this type of no warning ambush. The raw material to make explosives was easily obtained and plentiful. Mobile patrols were easily targeted, the road system had thousands of culverts and bridges, and patrols could easily be drawn in with anything from a fake road traffic accident to a follow up by the Security Forces to another incident.

In just one day, Sunday 3rd March 1974, 8 UDR had one part-time soldier killed in a landmine explosion near Cookstown and others seriously injured, and a few hours later near Dungannon a mobile patrol from the part-time company in Killymeal was ambushed. In all with just these two incidents we had 16 soldiers seriously hurt in Musgrave Military Hospital in Belfast and one dead. The Regular Army based at Castle Hill in Dungannon were caught in a landmine explosion the week before when a mobile patrol was ambushed.

The wrecked Land Rovers from these three incidents, five vehicles in all, were brought to the UDR base at Killymeal. I went to see our soldiers in Musgrave Army Hospital that night; I knew all of them not just as soldiers but friends.

I was in Killymeal two days later for duty when the CSM grabbed me and another soldier; he said that there was a health risk with the damaged Land Rovers and they needed to be washed out. The storeman gave us each a bucket, mop and disinfectant. This was the first time I had looked into these damaged, totally wrecked vehicles; I saw my friends' blood and for the first time the distinctive smell of brains splattered on the front passenger well where my friend had died. The risk was seemingly of meningitis. We hooked up the fire mains hydrant; a bucket and a mop just wasn't on.

I went on the security cordon detail for Corporal Moffett's funeral the next day.

The effect on morale in our Company was plain to see, resulting in the Company Commander calling us on parade: was it mutiny to question what commanders were doing, had they got the tactics right? We got over it, we always did our duty; this was a dangerous area both on and off duty and worse was to follow from landmine attacks on the Security Forces in Tyrone, thankfully not our Battalion.

Arnie Ferguson[1] commanded J (later D) Company; his recollections of a day in February 1976 also set the scene:

As I was briefing the patrol for a normal VCP operation one of the members said that he saw what he thought was a man acting suspiciously in a field just outside Eglish. I then identified the field having done many patrols in the area myself and one thing came to mind that there was a culvert under the road at that field. Our task area did not include that field but I got permission from Battalion Ops to include it for that night.

Using the information of the area where the suspicious man was spotted and the possibility of a firing point location, I reckoned we had enough dead ground to crawl the 200 metres from the VCP we would set up as cover.

It was last light as we set up the VCP. Armed only with a small torch, myself and the man who reported this started the long crawl to where I knew there was a culvert. Thankfully the grass was dry and there were no cows in the fields. After what seemed a very long time I came across a patch that had been recently walked over and we could see the entrance to the culvert. I crawled closer and took out the torch, and with the minimum of light looked into the culvert. If I would have had a heart monitor on it would have went off the scale because staring at me was several white plastic bags filled with something and an electric cable coming from them and under me back into the field.

I turned around and not a word was spoken as we started on the long crawl back to the VCP. We mounted up and went back to the Battalion Ops Room to report what we had found and organise a clearance in the morning. It started

---

1 Maj Thomas Arnold (Arnie) Ferguson MBE UD 1941-: 8 UDR 1970-92: (R Irish until 1994): GOC's Commendation: Building Contractor.

at first light; the device consisted of 200 lbs of home-made explosives with the command wire dug in, but no firing pack. One man's alertness had saved lives.

Cappagh/Galbally 7th September 1982

On 7th September 1982 B Company discovered a large landmine at Cappagh. It consisted of five milk churns, each containing 80 lbs of ANFO. Close by, a red Honda motorcycle 250 cc was hidden under bushes with wires leading to the land mine. A separate report provided more detail:

> At 2250hrs on 1st September an off-duty soldier reported five shots in the area of Kilneslee; this was confirmed by a neighbour.
> About the same time a confidential telephone call was received: 'I was ringing about not travelling round the roads in the Galbally/Cappagh area. I just wanted to ring again and say please don't travel on these roads by foot or car, it is dangerous and don't mention on the media about this call as our lives would be in danger.' The RUC believed the call to be genuine. It was decided to restrict all movement in the area while the RUC tried to get further information and the military researched and checked high risk routes.
> On 3rd September, the headmaster of St John's the Baptist School in Galbally reported a break-in during the previous night; school equipment was taken. This was treated as a come-on. It would have been initially investigated by Pomeroy RUC and therefore gave direction to research on where to start route checking. Discussions with the RUC about vehicle movement revealed the most likely route for the RUC would have been Gortavoy to Galbally across the land mine; this road is also the most easterly one in the sub-division and the RUC tend not to cross boundaries therefore increasing the use of the road. New policemen to the Pomeroy station have not yet familiarised with all the minor routes and therefore use the most likely to get from A to B. This route is also on the interface of a high risk land mine area, again a tendency to use it; military patrols were foot patrolling in the Galbally area on post office delivery days and there had been a previous device on this road in 1974. It was therefore planned to check this route. B Company were to check it on 7th September.
> On 6th September, a man rang the RUC and stated he had seen equipment he believed had been stolen from the school in an old derelict he used as a store. This was treated as a come-on in line with the previous assessment.
> On 7th September, a telephone call was made to the RUC from a Cappagh call box; it was garbled and incoherent. The only words identified were O'Neill's crossroads. This was not consistent with previous assessments and it was decided to treat it as a separate clearance.

B Company approached the task by concentrating on the high ground east and west of the road. The aim was to check for likely firing points, moving in a southerly direction, then returning north checking culverts. At 1010 on 7th September a command wire and recently used firing point were found. While cordoning the area, the patrol discovered a motor cycle which was camouflaged and, nearby, human excreta.

The patrol believed they may have forced those on the firing point to leave on foot and therefore the ARF (Airborne Reaction Force) and Groundhog (tracker dog) were tasked but the dog was unable to pick up a trail other than to follow the command wire.

RUC followed up the VRN of the motor cycle and five people were arrested under Section 11 but subsequently released.

By 1630hrs on 7th September a firm cordon had been established and was further strengthened before nightfall. Air reconnaissance missions were flown and the images studied. At 0830hrs on 8th September route clearance started to the ICP (Incident Control Point), completed by 0930hrs. Work then started on clearance of the firing point and motor cycle. This was completed by 1823hrs. Royal Engineers Search Team then started clearance to the culvert ICP; this was called off in fading light at 2110hrs and restarted at 0730hrs on 9th September by again checking the route to the filter ICP. By 1900hrs the whole area had been cleared.

The find consisted of five creamery cans each containing 40 kgs HME and 2 × ANNIE booster bags, one commercial detonator in the middle churn, a command wire approximately 275 metres in length (twin core, black in colour: it followed the hedge and fence and was not dug in), bell push consisting of four PP9 batteries taped with black and blue tape (standard bell push attached), one plastic bag containing one pair of rubber gloves and one lemonade bottle in a hole by the motorcycle, the hole also contained two crash helmets; motorcycle was 250 cc Honda Dream.

Prior to the start of the planned route checks it was decided to fly air reconnaissance over all likely firing points. Though not confirmed it is believed that the terrorists do not sit on the firing point 24 hours a day. The start point for the air reconnaissance was the subsequent firing point and it seems we were too early. The landmine was extremely well put together and to quote the RESA (Royal Engineers Search Advisor) 'that was done by a combat engineer'. The condition of the firing point suggested it had been in use for a week. This is consistent with earlier assessments.

The Company Commander, Jay Nethercott, outlines the operation:

The area known as Cappagh was a stronghold for a very aggressive PIRA unit who were readily supported by an element of Republican sympathisers from the community. There were no commercial targets within the area; off-duty security force members did however reside on the periphery and were vulnerable to attacks from this gang, along with Security Forces patrols and Police stations in the villages of Pomeroy and Ballygawley. It was deemed to be an area of high risk. It was, however, important that normal policing by the RUC from Dungannon and Ballygawley be allowed to take place in Cappagh and for that to be possible the military were tasked with providing a 24-hour presence of support patrols throughout this area.

This PIRA unit were a cunning, aggressive gang who preyed on soft targets. One such incident involved the police in Southern Ireland, the Garda, being informed of the death of a close relative of a family from the Cappagh area. The family asked that the Garda phone the RUC in Dungannon, who, as the family did not have a landline telephone, agreed to go to the home late at night and pass on the sad news of the passing of the relative. When the single police car patrol arrived at the isolated farmhouse, they were gunned down and murdered by a PIRA gang. All patrols were monitored by PIRA and their sympathisers, who would count the number of soldiers and police deploying to and from the Cappagh area, their patrol routes and routines, and this was all collated by PIRA. To set a patrol pattern or routine was to invite an attack by the terrorist.

Sometime over 5th or 6th of September 1982, a message was received on the Confidential Telephone from a female caller saying that it was dangerous for the Security Forces to travel on the Galbally Road. The caller did not want anyone to know this call had been made for fear of reprisals from the PIRA. You have to treat information as real and genuine but you also have to consider that PIRA are possibly controlling this, either to have more resources put into the area, thereby allowing them to operate freely somewhere else, or, when the Security Forces deploy to clear the route, booby-traps or attacks are intended on the patrols and agencies such as ATO, both deploying to or from the target area. With some twenty miles of what could be classed as the Galbally road involved, the potential for innocent lives at risk was considerable if there was a bomb on the route.

We therefore made a plan to deploy Stanley Gordon's platoon for a route check of a section of the Galbally road, deploying after first light by helicopter. They were briefed about the Confidential Telephone message and this type of task was a daily part of a military patrol in Cappagh. It was an excellent platoon, well versed and highly successful in search and rummage patrols and with an intimate knowledge of the ground and local suspects. Stanley led the route check. They were successful in locating a landmine in a culvert, the firing point and command wire and the getaway means, in this case a motorcycle. After an initial follow-up, Stanley was stretched with a road to seal and a firing point and getaway route to secure. Any further follow-up was tasked into the area from Dungannon by helicopter, looking for suspected terrorists and providing additional cover to Stanley's operation which was now on a cordon.

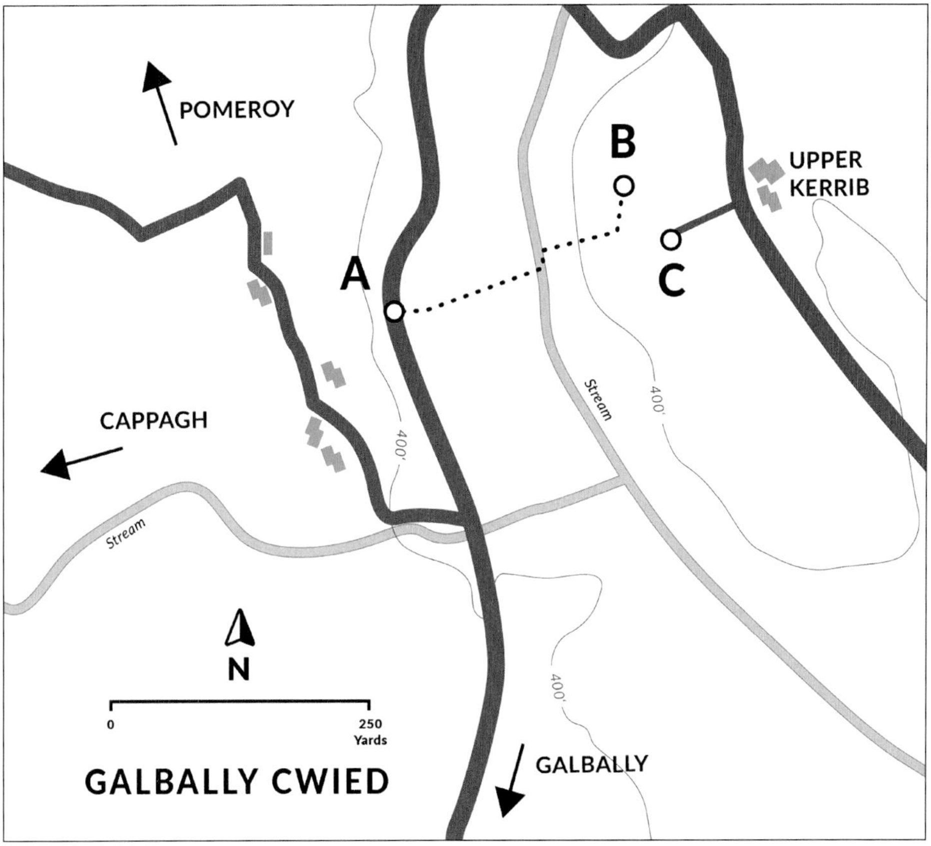

PIRA Landmine Attack Galbally
A: IED, B: Firing Point, C: Getaway Motorcycle Found

Route of Command Wire – CWIED at Cappagh/Galbally

Dean McGucken[2] discovered the device:

> I joined direct entry full-time in 1979 and attended the first Permanent Cadre recruits' course held at Ballykinler and after passing out was attached to the Ops Platoon based in Cookstown which then very shortly after this became B Company 8 UDR. I was a young man; local employment opportunities were poor and it was a career choice to serve full-time. I remained operational with B Company until the early nineties and retired as a Warrant Officer Class 2 in 2007, after serving my full complement.
>
> My experience gained on anti-terrorist operations in East Tyrone was put to good use. I became an instructor and also worked in England with the ATO and Royal Engineers, training and advising their teams on search operations. We devised and set simulated booby-traps and secondary devices as training lessons for these teams, with most of my information gained first-hand from my operational experience in East Tyrone. In the course of my service I witnessed and saw at first-hand some of the most despicable acts of terrorism from INLA and PIRA and the UVF, enacted against soldiers, police and the civilian population. Time has not lessened the effect that the depravity of all this has had on me.
>
> Victor McNickle[3] had a big influence in my early career and very soon I was put forward for an NCOs' course which I passed and I was promoted, serving as a team commander, with Stanley Gordon[4] my Platoon Commander, based in Cookstown.
>
> This was, without doubt, the most rewarding time of my career serving in B Company; they were an amazingly talented, highly motivated, very experienced Company. The bond among us all was legendary, even to this day. Now most of us are heading to our senior years and although we are dispersed far and wide throughout the world, that bond is still there.
>
> Our patrolling effort was directed against known terrorist members, ASUs and their munitions and we worked tirelessly in areas that were deemed high risk. We were expected to know from memory the names of suspects, where they lived, what vehicles they used, who they associated with, where they worked, what incidents their names were linked to. Commanders tested our knowledge daily using simple Kim's game type scenarios. Likewise, you had to know the ground, the location of past incidents, escape routes and firing points, threats on the routes we used and location of culverts under roads, for example. You felt sorry for new members joining the Company; the learning

---

2 WO2 Dean McGucken 1958-: 8 UDR 1979-92: (R Irish until 2001).
3 WO2 Victor McNickle BEM 1943-: 8 UDR 1971-92: (R Irish until 1999).
4 CSgt Stanley Gordon BEM 1957-2002: 8 UDR 1976-92: (R Irish until 1999).

curve was steep and their training in this was relentless until they had it. Our lives depended on each other.

After every patrol it was my job to complete an honesty trace on routes used, tea breaks, lie-up and rummage points, VCP locations, routes checked, drop-off and pick-up points, transport used (whether green, civilian or helicopter). There was no right or wrong, no one was criticising you for patrolling methods. This was all passed to our company lines; Intelligence Cells would review and identify obvious hot spots, over-use of routes and VCP points for example. It was all about lessons learnt. When you got this wrong, soldiers died. Jim Patterson,[5] one of our team commanders, related his first patrol when serving as a part-time member in Cookstown to us. He said:

They were deployed to Dungannon in Land Rovers, it was a Sunday, eight soldiers to a Land Rover and they were tying up with other part-time companies for a range day at Gortin, 30 miles west of Dungannon.

The Regular Army, deployed in Dungannon, were on mobile patrol and went out to the west side of Dungannon, along the route given for the UDR to use. Although this had not been arranged, it was by chance that the Regular patrol went first. A mile from the town their patrol was ambushed; a huge landmine was detonated by PIRA and four soldiers died at the scene. The UDR were redeployed to assist. He (Jim) provided cover for the agencies to clear up the scene and watched as the soldiers' remains were put into body bags by his patrol and removed from the scene. The Company Sergeant Major of the Regular unit saw one of his soldiers' berets floating in a pond close to scene of the explosion and walked out into the water to recover the beret, gently brushed it down and took it with him. Jim never could get that scene out of his mind.

Dean McGucken continues:

Cappagh was a PIRA stronghold. Some of the most notorious killers from East Tyrone PIRA lived in and operated in this area. When we started to learn this area as B Company, we initially just saw the whole community as terrorists, but very soon our commanders taught us who the real threat was from, who the terrorists were, and out of the whole community probably only 10 people were our real targets of interest. The rest of the local community had to suffer them too. We got to know everyone, we had more friends than enemies, although they never could or would be seen talking to us. We had all sorts of skills in our company – farmers who could help with lambing, mechanics who could help with a breakdown. Some very isolated elderly people were just glad of a chat.

---

5   Maj James (Jim) Patterson 1961-: 8 UDR 1979-92: (R Irish until 2007 then Royal Australian Defence Force): GOC's Commendation.

We were part of the community's daily life, not by choice of course. Bits of info would be passed, say at a VCP; you had to be able to read between the lines of: 'What are you boys at, racing up and down the Galbally road at 2 in the morning? Have you no home to go to?' What they were really telling you was: 'Don't go down the Galbally road' and so on. It was one of the best areas to get a home-made soda farl (bread) and Cappagh was the best by far, voted by all of us, along with some quality poteen. We never told on local poteen makers or hindered them on delivery nights. It was rural life for generations in Cappagh.

We were tasked by the Company 2 I/C to carry out a route clearance on a road running east from the village of Galbally to the main route leading to the village of Pomeroy. We were setting a pattern. We were using our civilian vans to deploy in and out of the Cappagh area and for occasional green vehicle patrols and the police were using mobile car patrols for normal policing duties and anti-terrorist duties. We did not have access to police information about their patrol patterns and I doubt if they collated the information anyway, so we added a third of our activity, just as a rule of thumb, I was told.

The clearance operation was planned by Stanley Gordon. We would use four teams, sixteen troops in all and deploy by helicopter to the start point near Galbally village, patrolling east, out to the safer area of Donaghmore, so if 'helis' were not available, later extraction could be by other means.

Formal orders were given, search equipment distributed and radios checked, although to be honest, radios weren't usually effective in this area and we had little faith in them. I was on the road checking culverts on the south side, Davy Wilson[6] and his team opposite us checking the north side. A team either side on the flanks was checking for command wires 200 to 300 metres out and for possible firing points. Visual control had to be maintained by all four teams. We took this work very seriously, slowly and meticulously. It did not matter if we only managed one mile or four miles in a day. We had to be careful going over wire fences as one householder had wired up the fence around his house to the mains electricity.

We had long given up using the 50 thou scale map for patrols. Now we used air photographs or Ordnance Survey large scale maps, and our local knowledge was even better than those. Stanley cut an air photo in two along the road in question and gave one side to Davy the other half to me, the flank teams had their own air photos.

It was a straightforward op, two men either side of the hedgerow on the road; don't get too far ahead if one team is having more difficult ground to cover. The pace is set by the slowest team, just as a wolf pack travels. I spoke to Davy as

---

6 Cpl David (Davy) Wilson 1951-: (Inniskillings and R Irish Rangers 1966-78): 8 UDR 1979-92: MID GOC's Commendation.

we approached a large culvert that we knew was just ahead of us. We couldn't raise the flank team by radio, wanting them to look from the high ground with the binos into the culvert first, so Davy and I went to the opposite ends of the culvert to look in, agreeing to tell each other what we could see, just by shouting through the culvert to each other. It was dark inside the culvert and I got my torch out to look through and saw creamery cans all wired up. Realising it was a bomb and Davy seeing the same from the opposite side, we just shouted 'Run!'

CWIED in Culvert

Well, I took off up the steep hill, running as fast as I could, shouting about a bomb. In my head was the five Ds, actions to take on discovering a suspect IED. I couldn't remember the first 'D'! I got to Stanley, shouting about the creamery cans and he was laughing and said: 'Calm down'. He had found the firing point and couldn't raise me on the radio to tell me to hold. Anyway he congratulated me on my turn of speed up the hill!

Things happen very fast, although they seem to be in slow motion. Stanley was more interested in following up terrorists escaping from the firing point, but we could only afford a team of four to go and hunt out their escape route and we sent them on. Best guess on our local knowledge, their brief was not to go out of sight because of the radio problems.

The road had to be sealed, the firing point sealed for safety and then forensic is your next worry and potential of secondary devices. The firing point was well used, the grass flattened, an area they used as a toilet was visible; all good evidence for the police to gather and we would not contaminate. The away team reported a hidden motorcycle, so that was another scene to preserve.

Stanley called a halt to potential follow ups. This now was a major clearance operation which would not happen today. We were not going home for a while.

It was a thousand pound landmine. If a police or military patrol had been caught, it was certain death for the patrol. A PIRA operation had been thwarted. When we went home the next day, I looked up the five Ds. The first 'D' was 'Detect'. They were 'Detect, delay, discuss, dominate, dispose'. I have never forgotten them and a few years later I was lucky to survive a landmine attack on our mobile patrol near Dungannon. It was a dangerous area to operate in.

Jay Nethercott again:

This then moved into a Company sized cordon and clearance operation which, when all agencies were tasked (ATO, RESA and search dog), and their availability confirmed, a planning conference was held at Killymeal in the early evening of the 7th.

B Company Team with the Explosives
L-R: Private Tom Espie, Lance Corporal Deko Anderson, Sergeant Stanley Gordon and Private John Ferguson.[7] (Team who found the command wire and motor cycle, and secured the firing point)

---

7   Pte Thomas (Tom) James Espie 1960-: 8 UDR 1980-87.
    WO2 Derek (Deko) James Anderson 1960-: 8 UDR 1978-92: (R Irish until 2000).
    Pte Henry (John) Ferguson 1952-: 8 UDR 1971-92: (R Irish until 1997).

The most important people to attend the planning conference and speak to the agencies are the soldiers who found the bomb, detailing the routes they used close to the scene of the bomb, what they actually saw and did before and after. With this information and an intelligence update from the RUC, we would proceed on planning a clearance operation for first light on the 8th, with a briefing at Killymeal. Full helicopter support was required, was allocated, and routes in and out secured for the road movements of ATO and police. Reserves are held in case the operation extends if problems develop on the ground; thus fresh troops are available to continue for as long as it takes until ATO declares the area safe, the explosives have been destroyed and forensics have completed their work. In this case, because we had such a detailed brief by the soldiers who had found the bomb, this operation was straightforward and was concluded during the daylight hours of the 8th. More information became available on the 8th from the police, who, prior to the find, had been informed by phone about a break-in at a local school at Galbally and disclosing where stolen property had been dumped. This was all a ruse to lure a police mobile patrol into the area of the Galbally road; the landmine had been placed on the route the patrol was likely to use.

We always had a de-brief after an incident; it was a very informal affair. The purpose was not to apportion blame, it was to review our procedures, analyse how and why problems occurred, and see if lessons could be learned at command level, patrol level and improve the effective use of all agencies. Forensics, preserving the scene and gathering evidence were increasingly important issues, as was the timely passage of information among all groups. The information about the break in at the local school and the location of stolen property might have changed the action taken initially. Against that the military were there to support the RUC to allow normal policing to take place and that as a mission statement was achieved.

Pomeroy 28th February 1985

A C Company foot patrol entered Pomeroy along the Carrickmore Road when a blast bomb was detonated by command wire. Private TW Harkness[8] was killed. Private G Patterson[9] was injured (shrapnel in the arm). With a radio breakdown, Lance Corporal Marks[10] commandeered a car and drove to the RUC Station to report the incident and secure assistance.

---

8   +Pte Trevor Winston Harkness 1949-85: 8 UDR 1970-85: Farmer: GOC's Commendation (posthumous): Killed 28th February 1985.
9   CSgt Gary Patterson 1965-: 8 UDR 1983-92: (R Irish until 2007): MID: Milkman.
10 LCpl Melvin (Sparky) Marks 1962-: 8 UDR 1980-90: MID: Joiner.

This was a six man foot patrol. As they came close to the village and were passing the Roman Catholic Church, there was an explosion at the base of a telegraph pole. Trevor was hit by a piece of shrapnel and died instantly. It is believed PIRA saw the patrol some distance away and had time to set up a portable landmine and roll out the command wire (only 35 metres long). Trevor was a part-time soldier working during the day on a farm and in the evenings doing his bit to help with the security of the area. He left a wife and young family.

Brian Hamilton[11] was the patrol commander:

> It was 28th February 1985 and it was a night patrol. Normally we'd work in teams of four, but that night, it was two teams of six. We were dropped off at the Carrickmore Road by covert vehicles and we were coming walking in towards Pomeroy. We had set up a short VCP to begin with. You're just coming in on that straight road from Carrickmore past the Parkview Estate.
>
> It was the same night that the policemen were murdered in a mortar attack in Newry and, because we had bad 'comms', my plan was to go down to the RUC Station at the bottom of the town to find out more, because we couldn't get through to them on our radios. But then that didn't happen.
>
> We were just at the side of the Parochial House when it happened, at that small laneway, just opposite Reggie Ramsey's and near the chapel. That's close to the town centre. The patrol had been on the ground for between one and two hours before the attack and had carried out several VCPs. We hadn't noticed anything suspicious prior to the explosion, so we all reckoned it must have been set for somebody else, although they probably could have set it up fairly quickly. I don't know. We were well spaced out; there were two men at the front, Melvin and myself in the middle and then Trevor and Gary bringing up the rear.
>
> Our major problem that night was that the radio was on the wrong frequency, so someone in 6 UDR in Omagh got the ambush call first. Trevor died instantly, hit by a piece of shrapnel, so nothing could be done at the scene. Everything goes still for a moment or two while you try to work out what's going on and I went back to check on Trevor. It was only a few seconds after the explosion, but he was obviously dead and when I tried to take the rifle off him, his fingers were rigid around it.
>
> We heard and then saw a car escaping from the scene within a few seconds, from where the command wire would have been. The car sped off. It was at a distance of about two hundred yards away from us. It went away so fast we could only see the tail lights and in the dark we couldn't recognise what kind of car it was. You couldn't risk firing a shot in case it hit somebody else.

---

11 WO2 Robert (Brian) Hamilton BEM UD and Two Bars 1948-: 8 UDR 1971-92: (R Irish until 1999): Farmer.

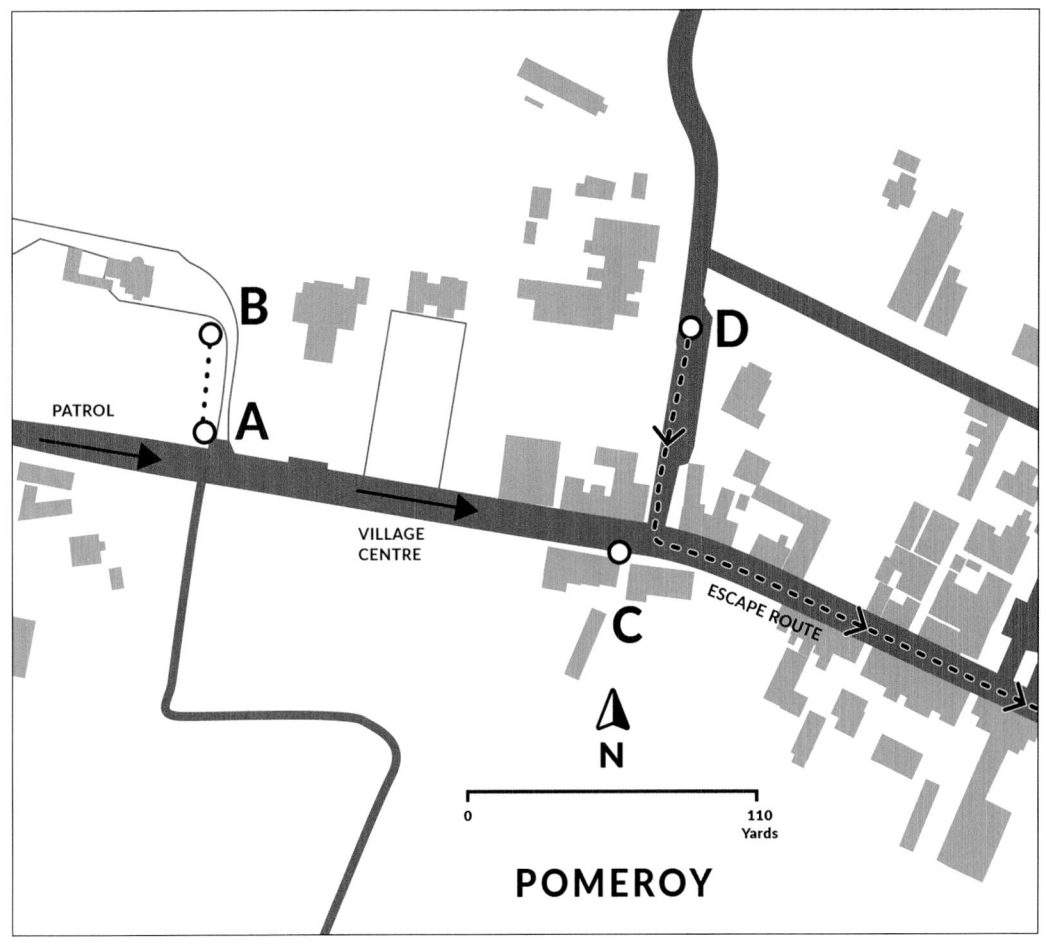

PIRA Attack on Patrol in Pomeroy
A: IED, B: Firing Point, C: Ramsey's, D: Getaway Car

We couldn't contact the other patrol, because we had no communications, though they would have heard the explosion and they would have seen the car speeding off and they made their way down towards us. Melvin's father, Jim Marks,[12] was in the other half of the patrol. Melvin did good work that night; he took over for a short time and ran for help. I rang Cookstown from a neighbouring house – I never found out what the people were called – I asked to use the telephone and they obviously knew that something had happened outside.

I think all the fellas, bar Gary, who was injured, were back to work next day and we had to start preparing for a funeral. Unfortunately, that's the way it was then and life had to go on.

---

12 Cpl James (Jim) Marks BEM 1933-: 8 UDR 1970-92: Butcher.

Melvin Marks takes over:

> The night of the incident, there were six of us in the patrol and Brian Hamilton was the Patrol Commander. We were dropped off by CPV (Covert Patrol Van) on the far side of Pomeroy at the top of the town and we came down the street past the Parkview Estate, heading towards the Police Station. We had been patrolling the whole evening but by then it was fairly late on, about half past ten or eleven o'clock.
>
> What helped us was that we were well spread out, maybe ten or fifteen yards apart. Brian and me were the two middle men of the six-man patrol. We had stopped for a couple of minutes and I had been leaning up against a telephone pole and when Brian said: 'Let's go', we moved off and the next minute, all I heard was 'Bang!' When I looked round, all I could see was dust and smoke and bits of trees. Then it sort of cleared a bit and I could see Trevor lying on the ground. I tried to get a pulse but I could get nothing. I said to Brian: 'I think he's dead'. Apparently it was just a wee bit of metal that hit Trevor on the back of his neck and cut his spinal cord.
>
> The radio wasn't working right so I ran to a house across the street and rapped the door and said: 'Would you please take me down to the Police Station, because there's been an incident?' I wasn't sure whose house it was – you just run and try to get help, you know? He was a good fella and he took me down to the Police Station and they came up to us. Gary Patterson, who was the other man at the back of the group along with Trevor, he was hit with shrapnel in his arm. After a few minutes, he was up and walking about, but he was dazed and shocked.
>
> They reckon the firing point was no further than fifty yards away from us. The Provos knew we were in the area so they just set the device in beside the pole and there was a command wire. It was handy enough to just plant it. If you were looking towards the town to the right, you had the housing estate and if you went to the left where the command wire was, you had farms and hedges and the like. Then they went out onto the back road and got away. They had plenty of safe houses. That night, it was lucky that there was no gunfire as well, because if there had been gunfire, they would have got us all. I was waiting for that to happen.
>
> The police sealed the whole area off and they phoned to different agencies from the station. C Company brought us back in to Cookstown and B Company took over. There was another patrol in the area at the same time and my Da was in that one. We were never sent out on the same brick at any time. He said he was glad to hear my voice.
>
> We didn't have any counselling. The only thing was, when we came in, they said to me: 'Here, have a drink and then just go on home and try to put it out of your head'. That was all I got. I went on to work the next morning and I was

back on duty again fairly soon after. But it never goes away. You get flashbacks all the time. Sometimes it just hits you, out of the blue. I'm not being selfish, but I sometimes think 'That could have been me'. That was the scary bit – that I had just been leaning up against that pole a couple of minutes before. I did ten more years after that.

Gary Patterson, one of the youngest men in the Battalion during that time, recalls:

I joined part-time in Cookstown on 1st July 1984. I was a milk roundsman during the day and a part-time soldier at night. I did my recruits' course and went out to do my normal, day-to-day job. On my very first patrol after my recruits' course, we were round the side of the camp doing base plates and I got into a row with some undesirables that lived two streets away from me. So there was my card marked with the first kick of the ball!

Thereafter, things ensued; they 'dicked' me and followed me. There was one individual whose job it was to follow me from the Milk Marketing Board to Monrush, at the top of Cookstown, which was my run. Ultimately, the police arrived. The thing that triggered it was when I set a pint of milk down on a certain doorstep and looked up and there were two individuals standing there in a dark alleyway. I came back and reported it and then, a couple of mornings later, I was about to set the milk down on another part of the estate, when the police arrived, 'scooped' me and took me down to Cookstown base. And this was about five in the morning. There was the Commanding Officer, Mr. Wilson, the IO at the time and a couple of senior policemen, saying: 'You're leaving the Country'. I said: 'What do you mean? I'm only in the place ten minutes!' They said the information had been passed on, they had reason to believe, and so on.

The old COIN (Counter Insurgency) packages were on the go at the time and Omagh was going to complete their two weeks in Lydd and Hythe. They pulled up at the gates and lifted me and I disappeared into the sunset on a boat from Larne to Stranraer with 6 UDR out of Omagh. I worked in their stores, but I was in contact with the Commanding Officer and he asked me to come back and see him. I came back at the end of the COIN package but that had got me out of the system, got me out of the Company, and when I came back he offered me the option of going full-time or leaving. I said I'd always wanted to go full-time so he told me I'd work in Cookstown camp during the day but I had to complete my part-time duties. And my last part-time duty with my platoon was the 28th February 1985. I was supposedly coming back for tea and sticky buns but instead I was blown all over Main Street, Pomeroy! That was also the night of the mortar attack which killed the policemen in Newry.

We went out on patrol and we were dropped off up the Carrickmore Road outside Pomeroy and we were foot-patrolling in, doing a rolling VCP. We stopped Tony Armstrong[13] and those boys in the car, and suddenly, 'Ping!' all the top brass from that neck of the woods were in the area. The boys did a full search and we walked towards the town and stopped at Lagan Transport, because the base plate in Newry had been on the back of a low-loader lorry. Brian Hamilton was in charge and told us to have a nosy around to make sure there was nothing untoward.

But as we were walking across the road still in the darkness of the countryside, just about a hundred metres away from the first street light on the edge of Pomeroy, a voice said in my head: 'Get to the other side of the road'. Originally, the whole way along the Carrickmore Road, Trevor had been on the right-hand side and as he went to check the lorry, something (I swear to Almighty God) said in my ear: 'Get to the other side of the road'. It was as clear as if you were saying it to me now, and just thinking about it makes the hairs stand on the back of my neck. I did my cover with the others as they were checking the base plates. So I moved across and Trevor said: 'I'll stay here'. One hundred metres down the road, 'Bang!' off she went. It was at the base of a telegraph pole so whether they had dug it in, knowing we were coming into the town, I don't know.

Trevor's SLR was down through his centre, he was walking and carrying properly, but the gas plug of Trevor's SLR sheared off, went up and cut the spinal cord at the back of his neck, then came straight across the road, went in through my left elbow, out through my left elbow and into my ribcage.

I fell over the little wall at Ramsey's house. When I got myself upright, with tinnitus and all the rest of it, I went: 'What has happened here?' When I looked over the wall, nobody was to be seen. Just then, as the dust started to settle, I saw Tony McCaw[14] a few metres down on the left-hand side, Brian was in the gateway into Ramsey's house and when I looked across the road, Trevor was lying there. I didn't know whether to go over and see him. My fear was that people were going to empty out of the estate and give us a kicking. And then … do I shoot these people in the heat of battle? What do I do? All this was going through my head.

The command wire ran from the telegraph pole into the back of the chapel, but they were shrewd enough – darkness was their ally, so even if the command wire had been luminous, we still wouldn't have seen it, the way they had laid it.

Melvin Marks ran and got Ramsey's car, went down to the police station and brought the police back up to where we were. But while he was away and things started to settle, in those few seconds, this massive pain shot through the left-hand side of my body. When I took my glove off the blood started running out

---

13 Thomas Anthony (Tony) Armstrong c1954-: Pomeroy: Sentenced to 12 years' imprisonment (1979) for causing an explosion and possession of explosives in Gortin 1974, Coalisland 1975 and 1978 (*Tyrone Courier* 17th January 1979).

14 Pte Anthony (Tony) McCaw 1959-: 8 UDR 1983-92: (R Irish until 1999): Butcher.

onto the ground and I realised something had gone wrong. Melvin came up with the police and they set me in the back of the car, the policeman got the First Aid Kit out, cut my jacket open and did his immediate first aid. I told him there was something wrong with my side, so he got the jacket partly off and he could see that something had driven into my ribs. He was concerned I had punctured a lung because my breathing was heavy, but it was just the shock.

I have a blank for a while then until I realised that an ambulance had arrived. The big ambulance paramedic put me into the wagon and said: 'We need to get you to hospital, son' and drove off. All the way from Pomeroy, I could see the lights of a car following us and as we were coming into the outskirts of Dungannon, I said: 'By the way I don't have an escort. I'm here on my own in uniform and my gun's lying back on that street in Pomeroy'. He says: 'You know what, Gary? You're right, son'. So he got on the radio and he drove round the roundabout here in Dungannon eight times so that the police could get out of Quarry Lane and get round to the South Tyrone Hospital. But there are two entrances to the South Tyrone and they went to A&E at the back and he drove me up to the front doors!

As he reversed up, he went: 'The police are here somewhere, Gary!' At that point the car that I had seen following us from Pomeroy also reversed into the doors and these two individuals came along, no hats, nothing to identify them and I didn't know whether this was Coyle and Armstrong, coming to finish me off. I went: 'Shit, they're coming to get me. Drive! Drive! Drive!' So when the policeman put his head round the door I swung the boot and left a big mark of Kiwi polish down the door of the ambulance.

As I was going in, the ambulance paramedic says: 'By the way Gary, don't say anything, but they're all the other side in here' and I says: 'What d'you think, will this give it away?' My coat was in shit order, the blood was pissing out of me and next thing, this crowd came running round with a trolley. This real arrogant Sister says: 'It's OK. What's all the panic? He's walking. There's no panic'. At that point, he said: 'You're on your own, son!' and off he went!

So they put me on the trolley and took me round and set me in a chair to try and undress me. I had the combat jacket, the jumper, the KFs (Khaki Flannel Shirt) the whole kit on. There was one at the shirt, one at the boots and hands everywhere. So I stood up to say: 'I'll do it' and some boy grabbed me by the hair, pulled me back into the chair, 'Sit there, we'll f***in' do it'. Next thing, the clothes off and I was lying, naked as the day I was born, on a slab. At that, they came at me with all these needles for lockjaw poisoning and all that. I think I had eight or nine injections some into my groin, some into my neck and that was me out of it. When I came round, Robin Ferry[15] was standing next to

---

15 WO2 Robert (Robin) James Alexander Ferry 1944-: 8 UDR 1977-92: (R Irish until 2002): GOC's Commendation.

me. He was Duty Officer at Killymeal and he came up to keep an eye on me. In the haze of half consciousness, the hospital told me they wouldn't be operating on me and that I was being sent to Musgrave (Military Hospital).

I don't remember the journey or going into theatre but I do remember next day having a huge injection needle under one armpit and another under the other armpit, and fifty-seven stitches in my left arm, both internal and external. They removed the piece of shrapnel from my ribcage and I had six stitches there. Oh, and I was in plaster from shoulder to wrist.

When I first woke up, I remember seeing Sir Douglas Hurd (*Secretary of State Northern Ireland 1984-85*) standing at the end of my bed. He had been visiting the injured from Newry Police Station, who were in the next ward to me. I can remember looking up through the haze, seeing this group all round me and going: 'I'm going to be sick!' and I sent a technicoloured yawn down the bed. He left quickly and I passed out again.

I didn't get to Trevor's funeral but a lot of people came in to see me. When I came out of the first operation, the first man in to see me was Brian and when he saw all the wires and tubes and plaster, he walked back out again, totally shocked.

Thereafter, I was in and out of hospital quite a few times and I had four operations to keep an eye on the wound. They thought I'd need a skin graft but it knitted of its own volition. I went to see various psychiatrists as well. There was a very good group in Musgrave Park Hospital Military Wing and I went to Lisburn to see the psychologist a few times. Albert Cooper's[16] wife was in one of the groups sometimes.

Battalion Headquarters, Dorothy Meenagh[17] and the Welfare team were all very, very good at organising these visits. So Post Traumatic Stress Disorder was now in bold type on all my medical documents throughout my Army career because that was only the first – I was blown up three times and shot at once.

When I was back doing light duties, I was on the guard at Killymeal House and I remember lying on the bed in the guardroom. I kept going back to the same dream where we were involved in the incident at Tyrone Brick and in the dream, we were going along in the Land Rovers, a good distance apart, but when the landmine went off there was an HGV lorry coming tossing through the air. Because of that, I always kicked everybody out of the bunk above me.

I wasn't too bad after Pomeroy, but then after the next one and the next one, the flashbacks all accelerated. When I was involved in the second incident, the 1,000 lb landmine at Tyrone Brick, the ambulance man who lifted

---

16 +WO2 Albert David Cooper 1948-90: 8 UDR 1970-90: MID (posthumous) GOC's Commendation: Businessman: Killed 2nd November 1990.
17 Cpl Dorothy Phyllis Meenagh 1946-: 8 UDR 1982-92: (R Irish until 1998).

me off the ground was the same big paramedic. And as he was lifting me up he said: 'We'll have to stop making a habit of this!' The third one was a blast bomb at Powerscreen International, down at Edendork Crossroads. After that you start to out-think stuff a bit too much. I remember saying to someone in the Guardroom one day: 'Why did I survive and Trevor didn't? Why not me?' because the guilt started to really rain in on me then, that man had family and he won't see them growing up and I'm a young cub of eighteen – the world won't miss me. That type of thing was all going through my head and building up. But those men in the Guardroom, who could have been dismissive, sat me down and let me get it out. I miss the boys and the craic but they always had their soft side.

A lot of the time, there's all the craic and slagging and winding each other up, but on this occasion they didn't. You could have been the hardest man on the planet but we all knew what people were going through because we all grew up in this bubble and when you needed to be serious or sympathetic, you could adapt your compass to the right settings. When the Tyrone Brick bomb occurred, I was married one year. That day was my wedding anniversary and my wife had announced she was pregnant with our daughter a couple of days before. I was supposed to be on leave that day, but because they'd messed up the leave, they said to do the training package in Dungannon (we were based at Cookstown) and that would be my mandatory training over for the year, then go on leave. Fair play to 'Gibby' (Derek Gibson,[18] who was driving the Land Rover) that day, he did a good job. He was a good pilot.

I went full-time on 1st March 1985 and went to B Company. I served my colour service until 28th February 2007 and finished as CQMS in Armagh. I hated leaving the job because I loved every second of it. When I became Platoon Sergeant and then CQMS and went behind a desk, it became a more 'normalised' routine and prepared me to some extent for when I went back into the big, bad world.

There was a lot of stalwarts at the head of B Company who knew their stuff and knew the right people in all the right places.

Jay Nethercott[19] adds:

At that time of the ambush of Brian's patrol in Pomeroy, I was Company Commander of the full-time, B Company 8 UDR and we were already deployed on an operation in the Cappagh area, south of Pomeroy and I then got the call

---

18　Pte Derek Gibson 1962-2020: 8 UDR 1980-92: (R Irish until 1998): MID GOC's Commendation.
19　Maj William James (Jay) Nethercott MBE QGM 1952-: 8 UDR 1971-87: (5 UDR 1987-92, R Irish until 2000): MID.

that I was to extract from that and go straight to Pomeroy, where we knew that some incident had happened. We had no real knowledge about the extent of it.

I extracted from the patrol I was with and took Tom Finlay,[20] one of my platoon commanders, and we went in a 'civvie' car up to Pomeroy. I went straight to the ICP and met with Brian. It was then that I was met with the reality that there was one dead casualty and one injured casualty who had been extracted to the hospital. Brian was in good shape, the cordon was fine, there were no problems with that; everybody was functioning as a patrol even though this incident obviously shook them up. So I was happy enough that they were able to function as a proper cordon and I had given directions then that the operation we were involved with was to be stopped and the lads make their way up to me, to Pomeroy Police Station initially, and I left it to those guys to sort out their own extraction. These are not easy things to do, but I didn't give any advice on routes; these guys knew their job. They would meet me at Pomeroy whenever they would get there. And they would do it with some urgency.

Although we had no mobile phones or anything like that, I remember I phoned back and told them to ring the Company Sergeant Major; he was to deploy to Pomeroy and to get the Storeman, 'Pal'. We always had a vehicle set aside in Killymeal, where our headquarters was, full of odd bits and pieces that we would use for cordon and search or whatever sort of incident we might be involved in. I 'stood to' the Reserve Platoon and it was to report to Killymeal and wait for further instructions. They would be two, three hours away from me. I then went down to the police barracks. Obviously, it was going to be a handover to me at some stage to complete the clearance operation for this incident.

Down at the police station, I met with the Commanding Officer and Albert Turner,[21] the Company Commander of the platoon that had just been hit. We had a bit of a discussion about things. I knew that really they wanted me to get that patrol extracted as soon as possible. We agreed on some sort of time scales, I was going to have to hold them until I got my own team up there and there was a lot of pressure on the Commanding Officer and the Company Commander, who were going to have to go and visit Trevor's wife in Cookstown, so I took on the full role of getting this sorted out. I was quite surprised when I was speaking to Brigade, that In this situation ATO, who would be required to do the clearance operation, would deploy that night, so that gave me a full night time clearance operation – not a problem (we were well used to dealing with ATO and clearing up scenes at night anyway).

---

20 WO1 (RSM) Thomas (Tom) Finlay BEM 1954-: (R Irish Rangers 1972-79): 8 UDR 1979-92: (R Irish until 2007).
21 Maj (Albert) Samuel Turner MBE UD 1932-96: 8 UDR 1971-91: Second in Command 8 UDR 1985-91: Meat Inspector, Ministry of Agriculture.

The biggest problem we had was how to get an ATO team moving by road to the Pomeroy area, bearing in mind that there had been a serious incident in Newry that night. A police station had been mortared and there were multiple casualties there. Our own area was a hotbed of IRA activity, so you were always worried about a secondary device along the routes. This small device, although successful from the PIRA point of view for it had killed a soldier, could have been a draw for us to deploy to the scene and get caught in a landmine attack. So we had to agree some routes that we could try to move ATO along by road. Those routes had to be secured and patrolled and checked. Some you would do by helicopter, some (in this case) by the Reserve Platoon, to get ATO eventually to me. The only advice I gave back to the base was certain routes that I would NOT use. After that, I left it to them to make their own plan and get those resources to me.

The lads who were on the operation we were involved with to the south arrived fairly quickly. They came in by van. We had our own extraction plan always available to us so 'civvie' vans were used. They were only about ten miles away and as soon as I had my own team in place, I knew I could extract Brian, we would take over the loose cordon that was there at the minute and get him back to the police barracks with his men. He had left with twelve men and he was going home with ten, so it was important at that stage to get them back to their own base in Cookstown as quickly as was feasible. An extraction plan was made; again the likelihood of another landmine attack was pretty severe, so we had to work out a route to get them extracted, again using civilianised vans and then it was up to the clearance operation.

These are clinical, textbook type things, and we were well-rehearsed in them. The Company Sergeant Major was my Search Team Adviser. Within the platoons we always had a fully-operational search team. The Reserve Platoon coming in brought ATO to us and I didn't need their full strength, I just needed their search team. They were sent back to Killymeal to rest up. In your head, you have no time scale of how long this is going to take, but it will always take many hours before these things are cleared up. As it was, we worked throughout the night. The sad thing was that, right through that night, we just looked at Trevor's body lying at the side of the road and there's nothing you can do about that. You just have to be clinically aware of the main operation, which is to clear things up. And of course you will get the remains lifted and taken back to a morgue at some stage. You just put it out of your mind and get on with the job. The search teams cleared the area with the search dogs and ATO cleared the scene where Trevor was. We then worked the command wire back to the firing point and, again, you have to be very careful of the likelihood of a booby-trap in the cordon position or at the firing point. ATO cleared that eventually and there were no secondary devices.

In the early hours of the morning, the operation was well advanced and now we were left with the police to come in and hold the scene for CID, because evidence is key all the time and you must try not to corrupt any evidence that may be at a firing point or along the command wire or where they had planted the small device. People that we'd had to move out of their houses were then able to move back in and in the early hours of the morning we extracted Trevor's remains and they were removed to a morgue.

To all intents and purposes, that was my part in the operation finished. It now became a daylight CID/police follow-up and that was it really. Over the next few days, we picked up on the operation we were involved with down in Cappagh and continued with that and then the funeral was organised. We were all involved with the funeral, because, like everything else, funerals were not straightforward either. There's the likelihood of an attack on a dignitary or at a police cordon point, so we had a lot of clearance operations to do for Trevor's funeral.

I never really had the courage to go and see the family. I knew them very well, I knew the young family and obviously we saw them at the funeral. He was the most modest, nicest guy you could ever have met. Some years later, when Beverley Weir did the Book of Remembrance for 8 UDR, we were interviewing the families who had lost members and I was helping with that. I met Trevor's daughter. She was just a child when he was killed and she asked about her father. I said yes, I'd been at the scene. She said that as a child she had never been told anything. When people arrived at the house that night, the children were shooed away. They knew something dreadful had happened but it was never really discussed. Just Dad never came back. Then all the people at the funeral and that…. and then life rolled on. She said that now, as a young mother herself, she was wondering: 'How will I tell my children about their Grandad. And how do we make sure not to let hatred come in on it?' I asked her did she want to know the full details of the whole incident and what I had seen because it had never been discussed. She said she wanted to know everything and I explained everything at the scene, what it was like for her daddy and the fact that there wasn't a mark on him. Just this sliver of metal had gone through the back of his neck and he would have been dead before he hit the ground. She was anxious to know these details. It was the first time she had heard them and I had been there in the aftermath. And that was it.

8

Vehicle Checks

Terrorists relied on vehicles for reconnaissance, liaison, movement of weapons and explosives, and for their attacks. 8 UDR mounted numerous Vehicle Check Points (VCP) to interdict this vehicle movement, as part of everyday operations. VCPs were deliberate and snap and set up by both mobile and foot patrols. In both cases the aim was to establish a chicane, no problem with a mobile patrol but if on foot it had to be done by controlling vehicle movement through the VCP.

Siting a VCP required considerable experience and tactical awareness. If it was too obvious the terrorist vehicle could easily evade or avoid the VCP. At the same time every effort had to be made not to lay VCPs in the same place and so risk an anti-personnel IED.

When a vehicle entered the VCP its licence plate was checked by radio with the database. This revealed if the vehicle was stolen or of interest; in the latter case instructions might be given on whether the vehicle should be searched or not, and if to be searched what to look for. A large number of these checks were made by VCPs and observation posts every day and these could be analysed to identify patterns or breaks in patterns of movement, invaluable to the overall intelligence gathering effort.

If there was suspicion about the vehicle a long car check could be done to ensure the plate and vehicle matched and confirm ownership. Again this was done by radio.

The next step was to check the driver and passengers, initially done by a combination of profiling and gut feeling. The driver would have his driving licence which included a photograph. This could be checked over the radio against the personality database. If the driver was in any way suspect then the passengers would also be checked and their sighting logged and reported. Such associations also helped the overall intelligence effort.

The final step was to search the vehicle, having kept a close eye that nothing was thrown from it whilst waiting to enter or in the VCP. This took time especially at night and in bad weather. All the time a balance had to be achieved between interdicting terrorist activity and causing excessive disruption to the quality of life of everyone else.

A snippet of information gleaned at a VCP very often led to success by the Army or RUC. It could have been an association in the vehicle or the time and direction of travel, and the information might not have been suspicious to the patrol at the time; it was when collated with other information that it produced intelligence on which an operation could be mounted. So every opportunity was taken to check vehicles especially those that seemed suspicious.

VCPs were dangerous operations; on 20th April 1976 Lance Corporal McCreedy[1] was killed and another soldier injured by a speeding vehicle while on a VCP at Minterburn south of Aughnacloy. Occasionally, very occasionally, a vehicle driver tried to break through a check point. The soldiers were then faced with a difficult decision that had to be taken almost instantaneously, often at night and in bad weather. On 13th May 1973 in just such a situation Kevin Kilpatrick[2] driving a van, broke through a VCP in the Ardboe; he was shot and killed.

Black Lough (Dungannon) 22nd March 1983

A Platoon of D Company stopped a yellow Cortina at the Black Lough. The driver ran off. A search of it located a milk churn with 70 lbs of explosives already primed.

A fuller report observed: A foot patrol of 8 UDR was carrying out a snap VCP on the Dungannon-Eglish road. During a slight build-up of traffic a car, Yellow Ford Cortina VRN JIA 5420, was abandoned. The patrol did not see the driver leave the car. The patrol commander on checking the car found that a milk can was situated behind the driver's seat. He withdrew and cordoned off the area. This was at 2055hrs. Nightsun, Groundhog (tracker dog) and ATO were tasked. The area was declared clear at 0210hrs and the cordon was lifted at 0220hrs 23rd March. The find consisted of one milk churn with 25 kgs ANFO, two booster bags ANNIE (four kgs approx in each bag) and 21 feet Cordtex.

The *Dungannon Observer* (25th March 1983) reported that three young men abandoned the car and ran across the fields

Joe Kerr[3] was the patrol commander that night:

> We had some lucky escapes when on patrol near Dungannon, especially with landmines. This was a favourite of East Tyrone PIRA and caused multiple deaths and serious injuries of Security Forces caught in this type of ambush, a devastating scene to witness or be involved in.
>
> Once we were on foot patrol on the Old 'Caulfield road on the south side of Dungannon near Lisnahull. It was a night time patrol and we had been dropped off by the Land Rover patrol earlier. We were patrolling into Dungannon, carrying out vehicle checkpoints, and we would be picked up again on this

---

1 +LCpl Robert James McCreedy 1934-76: 8 UDR 1970-76: Farmer.
2 Kevin Kilpatrick c1952-73: Coalisland: Mechanic: Shot and killed in the Ardboe driving a van with three volunteers on board when they drove through a checkpoint operated by the UDR (Gerard Magee, *Tyrone's Struggle*): Described as OC 1st Batt A Company Tyrone PIRA (*Tyrone Courier* 23rd May 1973).
3 Cpl Joseph (Joe) Henry Kerr 1942-: 8 UDR 1971-92: (R Irish until 1997): MID and GOC's Commendation: Factory Operative.

road by the Land Rovers later in the evening. We had stopped on the road; I was with Hugh Jennings[4] and we went for a pee on the side of the road before the Land Rovers would pick us up. I remember saying to Hugh that there was a very strong smell from his urine and asked was he all right. 'Aye', he says, 'there is a very strong smell' and just at that moment the radio informed us that the pick-up would be in two minutes.

We moved onto the road as the Land Rovers came to us. As I put on the red stop light to let them know where we were, a detonator went off. We were on top of a culvert and a landmine with a command wire leading back towards Lisnahull housing estate had been detonated by the terrorists. The command wire was later discovered by Archie Roleston.[5] The main charge failed to explode and we learned later that the water from the small stream running under the road had got into the main charge and that was the strong smell of urine I and Hugh had smelt. We always referred to that culvert as 'Captain Val' after the officer on patrol with us that night, Captain Val James.[6] If the main charge had gone off, we would all have been killed.

On the evening of the 22nd March 1983, I was the patrol commander of a mobile patrol operating on the east side of Dungannon, carrying out VCPs on routes leading from Eglish, Benburb and Aughnacloy into Dungannon. There was a high threat of a terrorist attack but no specific intelligence. They were relatively busy roads with vehicle traffic which would normally ease after 2300hrs. We were carrying out snap VCPs on the Eglish to Dungannon road about a mile out of Dungannon. There was a build-up of traffic at the VCP on the Eglish side, probably four or five cars waiting, when the stop man heard a car door slamming. On further investigation by the cover man, the last car in line, a Yellow Ford Cortina, had no occupants. When he looked into the back he saw a milk churn and wires. The terrorists had scarpered and this was a bomb.

The immediate concern was to move civilian traffic away from the VCP, secure and cordon the suspect vehicle so that civilian traffic could not pass by and create a sterile area of 300m. Next was to formulate a plan for a follow-up, tasking the Nightsun helicopter and back-up patrols to assist in searching the immediate area of fields, looking for people moving on foot back in the direction of Eglish, where the suspect vehicle had approached from. The ATO was tasked to clear the vehicle and defuse the bomb which was ready to detonate and probably was heading to a target in the commercial area of Dungannon. A

4　LCpl Hugh Jennings 1934-1989: 8 UDR 1971-85: Factory Operative.
5　WO2 Archibald (Archie) Roleston BEM UD and Bar 1942-: 8 UDR 1970-92: (R Irish until 1997): Agricultural Engineer.
6　Capt Charles Thiepval (Val) James UD 1924-2008: (RN 1940-49): 8 UDR 1972-85: MID: Office Manager DHSS: 8 UDR Signals Officer when it became operationally responsible for East Tyrone.

The Yellow Cortina

70lb bomb of quality HME was successfully defused. Another terrorist attack thwarted and a much better feeling of success compared to the night the detonator went off.

Coalisland 20th April 1985

Sergeant David Kirk[7] recalls, but first some background:

> I enlisted in Omagh in 6 UDR in February 1971 when I was 26 and served in Dungannon. Then after about eighteen months, in 1972, it became J Company 8 UDR, 'Shining J' as it became known because there was a shooting team, and nobody could touch us; and one night somebody stood up and said: 'We're Shiny J' and it stuck! I spent a few years in Northland Place; when it closed I then went over to Killymeal in '78-79. That was when we became D Company.
>
> I did 28 years part-time and finished on 28th December 2007. Prior to that I had been in the Territorial Army in Enniskillen for six years. In civilian life I was a civil servant with the MOD for 20 years. Before that, I had worked in Moygashel until it closed and then I worked as a driver for Securicor. I had a few nasty experiences with them. During the workers' strike in 1974 I had to go to Coalisland along with two others with the broo money, for the dole

---

7 CSgt Robert David (Davy) Kirk BEM 1943-: 8 UDR 1971-92: Factory Operative.

office. When we got to Coalisland, we couldn't even see the dole office for the crowd out round the square. They let us drive in but then we had to get out! There I was, known in Coalisland and part-time UDR! I very quickly put my helmet on and pulled a scarf round me.

I had been living in Moygashel, but then I moved to Ivy Bank Park in Donaghmore, in among the Provos! We stayed there for six years, until a man from SB told me about a letter that had arrived with my name on it. I went to see the Commanding Officer and he said: 'I take it you're going to resign?' I said: 'No, why would I?' We talked it over and I was advised to move. But I said that if I got out it wouldn't be in the middle of the night; I wanted to go under my own terms. About two days later, my neighbour, Tom Gates,[8] was shot. They shot and wounded him right in front of the house I had just moved out of. I was called in and told that it had been intended for me.

I went to live in Ballinakelly in 1994. We had a wee bit of trouble there at the start. The Provos would reverse a car into a lane opposite the house at night and sit and flash the headlights at the house, just to let you know that they knew who you were. I lived then in Coolhill in Dungannon for eighteen years, although there were things happened that I didn't like. I don't agree with all this Loyalist stuff and painting of slogans and flags flying all over the place.

The evening of the find at Coalisland, I was a Sergeant, a section commander on a normal Saturday evening patrol. I briefed the boys on what we were going to do and we split into two groups of six. Colour Sergeant Roleston was in charge of the other group. We were dropped off at the chapel and he went along the Ferry Road and I went the Kingsisland Road. We were two foot patrols within distance of each other if anything did happen. We had been out for an hour, maybe an hour and a half, when we came to Kingsisland chapel. We had a fella with us who had been a sergeant but he handed in his tapes. I saw him coming walking back and he said: 'There's a car away round to the car park at the chapel there'. I went up to it and there were three men. We knew a couple of them. I then brought the rest of the patrol in. Tom McMullan,[9] who was a Lance Corporal, was searching the car. One of the men kept coming over beside me and talking and talking. I didn't want to talk to him at all, so I kept walking away from him. But he kept following me and all of a sudden I saw a glint underneath the trees. I looked down and there was a sawn-off shotgun lying half hidden.

I said nothing and just moved on and he kept following me, until I said: 'Right. On the ground. The three of them'. We put them down and radioed that we'd had a find. We had always been taught that you don't walk around

---

8   Sgt Thomas (Tommy) Henry Gates 1943-: 8 UDR 1971-85.
9   LCpl Thomas (Tom) William McMullan 1952-: 8 UDR 1975-92: (R Irish until 1999): Engineer.

the area where you see something. So I marked the path that I had walked with your man and that's the path they used to approach the scene. The police came then. I didn't tell them what I had seen; I hadn't even told my own men what the object was, but I told them not to let anyone move. All of a sudden we heard this sound and one of the suspects was actually lying there, crying. We moved him away a short distance from the others in the hope that he'd talk but they made sure to warn him before we moved him that he wasn't to talk! Then the Commanding Officer came out and wanted to go up to see the find but I wouldn't let him. I told him I was the only person who knew what it was and that everyone had to wait until SOCO came. SOCO did his bit and then ATO came. There was a sawn-off shotgun and special cartridges. The other part of my patrol was sent to do some searching around in a boggy area nearby and they found a car which the IRA had been using to test what it would take to penetrate the doors.

The three men had been driving in our direction, they had seen the checkpoint and pulled into the car park to throw the gun out of the car. When the forensics were done, a lot of incriminating evidence was found, including pieces of glass in one man's top pocket, from a robbery in Coagh, where they stole the gun.

The three of them were arrested and they didn't come home for two and a half years. One of them was Thaddeus Donnelly.[10] We had never heard tell of him before that. The other two were McLernon[11] and McStravog.[12]

When we went to camp some time afterwards, they were using the whole episode as an example for training for the whole Battalion and for the Regulars too. Many times we were out doing VCPs with the Regulars and they would be stopping every tenth car for example and letting people through that they should have been stopping. They didn't think who could have been in the other nine cars. Obviously they were good at ground coverage, but the UDR had local knowledge and could read the situation better.

---

10 Thaddeus Donnelly c1965-: Coalisland: Unemployed: Sentenced (1986) to five years' imprisonment for possession of firearms in suspicious circumstances (*Mid Ulster Mail* 21st November 1985 and *Democrat* 26th June 1986).

11 Brian McLernon c1965-: Coalisland: Unemployed: Sentenced (1986) to five years' imprisonment for possession of firearms in suspicious circumstances (*Mid Ulster Mail* 21st November 1985 and *Democrat* 26th June 1986): In 1989 following an RUC operation sentenced to 18 years' imprisonment for possession of firearms with intent to endanger life (*Mid Ulster Mail* 28th December 1990).

12 Hugh McStravog c1963-: Coalisland: Cutting Technician: Sentenced (1986) to five years' imprisonment for possession of firearms in suspicious circumstances (*Mid Ulster Mail* 21st November 1985 and *Democrat* 26th June 1986): In 1989 following an RUC operation sentenced to 16 years' imprisonment for possession of firearms with intent to endanger life (*Mid Ulster Mail* 28th December 1990).

All six of us had to go to court in Belfast, but I was the only one who was cross examined. You had to give evidence in full view of the court and there was a big crowd from Coalisland there. They gave my name – no 'Witness A' or anything like that. They claimed that we had harmed them but I took the attitude that if you tell the truth you've nothing to worry about. We couldn't believe it when the judge gave them five years apiece.

Then one night we stopped a van and McStravog was in it. I says: 'Are you home from your holidays?' and he says: 'I didn't enjoy it'. I said: 'If you'd been a good boy you wouldn't have been there!' He went to drive off and then he got out and came back to me and he says: 'Just one wee word – I'll never be back in again'. I asked him how I should take that. He didn't speak, but then about a fortnight later he was arrested again!

Would I join up if I had to do it all again? Yes!

Coalisland 29th December 1989 and 3rd January 1990

On 29th December 1989, a six man patrol of B Company commanded by Corporal Thomas Martin[13] arrested three men in a car (in Coalisland) in possession of two drogue bombs (IAAG). The men arrested were Brendan Campbell,[14] Tony Doris[15] and Martin Gervin.[16] They were charged with terrorist offences including possession of the IAAGs; Gervin was also charged with the murder of S/Sgt Froggett who was shot dead from the mast of Coalisland RUC Station in September 1989. As a result of information from these arrests a planned search was mounted on 3rd January 1990. One of the search teams found a deep hide containing three weapons.

---

13 WO2 Thomas William Harpur Martin 1965-: 8 UDR 1985-92: (R Irish until 2007): MID.
14 Brendan Campbell c1969-: Coalisland: Unemployed: Sentenced (1991) to 20 years' imprisonment for possession of two drogue bombs with intent to endanger life (*Tyrone Courier* 10th January 1990 and 11th December 1991): Released under Good Friday Agreement.
15 Anthony (Tony) Doris 1969-91: Coalisland: Charge of possessing two drogue bombs with intent in December 1989 withdrawn (*Mid Ulster Mail* 22nd November 1990): Killed Coagh, 3rd June 1991: Tyrone Sinn Fein Committee described him (2015) as OC of his unit (ipolitics newsletter). In 1987 became an active volunteer and in 1991 made OC of Coalisland unit of East Tyrone PIRA (Gerard Magee, *Tyrone's Struggle* and Brendan O'Brien, *The Long War*).
16 Martin Gervin 1962-: Coalisland: Joiner: Sentenced (1991) to 16 years' imprisonment for possession of two drogue bombs with intent to endanger life: Previously sentenced to life imprisonment for aiding and abetting the murder of SSgt Kevin Froggett R Signals in 1989, and other charges including IRA membership. (*Tyrone Courier* 10th January 1990 and 11th December 1991): Released under Good Friday Agreement.

PIRA Operations in Coalisland Interdicted
A: Car/Terrorist and Drogue Bombs Captured, B: Venue Bar, C: Old Mill/Terrorists Captured

John Robinson[17] was B Company Commander at the time:

> As Company Commander of B Company 8 UDR in late December 1989, I was responsible for tasking patrols into the Coalisland area. In mid-December B Company's main effort was changed from west of Dungannon to the Coalisland area to replace the Regular Army Company that had previously been tasked there. The situation in this area had turned critical as the Regular Army Company were near the end of their tour and avoided patrolling in the centre of Coalisland; this encouraged the terrorist element to openly target the RUC reporting for and coming off duty in the Coalisland Station. Within a short time B Company operations in the Coalisland area were very successful.
>
> My aim was to keep up the pressure on the suspect terrorists in the Coalisland area by frequently tasking patrols into the centre of the town. On the evening of

---

17 Maj David John (JR) Robinson MBE VR 1951-: (2 UDR 1971-85): 8 UDR 1985-90: GOC's Commendation: (HQNI 1990-92, R Irish until 2007: Theatre Commander's Commendations Bosnia and Kosovo).

the 29th December, I tasked a patrol into the centre, commanded by Corporal Thomas Martin. They were deployed by Wessex Helicopter to the edge of the town just after 1800hrs and were to patrol into the town and provide a presence in the areas where the known suspects normally moved, so as to disrupt their activities.

Thomas Martin recalls his part:

My father, great-uncle, two uncles, brother and sister served in the Battalion; I joined when I was nineteen. I started part-time in Cookstown in April 1985, didn't stay part-time very long, and started full-time on 31st July 1985.

It was the time the Glosters were pulling out of Dungannon; they were coming to the end of their tour. Twelve of us were dropped into Coalisland, Trevor Brimage[18] was in charge of one six-man team and I had the other one. We were dropped off on the Washing Bay Road and were going to the town centre and Trevor's brick was going to head up to Shotgun Alley towards the Stewartstown road, to do a VCP up there. I had a policeman with me from Carrickfergus; he looked a bit like Errol Flynn, with the moustache and the swarthy skin.

We were heading in the direction of Brackaville crossroads and there's a bit of high ground, waste ground, in the V between the Brackaville road and the Derry road which goes to Newmills. From that high ground at the edge of the buildings, we had a barrage of bottles and stones coming at us from kids and we wondered what was going on, because although they didn't want to know you in Coalisland and you got spat on and all, we never encountered anything like that. I said they probably thought we were the Glosters and suggested that we should go round behind them and approach them from the other direction; there's a wee track up there that brings you round and into Bernie's Square (the town square, so named after Bernadette Devlin [*1947-: Member of Parliament for Mid Ulster 1969-74*] gave a speech there early on in 'The Troubles'). We came back in right in the centre of the town and there's a statue in the middle of the street and we came in at the front of it, stopped at the Venue Bar (there's a side street there takes you up to Bernie's Square), and as soon as we turned the corner I saw a car facing away from us, I think it was a Datsun Stanza, with the engine running and there was a fella standing with the driver's door open, one foot in the foot well, leaning on the roof, talking.

There was an individual between me and the car but even now I don't recall seeing him. I looked straight at the boyo standing at the car and I said: 'Young Steptoe! The very man I'm looking to speak to. Come here!' Brendan Campbell

---

18 WO2 Trevor Brimage 1957-: 8 UDR 1977-92: (R Irish until 2006).

from the Washing Bay Road, commonly called 'Steptoe'. Next thing, he bolted down a back alleyway, over beer crates and kegs, in at the back of the bar. I turned round and the man at the back of the brick was a wee man called Ronnie Campbell[19] who was a PTI and he had a punch like a fourteen-pound sledgehammer. I said: 'Ronnie, front of the bar and take every one of them. Anyone that heads out is yours. There's nobody getting out'. When I turned round, there was another one of my men standing stock still and pointing at two drogue bombs sitting on the back seat of the car (*James C Dingly writes in his book 'IRA: Irish Republican Army': Another development was the drogue bomb, which consisted of several ounces of Semtex packed into a tin can, with a throwing handle and stabilising fin, plus a small parachute designed to ensure the bomb landed right-side up on the armoured vehicle and detonated as intended*).

I told him to deal with that and he said: 'What will I do with him?' indicating the other individual. That was the first time I'd noticed the other man who was standing outside the car! 'Take him too', I said, 'We want to get Campbell. He's in that bar and he's not getting out'. I remember getting onto the radio, I think we were using Channel 9 at the time because the 'comms' down in Coalisland were terrible. Channel 9 was like Chat Net and I managed to contact Trevor Brimage. We had a couple of men on the upper side of the car on this wee narrow back street and we came round to the front.

At this time, Trevor and his brick were legging it in from the Stewartstown road (they were only five or six hundred yards away) and coming in past the old Coalisland Road mill. On the way past, one of the men, Walter Wilkinson,[20]

PIRA Drogue Bomb

---

19 LCpl Ronald (Ronnie) Campbell 1965-: (previously 7/10 UDR): 8 UDR 1988-92: (R Irish until 1994).
20 Pte Walter Wilkinson 1966-: 8 UDR 1985-92: (R Irish until 2007).

noticed something, so three of them went in to investigate that and Trevor and the other two came to me in the middle of the square and started sealing it off. In the mill, there was a man called Doris, who had studied chemistry at university and another man. Walter and the other two soldiers got them out of there and brought them with them.

At this stage, we were concentrating on Campbell in the bar. The bar was busy so I just wasn't going to walk in, and I remember Trevor having to climb up onto the statue in the middle of the square to get the radio to work! Anyway, the police arrived in quick time and asked what was going on. I told them that Steptoe was in the bar.

More police arrived and the cordon started to take shape. The Sergeant brought a couple of large policemen into the bar and Steptoe came out, apprehended by them. They had cuffed him and arrested him. Then we had to start moving back and clearing everything and the police took control and started getting the traffic moving again. The fella who was at the back of the car, the one I don't remember seeing to start with, was Gervin from the Killymeal Road, unknown to Security Forces, from a respectable family. The two of them were taken immediately to Gough Barracks in Armagh.

When they brought Steptoe out of the bar, Doris and whoever was with him were shouting at him: 'Say nothing, Brendan. We'll be all right'.

All of a sudden then 'The Bishop', Norman Black from CID arrived and asked: 'Young Martin, what's going on here?' I explained what had happened and said the suspects had been taken away. He said: 'Well, you'd better come with me. We're going to Armagh too'. I told Trevor and he just said: 'Cheerio!'

I arrived at Gough and Norman told me to take a seat in the waiting-room and someone would be with me in a minute. Then the door opened.

'You'll take a wee drink?'

I said: 'Like what?'

'Something … nice?'

I said: 'I'd take a wee Bushmills if you had one…. only joking!'

Next Norman came back in with a bottle of Bush and two glasses!

I said: 'Lovely, but what's this for?'

'You smoke, Tom, don't you?'

'Aye'

Back he came with two hundred Benson and Hedges!

I says: 'Norman, what's going on? Are we having a party?'

Next thing, a gentleman walked in and Norman stopped and said: 'Sir, this is the man here'. He was from the Regional Crime Squad; he came over and introduced himself and told me he wanted to have a drink with me. I asked what all this was in aid of.

'All in good time, young man. All in good time. What you did tonight, you'll maybe know some day'.

I asked again what it was about and he replied: 'I just want to get you a drink. Norman will take you back to Dungannon, but I just want to thank you personally'.

I went back to Killymeal and John Robinson, who was Company Commander, happened to be in the office and Trevor and the others were sitting waiting, when I came in and put the drink and the cigarettes on the table. Next thing, the Commanding Officer came in and said: 'John, I think the boys could all do with a drink'. Chalkie[21] went down to the Mess and he came back with a bottle of vodka and slammed it down on the table.

Information gained as a consequence of these arrests led to the whereabouts of a large number of hides in the Coalisland area, including the last place that the 12.7 was (*Soviet DShK 12.7mm Heavy Machine Gun*). The searches had missed that but they got 272 rounds of 12.7 armour piercing bullets. Several blue plastic barrel hides turned up, handguns, shotguns, a couple of AKs. Gervin and Campbell both got time.

There was a police changeover due to take place and the drogues were probably intended for them. The police would have come from Dungannon, arrived at the Police Station gates in Coalisland and drove in. The Provos had the timings sorted out for that, so Campbell was going to throw the drogues at the police cars.

I don't know why the kids were trying to distract us except that they were trying to draw us up the Brackaville road and that left the town centre free, but then I backtracked into the town centre. If I'd gone after the kids I'd never have got the find in the town centre. They probably thought it was the Glosters who wouldn't have known that there was a road up round the back of Bernie's Square. We knew about that locally and had been patrolling it for years.

John Robinson again:

Following on from this incident, working with the RUC between 29th December 1989 and 4th January 1990, I planned searches in several areas of Coalisland, which led overall to the finding of eight hides containing various weapons, ammunition (including heavy machine gun ammunition) and terrorist equipment. Most of the finds were as the result of a planned 8 UDR search on 3rd January 1990.

Robert (Chalkie) White recalls this search operation and other experiences:

---

21 CSgt Robert (Chalkie) William White 1957-: 8 UDR 1978-92: (R Irish until 1997): MID.

Then there was this time, in 1989, between Christmas and New Year, when Thomas Martin found the car in Coalisland with two IAAGs in the back. It was parked up an alleyway. I was the Search Adviser at the time and a couple of days later, I got tasked into Dungannon and was told by the police and the Commanding Officer that they wanted to do a search in this area in Coalisland at the back of Seán O'Farrell's[22] house.

Totally against all the training that you got at Chatham, to be careful in case of booby-traps, B Company used to get issued with strimmers and we'd cut the grass back, because if you can't see it, you can't search it. The information was pretty good, we had a fair idea of what we were looking for and where. I tasked the Engineers for a light-wheeled tractor, because there was talk of a manure pit and I thought we'd probably have to empty it. Looking at it from photographs, we could see that it was at the back of stables, so I knew it wasn't going to be a slurry tank, but rather a more solid dunghill.

It was mostly B Company doing the searching, along with four search teams from the Regulars who were in Ballykelly at the time and the cordon troops were all from Ballykelly as far as I can remember. They all flew in and secured the area and started the search. I got air photos, went to RIC, marked all the areas, and then gave the teams a NISR (Northern Ireland Search Record) with the search areas marked on it that they were to cover. It was as simple as that. They all started searching the area with dogs and everything and the light-wheeled tractor was tasked to the stables. B Company went in to search the stables and found nothing. They searched round the dunghill and found nothing there either, so we got the tractor to start moving all the manure out. I noticed that every time the tractor went in, there was always a certain point where the wheel of the tractor would keep going down into a dip. It looked a bit soft, so we stopped the tractor and got a metal pole and stood over the top of the pit and just pushed it down into the manure. It kept hitting something solid and bouncing off. So we got a spade and dug away the manure and sure enough, there was the top of a plastic barrel. The lid was stuck down but we wouldn't have opened it anyway.

We stopped searching at that point, although the search carried on all around, and we tasked ATO. He looked at the barrel and when he couldn't get the lid off, he put a ring charge of explosives round the top of the barrel and blew the lid off. Inside that barrel was three weapons, two rifles and one pump-action shotgun, along with magazines and ammunition. One of them was the weapon that was used by the IRA to shoot Staff Sergeant Froggett of the Royal Signals

---

22 Austin Sean O'Farrell 1969-92: Coalisland: Painter: Charged (1991) with possession of an assault rifle and an RPG-7 warhead with intent to endanger life (*The Courier and News* 1st May 1991): Involved in DShk (heavy machine gun) attack on RUC Coalisland: Shot at Clonoe soon after the incident: Killed 16th February 1992 (*Tyrone Courier* 19th February 1992).

off the radio mast in Coalisland one night. It went straight into the hide from that shooting and was sealed up. I can't remember what the other weapons were. I think there was an AK and maybe a shotgun, but I can't be sure (*there was one G3 rifle, one AK rifle and one shotgun*).

G3 and AK Rifles

B Company were searching a garden in Coalisland just a couple of hundred yards away from where the barrel hide with the weapons was found and one of the boys noticed a dip in the garden, just stuck the shovel in and found a barrel hide. We opened it (which we shouldn't have done) and in the bottom of the hide was a metal box with Soviet markings on it. I actually thought it was a site for an RPG-7 box, but we tasked ATO. He wasn't sure what it was, but his second-in-command had been to the Falklands, clearing up after the war, and he knew exactly what it was – a box of ammunition for a DShK 12.7 heavy machine gun. That was a very significant find; that machine gun was used to shoot up the police station. We also found a magazine for a pistol and a couple of hides of ammunition. That search went on for about three days and I think we had six or seven finds altogether. The hide for the DShK, the machine gun, was actually found by a Regular patrol a couple of years later dug into the side of a bank in Washing Bay. There were two big blue barrels; they cut the base off one of them and super-glued it to the other one to make it longer. It took us a good few hours to dig it out.

There's always a marker and that's easy if you know what it is. You have to see every hedgerow as a possible marker, so you have to search both sides one way and then come back in the other direction, so it's done twice. The most likely place to find anything was in a hedgerow or within two metres either side of it.

Thomas Martin was very successful; there was Moyboy road up in Pomeroy – it was Thomas Martin's team that started that off. There was a route search being done by the Regulars and Thomas' men were the flanking team securing the area. They were patrolling along and, although you weren't supposed to go into derelicts, they did anyway and one of the men found a booster tube in a cupboard, pulled it out and told Thomas. They went away to do Op Clean (the find had not been compromised so a covert operation could be mounted) and the area was out of bounds for three or four weeks. Then one night, my pager went off and I went into the base at Cookstown and Op Clean had been sprung. The Provos had gone into the derelict and put the explosives into the back of a van and were leaving the area when the military 'scooped' them. They pulled the van into a man's farmyard and tried to run away but they were all caught. Next day, we had to go and clear the van and the derelict.

9

More Off-Duty Attacks

No Let Up

Every soldier in 8 UDR was under constant threat and took measures accordingly. Some had been specifically targeted by PIRA because of where they lived or worked, or because they had come to notice for some other reason such as making an arrest. They had to live with this knowledge perhaps for many years, as did their family. When information was received of the time and place of an attack a covert operation could be mounted: other measures such as a house move could also be considered but the soldier and his family were usually reluctant to leave a home that their ancestors had secured generations earlier.

Luck and alertness played a major part as Dessie Gordon[1] describes:

> One day in 1989 the Provos took over a neighbour's house and hi-jacked their car. Leaving one terrorist they drove to, and parked up, near the end of our lane. They obviously thought I was going out on duty. However, I went out and began to work in the workshop. Keith Lennox,[2] one of our platoon members, arrived about 7.30pm to help me. At about 10.30pm our Alsatian dog, Duke, began to bark ferociously. I grabbed my 9 mm and ran out to the yard, spent a few minutes, the dog went quiet and I returned to work. Twice more this happened: both times I went out armed with my 9 mm and Remington 870 Wingmaster pump action shotgun. Keith went to the other end of the yard armed with his 9 mm (we had both purchased Beretta 92SB pistols with a capacity of 16 rounds fully loaded, and nine rounds in the spare magazine). I rang into our base to check if any patrols were about, but there weren't. All went quiet and we worked away. I went to get some drink for us and it was then my wife asked why I was in Davidson's field whistling at Duke! She had been sitting in the back room styling her hair and would have been seen by the gunmen. The next morning all became clear; the neighbour's car had been seen leaving our lane at 7.15pm. The gun team had come back for a second try. The

---
1 Sgt Desmond (Dessie) Gordon BEM 1958-: 8 UDR 1977-90: Car Repair Business Owner.
2 Pte Keith Andrew Graham (Levers) Lennox 1969-: 8 UDR 1987-92: (R Irish until 1993): Car Body Repairer.

police tracker dog picked up their scent in the field. Five months later, the local suspected PIRA OC shouted at me, calling me by name: 'What about the night up your lane, only for the dog we would have got you!' If big Duke had been a service dog, I would have recommended him for the Dickin Medal! Only for him the terrorists would have been able to hit us in the workshop!

That was just one such incident: with experience, the security of some of those targeted was gradually improved but this was very difficult without further reducing their quality of life or drawing even more attention to them. Patrols were mounted to provide cover at high risk times and in the latter half of the Campaign these were provided by B Company with their much greater local knowledge; they might not have been able to prevent an attack taking place but often a quick follow-up produced success.

There was no let up from the constant threat, and the endless pressure to maintain vigilance.

Jeffrey Lamont 24th September 1987

Before Lance Corporal Lamont, C Company, entered his work premises, four armed terrorists had taken over the home and car of his employers. When he arrived he was struck on the head with a pick-axe handle. During the ensuing struggle, Lance Corporal Lamont drew out his PPW, fired three shots and hit two terrorists. He was knocked to the ground and shot twice at close range with a shotgun. An immediate follow-up by a B Company patrol followed a blood trail and a follow-up by RUC in the Greenvale estate resulted in two terrorists being charged with attempted murder and possession of firearms.

So much for one record; Jeffrey Lamont[3] tells his story:

> I joined the UDR on the 9th October 1984 aged 18 and was with C Company 8 UDR. My dad[4] also served for eight years in the same platoon and my sister[5] served for eight years in HQ Company at Dungannon.
>
> I remember doing a few training days in the base in Cookstown and going to the firing range in Gortin. I then attended a recruit training course for a week in the base, the training instructor was Wincie Watterson[6] and that was you, sorted and ready for the road. I was in 8 Platoon (one of four part-time

---

3   LCpl Jeffrey (Jeff) John Lamont BEM 1966-: 8 UDR 1984-90: Draughtsman/Architect.
4   Pte Henry (Harry) John Lamont 1942-: 8 UDR 1981-89: Factory Operative.
5   Pte Loraine Harrison (née Lamont) 1963-: 8 UDR 1981-90.
6   CSgt Winston (Wincie) Alexander Watterson 1947-: (Inniskillings/R Irish Rangers 1965-74): 8 UDR 1974-84.

platoons in the Company) with Colour Sergeant Robert Harrison[7] the Platoon Commander and Sergeant Dessie Gordon the Platoon Sergeant. 8 Platoon worked along with 10 Platoon, which meant you were on patrol practically every other night, so we were doing 12 to 15 duties a month. I worked full time in an architect's office and I started work with them around the same time that I joined the UDR. The office was in the old cinema building on the Fairhill Road in Cookstown, which was renovated into offices. There was 'the boss', myself, a secretary, and another draughtsman.

On the night of the Kildress incident, we had gone to check out car numbers in the car park of the Kildress Inn. We were mostly around the perimeter of the car park when a car drove in at speed and headed directly at our commander, trying to hit him. We thought it was an ambush. There were shots fired and one of the occupants of the car was hit in the shoulder. The car stopped and we administered first aid to the wounded man until the ambulance arrived.

Out of the five men on the patrol, we were all targeted by the IRA. Glen Espie was shot and wounded in March 1987, then there was my own attempted murder/abduction in October 1987, and Raymond McNicol[8] was murdered in August 1988. Neil Rea[9] ended up in Australia for a time and Alan Gourley[10] was just shifted from pillar to post, with different jobs and houses, and he never got time to 'take root' anywhere.

On another night, while on patrol near Drum Manor Forest Park, we had stopped one of the Neesons. We did the usual checks on him and filled in a log sheet. He said to me: 'You'll not be so smart the next time we see you.'

The evening before the incident on the 24th September 1987, the gun team took my boss and his family hostage at their house on the Fountain Road. They held him hostage to get the use of his car and the keys to open the office the next morning.

I left for work as normal from my home in Monrush between half past eight and nine o'clock. I went to work on a racing bike so it was easy to vary your route getting to and from work. I took a different route every morning. When I got to work I saw the boss's car parked outside the office as usual, but not the way it normally was. It was at an angle and he always parked dead straight. Then I saw that the door of the office was slightly open, which I thought was strange. I assumed he must be next-door getting office supplies and so in I went, although I was having doubts. I couldn't see what was going to happen, so I again assumed he must be next-door and would be back in a minute. I

---

7 CSgt (Robert) James Harrison 1940-: 8 UDR 1970-92: (R Irish until 1998): Supervisor.
8 +Pte (Raymond) Andrew McNicol 1957-1988: 8 UDR 1976-88: Engineer: Killed 3rd August 1988.
9 Pte Neil Rea 1963-2017: 8 UDR 1981-92: (R Irish until 2002): Businessman.
10 Sgt Alan (Goul) Keith Gourley 1961-: 8 UDR 1980-92: (R Irish until 1996): GOC's Commendation: Lorry Driver.

never thought they would take over the office. It was the last place I'd have thought of. I thought if they were going to attack me it would be either going in or coming out of the office, but not actually inside.

I went into the office and down to the kitchen at the back, set down my lunch box and left the bike out the back. Then I headed up the stairs. I had bought my own 9 mm pistol, a Bruno (BRNO), and I always carried it loaded in my pocket. When I got to the top of the stairs I did a U turn to go into the front office and that's when I got hit on the back of the head. There was another door into a small store room and this is where the terrorist was standing in the darkness; he hit me over the head from behind. I fell to the floor, semi-conscious, and as I lay on the floor all I could see was a mass of masked men all round me. All I could see was blackness, darkness.

I don't know how many of them there was but I guess at least four or five. I realised then that they were out to beat me unconscious and abduct me, so I

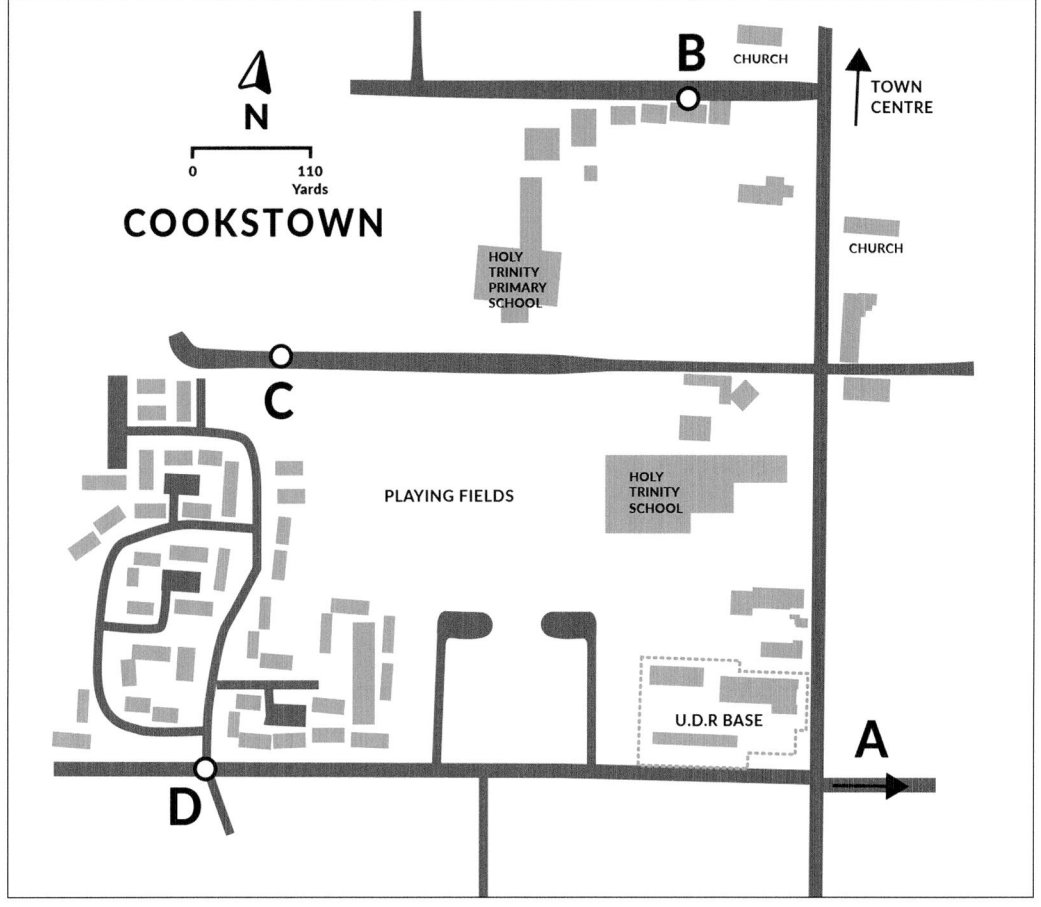

Attack on Private Jeffrey Lamont.
A: Employer and Family Held Hostage, B: Attack, C: Parkas and Weapon Find,
D: Terrorist Captured

kicked and fought them as hard as I could. I really was fighting for my life. My pistol was in my pocket, so I clicked the safety catch off and started to fire; I fired four shots and saw them running down the stairs before I blacked out. I didn't know whether I'd hit anybody or not. I was in and out of consciousness.

When I came round I was lying over beside the door on the landing and a fella came out of the back office with a sawn-off shotgun. I went for my gun which was lying on the floor across the landing but, before I could get to it, he fired and hit me in the right arm. He hit me with two shotgun cartridges at point-blank range. I blacked out again and when I came around I had moved from the landing to the back office and I was sitting with my back up against the wall. I don't know how I got from lying on the floor to being in the back office. I looked at the wound to my arm and thought what a mess. The secretary was in the corner, cowering under the table. Her hands had been tied up and she came over and I tried to get her untied but I couldn't. The terrorist that shot me was obviously there to keep an eye on the secretary while the rest were trying to abduct me and, when they cleared off, he was caught between me and the exit door. In his panic he had left a bag lying on the desk with guns in it but had taken my 9 mm pistol and it was never recovered.

A short time later a RUC officer appeared and I told him the guns on the table belonged to the gang. I can remember very little after that, other than the ambulance arriving. I was losing blood and I remember the ambulance man grabbed me under the arm to clamp the artery. That probably saved my life. I have never felt pain like it. I remember coming round and looking down at my arm and thinking: 'That's the end of that'. They brought me down the stairs on a stretcher and out the front door into the ambulance. People had gathered round, saying: 'What happened? Were they trying to steal something?'

Then I was taken over to the Mid Ulster Hospital in Magherafelt. Here, outside the doors of the operating theatre, one of the doctors told my sister and our Platoon Sergeant that I would likely come out without my right arm. I remember coming out of theatre and moving my fingers. They had stabilised me and my right arm was still there. The ambulance men were putting me into the ambulance. I can remember Elaine, my girlfriend now my wife, being there; she gave me a hug and a kiss before they took me to the secure wing in the Royal Victoria Hospital in Belfast. I was under 24-hour guard in the intensive care unit.

The terrorists had all run out of the office and down along Fairhill Road and then took left across the grounds of the Holy Trinity Primary School which takes you over into the Ratheen/Greenvale housing estate. There happened to be a B Company patrol in the area that morning and they caught the fella that I shot as he was coming out of the estate in a taxi. The RUC went into the house of a known IRA member and got boiler suits in the washing machine.

I think they arrested up to five men that morning. Mark Mulgrew,[11] the fella that I shot, got fifteen years for attempted murder. I was told that there was at least one Neeson.[12]

My arm was smashed right up to the shoulder. The bicep and forearm muscles were completely gone. There was a lot of nerve and tendon damage but I still had slight movement in my fingers. The surgeon had made it clear from the start that I would probably lose the arm. Fortunately, they worked their magic and saved it. I was in intensive care for ten days and in the Royal Victoria Hospital for a total of six weeks.

When I was discharged from hospital I had to have my wounds cleaned and dressed every day; this was done at home by my mum and Elaine. I had to travel back and forward to hospital on a weekly basis for about two years for physio and various operations on my arm. I went to Musgrave for a while and then to the 'Royal'. Two men from the platoon would escort me there and back. We had to go to Grosvenor Road RUC Station and they ferried us across to the Royal in a Land Rover. Even while I was in the hospital any visitors, like my mum and dad, girlfriend, sister and brother, all had to go to Grosvenor Road and they were escorted to the hospital in a police Land Rover. They told me on more than one occasion the police got a call about a stolen car or some other incident and they were told to belt up and stay in the back while the incident was dealt with. Mad Times!

Elaine, because she was my girlfriend, was also subject to harassment and verbal abuse from the IRA. She was harassed a number of times waiting on the bus to go to College in Omagh, and because of this she had to change her travel arrangements. On one occasion when I was there, a girl that was giving Elaine hassle spat in my face and called me the usual UDR bastard. When we bought a car she had to learn how to check a car for under car booby-traps, she had to make sure she didn't set patterns in her daily life, and she had to be aware of who the terrorists were. Elaine had to be as much security conscious as I was, not only for my safety but for her own safety as well.

I was medically discharged from the Army in January 1990. I had no contact from the Army other than the fellas I patrolled with. It was only by chance about ten years later that I received support from Combat Stress, Carolyn Arnold in particular was very helpful, and then later the UDR Aftercare Service.

---

11 Mark Mulgrew c1967-: Cookstown: Sentenced (1989) to 15 years' imprisonment for wounding the soldier (Lamont) with intent to cause grievous bodily harm, possessing firearms with intent to endanger life, and false imprisonment of two other members of staff (*Tyrone Courier* 5th July 1989).
12 Terence Joseph Neeson c1966-: Cookstown: Acquitted (1989) of similar charges to Mulgrew. (*Tyrone Courier* 5th July 1989).

David Wilson[13] was in B Company and involved in the follow up:

> That morning in question, our briefing was to do a dawn watch patrol in two Land Rovers, giving close protection cover for ODS (Off-Duty Soldiers). It was in Cookstown and my call sign was 63 and Stanley's (Stanley Gordon[14]) was 64. I can't remember who was with me; different days, different men, but it was always the men from Cookstown.
>
> You knew where all the ODS lived and where they worked and so if, for instance, Jeffrey was leaving his house at eight o'clock in the morning, you'd know where he was coming from and where he was going. It came over the radio from our Ops Room in Dungannon that there had been a shooting incident on the Fairhill. When we heard the message, we were coming up Molesworth Street which was about a quarter of a mile away, so we came into the centre of the town. I think it happened around half past eight, so we were despatched to it because we were in the area. The police would have informed the military immediately. There were joint radios and they could hear each other's conversations.
>
> Stanley Gordon was the Platoon Commander and he radioed to me 'Go round Convent Road' and he went up towards Greenvale. From our local knowledge of the terrorists in Cookstown, our instinct was to head for the Greenvale housing estate. If you go up Convent Road now it's completely different. You used to be able to go through a path at the dole office, but that's all blocked off now, although that's the way the gunmen made their escape and ran across the playing field into Greenvale itself.
>
> At the end of Convent Road there was a big high fence and there were three Parka Light coats hanging on the top of it and the steam was still coming out of them! It was a frosty winter's morning. They must have been taking the coats off while they were running and as they climbed over the fence they left them hanging there. So I radioed Stanley that they'd gone this way. He had come round and cordoned off the Greenvale estate. That day he only had about six men, and I was in the same boat.
>
> Anyway, we sealed that area off and the next thing the RUC came and they said they would take over and we were more or less in the background. We set up the cordon and then they came in and swamped the area. They did a rummage of the whole area and afterwards, there wasn't much left for us to do, so I was walking around back towards the Land Rover. I happened to look in under a pillar just in the corner and what was lying there? The shotgun and the baseball bat which the police had missed whenever they did the search. So I said

---

13 Cpl David (Davy) Wilson 1951-: (Inniskillings and R Irish Rangers 1966-78): 8 UDR 1979-92: MID GOC's Commendation.
14 CSgt Stanley Gordon BEM 1957-2002: 8 UDR 1976-92: (R Irish until 1999).

to the RUC man who was standing there 'By the way, there's a sawn-off shotgun lying there'. The gunmen had made their escape, dropped off the gun at the pillar and ran across the playing field into Greenvale itself. The policeman said he hadn't seen it. Then the forensic men came, took it all away, the usual thing.

I don't really know what went on over on Stanley's side of the cordon. The RUC had taken over at that point. Everything was all sealed off and then they did the follow-up searches. Just going by what you could hear coming over the net, we knew they had arrested someone and they had stopped somebody. The reason they saw Mulgrew was that he tried to get out of the estate in a taxi, but Stanley's patrol stopped it. One of the soldiers that stopped him seen a spot of blood on the ground and they noticed that his arse seemed very fat. He had a towel stuck on his arse where he had been shot. He claimed that he was the victim of a punishment shooting, but when they did the forensics, they knew it was a bullet from Jeffrey's pistol!

So Mulgrew was arrested, and two other suspects, Bell[15] and Neeson, were arrested in the vicinity. Another was got in one of the houses. It was said that when the gunmen made their way into Greenvale Drive, they went into the first house, up the stairs and into the attic and they had dug from one attic to the other, straight across the row of houses. Then they went through the four houses and came out at the door at the other end. Well that's what they said after the follow-up search. The wife of a suspect had washed their clothes and they took one of the washing machines for forensics. I think they arrested her as well for withholding evidence. There was one small coat, and you knew straight away whose it was. It wouldn't have fitted anybody else; one suspect was only about 4'11"!

When we finished that day, we all had to make statements and then eventually there was a court case. It was held in Crumlin Road (Belfast). We were escorted across a wee tunnel and we were in a different room but when the prisoners were brought out into the courtroom, they could see us and we could see them. Then when the sentence was passed, they just stood and laughed at us. We didn't have to give evidence because they already had the statements. It was the police who were running the whole thing; we weren't asked. We were just there in reserve in case we were called as witnesses. What really got me was when we were in court and the terrorists sitting, grinning and laughing at us whenever they knew they were getting away with it. And who mucked up the evidence? The police! They came to us every day nearly every week after it – have you got it all right? Have you got the story right? Yeah, we've got it right. Then when we went to court, who had it right? We had it right, they had it wrong.

---

15 Thomas James Bell c1957-: Cookstown: Charges of assisting people involved in a murder bid on a part-time UDR man were dropped (*Tyrone Courier* 2nd November 1988).

I joined the Inniskilling Fusiliers on 30th December 1966. They amalgamated on 1st July 1968 and became the Royal Irish Rangers. After twelve years I came out and joined the UDR in May 1978. I was part-time for 78 days and then went full-time and ended up doing thirteen years and two and a half months. I came out in March '92, just before the amalgamation. My release date wasn't until September but they let me away in March.

I served in Libya in '69 before anybody knew anything much about Gaddafi. Then we had the Cyprus conflict in 1972 when the Turks invaded the island. We were stationed at Nicosia airport and they actually shot all the planes out of the sky as they were taking off. We were up there along with the Irish Army. People underestimate the Irish Army; they are good.

That was peace-keeping, between the two factions. It was completely different to the UDR. We were trained in warfare, but when you came here, it was completely different. It didn't matter what you knew about Army tactics, UDR tactics were completely different!

Plus, you're dealing with a terrorist situation at this end, which, if you were a regular soldier, you never had trained for. A lot was based on local knowledge. You knew the people, where they lived, where they worked. At one time you carried a sighting list around with you. So if you stopped somebody, you could have a quick look or if you asked their name you could check it against the list. The only problem was if you had somebody from outside your area, then you had to do a car check.

But here, it was a different situation. At least in the Army, if you're fighting a war, you know who your enemy is, but here, you didn't know who your enemy was. It could have been your next door neighbour and in many cases it was your next door neighbour. People would say: 'Be careful of this. Be careful of that'. At the end of the day, there's only one way out of your house and that's through the front door and there's only one way up the road, and that's it. You can go out and search your car, do whatever you want, but you still have to go out to your car.

Maurice Murphy[16] was also involved in the follow-up:

I joined as a full-time member of 8 UDR in 1980 and after completing my training in Ballykinler was posted to the Ops Platoon based in Cookstown. On the formation of B Company I was based in Dungannon, serving with Tom Finlay,[17] my Platoon Sergeant. I have great memories of the strong bond

---

16 Pte Maurice Elliot (Murph) Murphy 1960-: 8 UDR 1980-92: (R Irish until 1994).
17 WO1 (RSM) Thomas (Tom) Finlay BEM 1954-: (R Irish Rangers 1972-79): 8 UDR 1979-92: (R Irish until 2007).

we had in the platoon and a high regard for the very professional and dedicated manner shown by all, in particular Tom Finlay.

Throughout my service East Tyrone where I was based was a hot bed of terrorist activity from PIRA, the INLA, and cross border murder gangs. Other members of my family served in the part-time element of 8 UDR and the threat to these soldiers when working in their civilian jobs was particularly high. My brother, serving part-time with the Cookstown Company, survived a terrorist murder attempt on his life mounted by East Tyrone PIRA when he was off duty travelling to his home.

Our role with B Company was to concentrate on suspected terrorist members, gather information on their activities whether at their home, socially or at work and looking at links to other known suspects and new associations. Ironically, when on patrol I was stopping and searching and logging the movements of PIRA members who had attempted to murder my brother and they would throw up smart remarks and, as they knew us anyway by name, their comments I suppose were meant to disillusion us. After completing a surveillance course in Ballykinler I moved to another platoon when the Company balanced out the requirement for each platoon to have search-trained teams, surveillance teams and intelligence gatherers.

We had an intimate knowledge of every vehicle, home and work location of terrorists operating in East Tyrone. It was our bread and butter responsibility for every soldier to know these details, not by referring to notes but carried in our heads. When an incident happened you needed to immediately be able to follow up with all these tools to hand. Invariably it was the difference between operational successes or failures for us on the ground.

Of course you had to know the same information about potential targets and at times our patrols would concentrate on defensive operations covering soft targets. That may have been normal police patrols, police and military bases, or off-duty personnel travelling to and from their work.

On the morning of this incident I reported for duty at the Cookstown base at 0430hrs. Stanley Gordon was the Platoon Commander; I had served with him for a number of years and he would lead our patrol. Without doubt he was an outstanding soldier who was very experienced and had many operational successes in East Tyrone, a very resourceful commander. Stanley was brilliant when dealing with known terrorist members, he had a great sense of humour and he would tie them up in knots verbally on every occasion. He delighted in in-depth conversations with PIRA members and was on first name terms with most; likewise they knew him too. It was an education to watch him at work. That same quick wit transformed to quick appreciation of incidents. He could assimilate information fast and immediate orders passed to his patrol, Operations cells, Police. Everyone reacted positively to his leadership and he was the man to have on your side in the middle of an incident.

Our task was to provide cover to off-duty personnel travelling to their work in the township of Cookstown. No specific target, just general cover and we deployed as a 12-man patrol in two Land Rovers, six men in each. This gave us the ability to drop off a 4-man team on foot patrol and still operate an 8-man two vehicle patrol in support and we had an intimate knowledge of soft target routines. We deployed from the base at 0530hrs. It was an uneventful morning, no sightings, nothing unusual seen and by 0900 the soft targets would be at their place of work. I guess we were all thinking of breakfast fairly soon. It was always the same; when do we eat and what time are we getting home? In 12 years of operations I could count on one hand the amount of times that plan worked out!

I was in the front Land Rover with Stanley and we were coming into the centre of Cookstown towards the main street when at the newly-installed traffic lights a police car jumped the red lights. I can remember Stanley shouting 'Move! Move! Move!' Following the police car we went to the Fairhill Road some three or four hundred metres away. We knew, stopping outside the shops, with the police activity, an ambulance arriving, people standing about, that an incident had happened and that Jeffrey Lamont, a part-time member of the UDR, worked in this area. Stanley went straight up the stairs of a shop following the ambulance man who he knew. We were out of the Land Rovers covering, a woman pointed out the direction men in masks had run past her. Stanley arrived back with us in seconds. Attempted murder, soldier alive but badly wounded, gun team escaped. Someone briefed Stanley on the woman's sighting.

Stanley told Davy to take his team of six and follow up the woman's report; he would take his team of six and drive immediately to the Ratheen estate in Cookstown, a good half mile away but one of the housing estates where suspect active PIRA members lived. The traffic was heavy and we drove the wrong way down the road against the flow of traffic. Arriving at the estate entrance, we set up a VCP. Davy radioed to say they had found three Parka coats and masks on a fence line, the steam rising out of them, informing us this was a likely route the escaping murder gang would take back to the Ratheen estate.

A car, I think it was white, approached our check point from the estate and we stopped it. The driver was asked for his licence, another male was in the back of the car. The driver said he was a taxi driver. The licence had some fresh blood on it from the driver's hand when he handed it over to our stop man and Stanley, busy on the radio, was quietly informed. We knew the passenger, a suspect member of PIRA from the estate, a man Mulgrew. He was asked to step out of the vehicle. There was blood on the seat and he had a huge wad of something pushed down the back of his trousers.

You are reading the situation as it develops from very sketchy pieces of information. A few minutes ago three men had tried to murder a member of the

UDR, they had escaped the scene, these two men were arrested by Stanley and held at the checkpoint. The Ops Room was briefed. You have to be very meticulous in how you handle evidence and suspects at any scene as cross-contamination can destroy a prosecution case. We were armed, had handled ammunition and this can cross-contaminate a scene which we knew from experience had resulted in criminals getting off at the courts in the past.

Very soon the RUC arrived with us. They were a DMSU deployed from Dungannon and we often worked together and they knew Stanley our commander very well, so there was no time wasted on silly questions. Their commander told us to hold this scene, confirmed local PIRA names in the estate and followed up immediately with house searches of known suspects. We were all fired up, the adrenalin pumping. Stanley had two important scenes to oversee and armed terrorists were loose in the vicinity. Local people were gathering, some not very pro the Security Forces and we had to have this injured suspect dealt with. As the follow up was in progress we were told the intended target was in hospital, alive, being operated on, and a UDR rep was at the hospital with the injured soldier's family there too. Excellent news to receive. It makes all the difference to know what is going on. It was up to the extensive follow up by the RUC to come up with more evidence. Shortly after this we were told East Tyrone PIRA had put out a statement on the media that they had carried out a punishment shooting in the Ratheen estate that morning. Stanley laughed. Mulgrew had tried to murder Jeffrey and Jeffrey had fought back and shot Mulgrew in the arse when he was running away!

The day progressed with us covering the RUC teams. Events of the morning became clearer and Stanley briefed us that it looked likely that the escaping murder gang had gone back to the Ratheen estate. Blood was found at one house on the trap door leading into the roof space. Dividing walls in the roof space of the terraced row he lived in had been removed, allowing easy access to other houses. The team had then moved over to another house and patched up Mulgrew, put all the clothes into the washing machine; this washing machine, with the clothes in it, had been seized by the RUC for forensic analysis. Mulgrew had got a local man to drive him out of the area to try and make his escape. An off-duty RUC officer at the time of the incident had saw a suspect running back to the Coolnafranky estate and a follow up by the RUC to that house arrested him, and he had fresh blood on his trouser waistband and belt.

We were all elated, the RUC had four men arrested, all suspected PIRA members, forensic evidence seized that was to prove vital in charging and convicting one member of this murder gang. Best of all Jeffery had fought off these four terrorists who had tried to murder him and against the odds had survived, although badly injured. We never got that breakfast and it was late in the evening when we were stood down.

The alert soldier who spotted the small amount of fresh blood on the licence was Derek Gibson.[18] He recalls:

> Stanley Gordon was in charge and we went down to Ratheen and cordoned the whole place off. I was stopping the cars coming out of Ratheen. I stopped a car and spoke to the driver and he got his wallet and there was wet blood on his licence. It was just a wee spot in the corner of it. I took the licence over and showed it to Stanley and then the police took over. Anybody who carries a licence doesn't have wet blood on it! I never heard nothing about the follow up. I just noticed the licence with blood on it, but that's all.

With cudgels they beat this young soldier
For their aim was to leave him dead
But the deed of the IRA murderers
Was to turn on themselves instead.
(Amy Gordon – extract)

Thomas John Hardy 13/14th March 1989

(Thomas) John Hardy[19] (born Donaghenry, Stewartstown 31st January 1941) joined 8 UDR on 2nd March 1970 and served in D Company. On 14th March 1989 he was ambushed by two gunmen as he drove his lorry into a loading bay at an abattoir in Granville.

Major John Robinson[20] was at that time Company Commander of B Company:

> B Company played an important role in the capture of a gun team and the recovery of weapons linked to the murder of Private John Hardy. The evening before the murder, a B Company patrol, operating in the Cappagh area had stopped a car with known terrorist suspects. Balaclavas, gloves and boiler suits were found in the vehicle and these were all commonly associated with use by terrorist gangs. Unfortunately, although the team requested the RUC to attend, this request was refused, and the known terrorists had to be released. However, the information recorded by the patrol was vital evidence and used to convict three of the team for the murder of Private Hardy.

---

18 Pte Derek Gibson 1962-2020: 8 UDR 1980-92: (R Irish until 1998): MID GOC's Commendation.
19 +Pte Thomas John Hardy 1941-1989: 8 UDR 1970-89: Lorry driver: Killed 14th March 1989.
20 Maj David John (JR) Robinson MBE VR 1951-: (2 UDR 1971-85): 8 UDR 1985-90: GOC's Commendation: (HQNI 1990-92, R Irish until 2007: Theatre Commander's Commendations Bosnia and Kosovo).

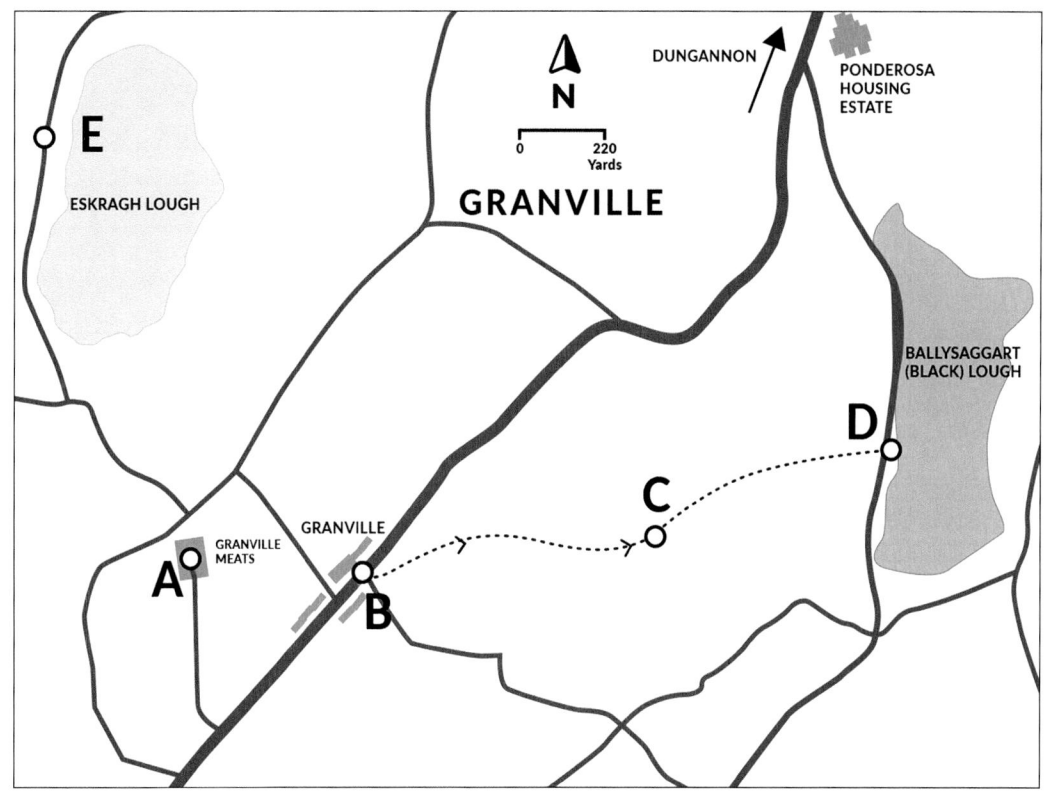

Killing of Private John Hardy and Follow-Up
A: Granville Meats, B: Car Abandoned, C: Weapons Found, D: Terrorists Captured,
E: Three more Terrorists stopped by RUC

On being informed of the shooting incident at Granville, two off-duty members of B Company, who were in Company Headquarters at the time, went in their own vehicle, with a military radio and armed with their own PPWs, to the scene of the incident. They found a crashed getaway vehicle and went back towards Dungannon, looking for people on foot. At the Black Lough, close to the Ponderosa estate, they apprehended three men, one of whom they recognised as Martin Bullock[21] who had been stopped by David Galloway[22] while on patrol the night before.

A follow-up search found two AK47 rifles in shrubbery close to the Black Lough. In all, six members of East Tyrone PIRA were charged with the murder of Private Hardy and a number of other related charges.

---

21 Martin Bullock c1951-: Dungannon: Unemployed: Sentenced to life imprisonment for the murder of John Hardy and 22 years for possession of weapons (*Tyrone Courier* 6th February 1991): Released under Good Friday Agreement.
22 Cpl David (Davy) Wallace Galloway BEM 1964-: 8 UDR 1982-92: (R Irish until 2004).

Corporal David Hogg[23] was on patrol the night before the murder:

> We were on the way to Altmore and I got a call from Galloway. He'd seen people going into a house in the wee orlits (*small housing estate*) in Galbally, on the right hand side as you come from Dungannon. He sneaked in and got underneath the window. He couldn't hear a lot, if he heard anything at all, but he came back out and said to me that there was something being planned. So he went south (Dungannon side) of the orlits and I went north towards Altmore. When they came out, I got them. There were four of them in a vehicle, one of whom was Martin Bullock. I knew him right away. They were heading towards Cappagh probably because that's where they hi-jacked the 'hit' vehicle. I got them out of the car. There were boiler suits, a shovel, gloves – they had everything in the car but the weapons.
>
> I was convinced I'd caught a 'team'. I told the Ops Room 'They've got everything here but the weapons'. I told them the police would come out. I did everything to egg them on, even to fight. That's all I wanted them to do. If they'd started fighting then I'd have had to arrest them and then the police would have had to come out. I wish I just said that they'd started fighting. I held them for as long as I could and I had to let them go. Ten minutes later, Ops came back on 'Have you still got those people? The police would like to see them'. It ruined the night. It was the inaction of the police that I thought was disgraceful. I was raging, to say the least.
>
> Whatever he (Bullock) told the police whenever he was questioned was contradicted by the log sheets in the debrief and that was evidence against him, and that put him away. His story didn't tie in, because I had logged the log sheets and the VCP pro formas. They told me that helped convict him, because he said he was elsewhere.
>
> None of us was called to court and I can't remember statements being taken. I think it was just taken off the log sheets.
>
> It was fortunate that the next day Davy Galloway headed out to 'The Ponderosa' because he was in Galbally the night before.

Kenny Ferguson[24] recalls:

> The incident took place on the 14th March 1989. John Hardy was ambushed by two IRA gunmen at the abattoir at Granville where he worked. John drove his lorry into a loading bay, the gunmen fired at close range and John died a short time later. He was 48 years of age. We were in Killymeal at the time

---

23 CSgt Thomas David (Boss) Hogg 1956-: 8 UDR 1976-92: (R Irish until 1998): GOC's Commendation.
24 WO2 Kenneth (Kenny) Ferguson 1962-: 8 UDR 1979-92: (R Irish until 2002): MID QCVS.

and Constable Stevie Oliver, who was a member of the RUC liaison team, and myself were heading out to recce a search area. As we headed up through Dungannon town centre it came over the radio that a shooting had taken place at Granville and we headed in that direction instead. Whenever we got to the scene, the police were already there and there was nothing that could be done at the actual scene, so we started searching the surrounding area.

The getaway car was found by a police car coming from Dungannon. It had crashed a short distance away, near Granville Primary School. The search took place in around the housing estates for people out of place, who might be on foot and a short time later it came over the radio that people had been caught jumping into the Black Lough, which was over the hill from Granville in the direction of the Ponderosa.

We headed that way; David Galloway and Ozzie Gordon[25] had come across men who had jumped into the Black Lough. The police arrived, they were arrested and taken away and a follow-up search was conducted between the crashed car and the Black Lough, which was the most likely route the gun team would have taken. Of the three who were arrested, one was Martin Bullock. I can't remember who the other two were.

Later on that evening, two AK47 rifles were recovered at the base of a large tree, close to where the men were arrested. A clearance operation was ongoing at the crashed car and was now diverted to the weapons find. ATO had this cleared very quickly and while that was being wound up, we were called to another bomb incident in Cookstown.

AK47s

If it hadn't been for the work of Ozzie Gordon and Davy Galloway, the murderers would probably have got away. They were making their way to the Ponderosa.

---

25 Cpl Alastair James (Ozzie) Gordon 1964-: (Irish Guards 1980-86): 8 UDR 1986-92.

Corporal Ozzie Gordon remembers:

> I joined the UDR in 1985 after serving six years in the Irish Guards. I joined the Army at 16 and then in 1985 I decided to come out because I had a young child and I was coming back home, and so I joined the Ulster Defence Regiment. I already had family in the Regiment; two brothers, a sister, and my father as well. And shortly after that, I had a younger brother who joined also. I served until 1992, the night of the amalgamation. My service was no longer required.
>
> I went straight into B Company. At that time, the Irish Guards weren't allowed to serve in Northern Ireland. They never came here until the very end, until it was over, which I loved telling them about! I found the UDR more exciting. It was what soldiering meant to me. Barrack-room life never suited me and that's the reason I enjoyed it more over here. Obviously, there was a drastic difference in discipline, but in a way, it worked. Apart from that, they were the best lads I ever served with. There was a closer bond. When I went into B Company, I was amongst guys I'd been to primary school with, guys I knew all my life, neighbours that type of thing, so that bond was there even before we served together. Trust was second to none.
>
> With reference to the John Hardy murder, I was on holiday for two weeks beforehand, so on that day, just before I was going back to work, I decided to leave the river where I was out fishing. I took my waders off, just had my welly boots on, jeans, hadn't shaved, and I went in to B Company to see what I would be doing the next day, what time we were going out and all that. So I took the drive over to Killymeal and went into the building. There was no one there; the lads must have been out on the ground, or whatever, and then I saw Davy Galloway. And Davy had a radio he was carrying. It came in on the radio that there had been a shooting at Granville Meats. That's all I remember. I asked Davy where that was; I had an idea, but I wasn't sure of the local Dungannon area, but he knew it well.
>
> He says: 'Right, we'll go for a drive'. So we jumped into the car, we were both in civilian clothes (I was a bit ragged looking), drove out by Moygashel onto the Ballygawley line and came back in to Granville Meats that way. And as we came round past Granville Industrial Estate, we came to a junction, where you turned right to go to the Black Lough. Just at that junction, there was an Astra car abandoned, with the passenger and driver's doors lying open, the car was running and the fumes were coming out of the exhaust. I can still see it now. There was two lads out of Op Ram (the police unit) who were standing there. The car must have skidded off the road onto this bit of grass. It was all mucky, so the terrorists had obviously done a runner from the car. If they had stayed in the fields, we'd have missed them! We drove on, towards the Black Lough and as we came up to the lough we could see three people, standing at a low wall, where the car parking area is, standing with their backs to the high ground. We screeched up in the car, I got out and I knew Bullock immediately. I think Davy

and I both said it at the same time: 'Bullock!' So I ran out towards Bullock and I had a 9 mm with me and all I heard was 'Stop! Stop!' and Davy must have taken out his ID card and shouted 'Security Forces!' because at this time, as I was running towards them, there was a Regular Army outfit coming down the field, through the hedging onto the road. So we more or less arrived at the same time.

As I say, the only one I knew was Martin Bullock and he had a red V-neck jumper on him and it was hanging away down, obviously soaking with water. They must have jumped into the lough to get rid of the forensics. The three of them were drenched. The guy in the middle I had never seen before. It turned out to be Dermot Moore.[26] He was the actual gunman at the time. Then the other lad, I can't remember his name. Well things got heated and I said a few expletives. I asked yer man his name in front of this Regular officer. They were trying to do it and I was trying to do it; then I was told to clear off. So we got into the car and went back into camp and that was it.

There's a clump of vegetation at the end of the car park and they had stashed the weapons in there and jumped into the lough. So the weapons were at the scene. Later on that day, two guns were found during a search, basically between the crashed car and the scene of the arrest.

Then shortly afterwards, I was sent to Ballykinler, which was their way of getting me out of the way. I had done my Instructor's Course and I became an instructor down there. Several months later (I've no idea of the time span) the CID came down to see me, a police officer on his own. He told me I would not be required to attend the court case. Moore and his solicitors had claimed that he was assaulted by an undercover soldier and all this nonsense. So they kept me out of it and we weren't allowed to be mentioned in court. I don't know what they said to Davy (David Galloway), who was also on the patrol the night before, but that's what they said to me.

What we did was instinctive, but Davy had the local knowledge. I'm from Cookstown and although I knew Dungannon quite well, I didn't know all the back roads. The one in the middle, it turned out that he wasn't even known to the Security Forces so he was obviously new. Bullock was a dangerous man. He was a killer.

David Galloway tells of his part:

I joined the 30th April 1982 when I was eighteen. I did six weeks' training in Ballykinler and then I was posted full-time to B Company. You were part-time

---

26 Dermot Patrick Moore c1966-: Dungannon: Factory Worker: Sentenced to life imprisonment for the murder of John Hardy and 22 years for possession of weapons (*Tyrone Courier* 6th February 1991): Released under Good Friday Agreement.

to begin with, until a slot came up for a course and I think I got a September slot. Before that I was a disc jockey in a roller disco. I served with 8 UDR for around twelve years until it merged with the Royal Irish, and then a further ten years with the Royal Irish Regiment. So I did the full twenty-two.

On the day that John Hardy was murdered I wasn't on duty. I went out in the car to get a loaf of bread and a pint of milk, and for some reason I decided to call in at the Company. I don't even remember why I went to Killymeal. While I was there, there was something coming in about the murder of a part-time soldier. I remember they were fussing about; the QRF had to go and get briefed and all the rest of it. There was me and Ozzie and it just clicked and we decided we'd grab a radio and go and see what could be done. We knew the local area and we knew what we were looking for. We knew that if we saw anything… we were looking for people coming away from it, Joe Bloggs or the soldiers (of the Regular Army) or the police wouldn't have known these people. We jumped into a Fiat Panda, which was my car of choice at the time! We got there quicker than the QRF because they had to go to the scene and then drive nearly a mile, although you couldn't go all that fast in a Fiat Panda. They were not the sort of car you'd use for a hot follow-up!

We drove as hard as we could go, out through Moygashel, along the main road and turned in at Granville, coming up towards Granville Meats. Op Ram were standing there with the road sealed. Ozzie had seen the car; it was sitting on the right-hand side. There was a minor road that turned off, which would take you onto the Ballygawley Road to where the Black Lough is. We got one of the policemen into the back of the car with us and drove on a bit further down that road. There was a wee primary school down there and we let him out there, though I can't remember why. We continued down and came out onto the old Ballygawley Road and turned left. Just as we turned left Ozzie says: 'There's Bullock'.

There was a wooden fence to keep people out of the water and they were getting over the fence to get into the water and I think there was one boy already in the water. (Ozzie added: that was Bullock. His jumper was soaking.)

But basically we just drove straight in and by the time I got the car stopped, the doors were open, Ozzie was out and was making his way towards them. I went to follow Ozzie but I just saw this Land Rover pull up and I could see the two boys on top cover (Ozzie added: I never saw them because they were behind me. All I heard was David shouting 'Security Forces! Security Forces!').

All I could think about was that this guy is going to kill us, he's going to shoot us! I knew Ozzie would be all right because he had the Browning out. But I thought: 'These boys haven't seen what we're at and they're going to mow us down'. So I just started shouting at them. I don't even think I showed my ID; it was maybe just my wallet. And I remember there was an English boy coming and shouting: 'Who the f*** are you?' Ozzie was questioning the terrorists at this stage and we said: 'This is the gun team'.

Both the terrorists and the Army thought we were going to kill them. They knew we were Security Forces but they hadn't a clue who we were. I've never seen hardened terrorists so afraid.

Ozzie added again:

I had a bit of a growth of a beard and my hair! I'd been on holiday for two weeks. Our adrenalin was pumping because we knew that was the gun team. There was no question about it.

David Galloway finishes the story:

Then the English officer basically said 'Get off side' and we decided we'd head back up to Killymeal. The police and all were starting to come down by then and I think the police QRF as well. A few months later we were told we wouldn't be required for the court case. Dermot Moore confessed; they couldn't shut him up in the police station, he was that scared that the SAS would come and he'd be killed. That's when they got the name because nobody knew his name. It must have been his first time out. What they called 'a blooding'.

I believe it's totally down to Ozzie scaring the daylights out of him. You might think they're hardened terrorists, but it must really have put the fear of God into them, how quickly there was people there. The other thing was, if they'd still had weapons with them. I'm not the best pistol shot in the world, but Ozzie was quite good. We didn't realise till afterwards that the weapons were in a wee clump of gorse about forty or fifty metres away. The follow-up search team with the tracker dog were able to track their route over the hedge, up the hill, and across the field to the Black Lough. The terrorists had made their getaway in the black Astra, but it got bogged in mucky ground at the junction as you turn in to the Eglish road towards the Black Lough. So they ran with their kit, threw off their headgear, gloves, whatever, and then threw their weapons into the gorse.

I remember when I got home my wife was ripping, because I forgot to bring the loaf of bread and the milk!

Moore worked with John Hardy and he took the afternoon off to commit the murder. There were two UDR men working at Granville Meats and they (the gunmen) tossed a coin to decide which one they would murder. There was a total of six people convicted. Those three[27] were convicted of murder, but the stuff from the night before was enough to convict some of the others.

---

27 Patrick Edward McGurk 1962-: Dungannon: Sentenced to life imprisonment for the murder of John Hardy and 15 years for possession of weapons (*Tyrone Courier* 6th February 1991).

Major John Robinson recalls:

> Corporal Hogg played a major part in obtaining convictions due to his meticulous recording of details. It was on the night of 13th March 1989 with the murder of Private Hardy the next day. When his patrol stopped the car he had tried to get the occupants arrested but the RUC said no and to let them go. He rang me at home when he was told this as he was not happy but I told him to ensure they were all recorded and let them go. What he achieved was to delay the move of the weapons into position for the shoot the next morning. All those in the car logged by Corporal Hogg were charged with the murder of Private Hardy; it was the proof needed that they did know each other when they claimed they did not.
>
> Dominic Nicholl[28] and two others were apprehended by police responding to the murder. They had crashed their car beside Eskragh Lough, having been panicked by the sirens of responding police vehicles. Rubber gloves were found in this car which added to police suspicion that they might be involved in some way. These three were separated at the scene, arrested, and during interview at Gough Barracks one admitted they had been travelling towards Dungannon to collect the weapons used in the murder and return them to a PIRA arms hide in the Galbally area. They had claimed that they did not know any of the three gunmen but Corporal Hogg's stop logs from the night before proved that at least one of them did.
>
> As a result of information gleaned from the interviews of those arrested, 8 UDR search teams uncovered a substantial and sophisticated PIRA arms hide on a disused farm. This included two more AK47 rifles, detonators, rifle magazines, ammunition and other terrorist paraphernalia. The elderly owner of the farm was charged with possession of the weaponry and terrorist equipment but was subsequently acquitted on a defence of duress. The searches went on for a number of days before the first barrel hides were found dug into a bank and under the pallets in a hayshed on which hay bales were stacked.

Bob McCammon[29] concludes this story which began with the brutal John Hardy murder and ended with further 8 UDR success:

---

28 Dominic Martin Nicholl c1965-: Donaghmore: Labourer: Sentenced to life imprisonment for the murder of John Hardy and 15 years for possession of weapons: He was arrested on the Dungannon to Aughnacloy road after crashing his car en route to collect the rifles after the shooting (*Tyrone Courier* 6th February 1991): Long Kesh H5A <www.irl.net>.

29 WO1 Robert (Bob) Norman McCammon BEM 1957-: 8 UDR 1976-92: (R Irish until 2000): MID.

About ten days after John Hardy's murder in Dungannon, the RUC gave us a task to search an area close to the village of Galbally looking for a terrorist hide and munitions. The area was centred on open farm land along the Pomeroy road out of the village and we were to concentrate around a small water treatment plant adjacent to the road.

I was in command on the ground and as Search Adviser I allocated the tasks to the search teams and our search dogs. All were very experienced soldiers and search trained. The weather was atrocious, very cold and relentless rain all day, and we found nothing. We debriefed back at Killymeal, sure that there were no hides or terrorist munitions inside that designated search area. However, it was agreed to continue searches in the area the next day.

The same grouping deployed early in the morning of day two, the weather conditions just as harsh. When we were on the ground I gathered the team commanders and we discussed our options. I saw no value in searching the ground we had already covered the day before, there were no hides on that land. The road climbed ahead of us going away from the village and on the high ground was an isolated farm; we knew the area very well so I deployed our teams to the farm. An elderly man lived alone at the farm house; he did not drive, had no tractor and the house, outbuildings and land were run down. He chatted away, offered us tea, was glad to see someone; as I chatted away to him the team leaders were assessing the ground looking for indicators, just the normal actions we were trained to do.

Two indicators were obvious – vehicle tracks were spotted going into an old hay shed and recently too. An elderly man living on his own, isolated with no transport, was a situation we had come across before in Coalisland, where terrorists had used an elderly disabled man's property to store explosives.

We started to search; Corporal Hogg, nicknamed 'Boss', started with the hay shed and the other team took the yard and outlying fields. There was no objection from the owner, he was very amicable. Everything has to be moved by hand when searching inside farm buildings. It is slow, heavy work. We had been at it for a couple of hours, the rain was incessant, when a soldier nicknamed 'Fingers' indicated to me (we used discreet hand signals to communicate to each other, a bit difficult for him as he had that many fingers missing). He was telling me Op Clean. We were trained to always keep a success and information very tight, even among our own teams, if you did not need to know don't ask. I reported back to Killymeal on a specific radio channel used exclusively for this type of situation.

Our aim was pass on a live situation to other troops who would develop the operation. The option for Op Clean was not taken and the search continued. ATO, the police and WIS (a specialist military weapons intelligence unit) were deployed. The rain stopped, the sun came out and Boss found other hides hidden under large heavy steel plates under hay bales.

When ATO had cleared everything I could not believe what I was looking at set out on the ground. There were two assault rifles (AK47s – now four AK47s captured from PIRA), two handguns, ammunition, detonators and detonator cord, timers and grenades. It was a major success against East Tyrone PIRA and all created from Boss and Galloway's suspicions on the night before John Hardy's murder when they noticed activity at Galbally, waited and stopped what was to be the murder team at a VCP. They logged the occupants of a car, noting they had gloves, boiler suits and were suspected PIRA members.

10

All Pulling Together

Cordon and Search

If the Security Forces could be quick to react to an incident and cordon an area they stood a good chance of pinning down the terrorists (at night with helicopters) and then catching them in a subsequent clearance. However, this often took many hours in all weathers – staying alert and wondering if a fish had been caught in the net.

The primary difficulty was making decisions where to place the cordon: if done quickly they would have to be made on limited information but should the decision be postponed until the situation was clear, the terrorists would be long gone. Assembling a large number of soldiers quickly and deploying them in a cordon was a challenge but often a degree of deception worked. A weak cordon deployed carefully and quickly often kept the terrorist pinned down until others arrived.

In the follow up to a serious incident, such as a killing, those who participated in such operations felt they were contributing, and this sense was all the stronger when they succeeded.

Chapter 1 covered a patrol action in 1973 which ended with a cordon and search carried out by the Regular Army. Ten years later 8 UDR was able to carry out such an operation on its own and be just as successful.

Annaghmore (by Coalisland) 2nd December 1982

At 1605hrs on 2nd December Mr James Gibson[1] stopped his school bus at Annaghmore (at the old and then derelict primary school) to let off some school children; he was travelling towards Coalisland. Two gunmen came to the gateway and fired through the open door on the near side of the bus hitting Mr Gibson in the head and upper body. The gunmen then walked around the building to a car, a blue Ford Escort that was parked at the back of the building. In attempting to get away from the gunmen Mr Gibson's bus ran into a ditch after a few yards. The car, which had been hijacked at 2300hrs on 1st December from the home of Peter Hughes, Moor Road, Coalisland (he

---
[1] +Pte James Gibson 1932-1982: 8 UDR 1970-80: Bus Driver: Killed 2nd December 1982.

was told not to report it to the RUC until 9 pm next day), then drove east on Washing Bay Road then SE towards Kingsisland. Ten .223 cases and a piece of wadding believed to be from a shotgun were recovered at the scene. (A woman who lived nearby said: 'All the youngsters on the bus were in hysterics. I took three of them into the house. They were in a bad state and they were all screaming'. *Lost Lives*)

At 1615 three soldiers travelling in a civilian car found the blue Ford Escort. At the car were three men; one was attempting to burn it by soaking a rag in the petrol tank and throwing it into the car, another was firing into the car with an Armalite rifle. On seeing the other car the men drove off in a brown Ford Escort Mk II, south towards Kingsisland.

The soldiers followed the brown Ford Escort. A man was waiting by the side of the road, the brown Escort halted, the men got out and one of them threw the Armalite to the man at the side of the road. The soldiers drove past and halted. All three fired their PPWs at the group of men (10 rounds in total). The three men drove off in the Escort towards Washing Bay, the fourth man ran into the bog, dropping the Armalite rifle. A bicycle belonging to the man who ran away was left behind at the scene.

The area was cordoned for follow up in daylight (*by now all four companies of 8 UDR were involved*). The man who ran away gave himself up at 0200hrs on 3rd December close to the scene. He was Kevin O'Neill[2] from Coalisland. The Armalite rifle was found to have a 7.62 short round jammed in the breech. It was one of East Tyrone PIRA's prestige weapons with a history going back seven years. It had been used 42 times and possibly 4 murders; it was last used against an 8 UDR patrol on 1st November 1982 in Coalisland.

Air Reconnaissance with thermal imaging and Nightsun were tasked during the night. At 0900hrs on 3rd December the search started in the immediate area of the contact and along routes thought to have been taken by the brown Ford Escort. It ended at 1620hrs. The following were found during the day: 0900hrs one blue boiler suit, one face mask and one pair of red woollen gloves; 0915hrs one green boiler suit by the side of the road; 0925 one pair black woollen gloves; 1015hrs one pair brown kid gloves; 1425hrs one sawn off under/over shotgun No P11184 (stolen in Stewartstown on 17th November 1980) under a plastic bag in a hedge against a telegraph pole. A further search on 4th December found a transit hide on the south side of the junction where the contact took place.

Mr Gibson had been on this run for three days; Ulsterbus drivers from Dungannon do one week in 39 weeks on this run.

Jim Gibson was born at Coagh in 1932 and after school worked as a postman before taking up employment with the Ulster Transport Authority. In 1955 he married Robina and they had eight children. His son, Glen, was killed in a motor cycle accident in 1977 and Robina died in 1979.

---

2 Kevin O'Neill 1963-: Aughamullen, Coalisland: Bricklayer: Sentenced to life imprisonment for murder of James Gibson, 15 years for possession of an AR15, 10 years for conspiring to have a weapon in his possession under suspicious circumstances, and eight years for membership of PIRA (*Tyrone Courier* 11th April 1984).

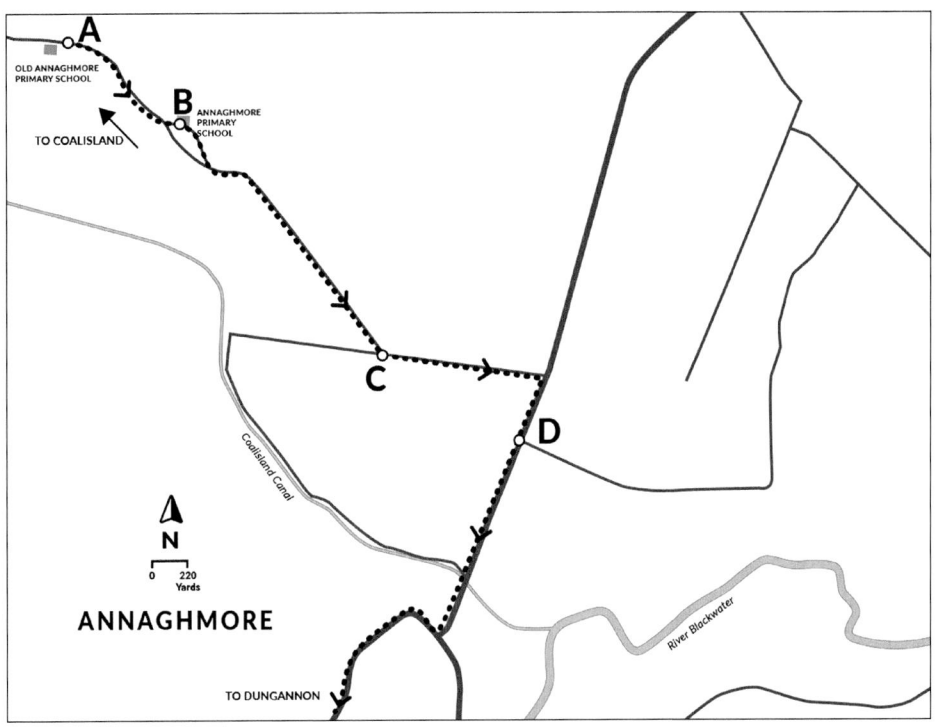

Killing of ex-Private James Gibson and Follow-Up
A: Old School, B: Cars Switched, C: Contact/Terrorist and Weapon Captured,
D: Weapon Found

At the outbreak of the troubles in 1969 the family was living in Main Street, Coagh and Jim was still working for the Transport Authority. While they lived there a bomb placed at Coagh RUC Station exploded just a few yards from their home.

Jim was at this time serving with the Ulster Special Constabulary; he joined the UDR in 1970 as a part-time Private serving in the Cookstown Company. During his time in the Battalion the Land Rover he was travelling in was caught in an explosion near Ardboe and he sustained back injuries. He left 8 UDR in 1980. In the Spring of 1982, the family moved to Dungannon so that Jim could be closer to his place of work at the Dungannon Bus Depot.

So much for a report at the time.

His son, Derek Gibson,[3] recalls:

> The day of my father's murder, I was on duty and out on patrol somewhere near Pomeroy. There was three bricks in the patrol and Jim Patterson[4] was in

---

3 Pte Derek Gibson 1962-2020: 8 UDR 1980-92: (R Irish until 1998): MID GOC's Commendation.
4 Maj James (Jim) Patterson 1961-: 8 UDR 1979-92: (R Irish until 2007 then Royal Australian Defence Force): GOC's Commendation.

charge of ours. It was late afternoon, because my father was doing the school run and his bus was full of schoolchildren. We stopped wee Mervyn Boyd[5] who was going home from doing guard duty in Pomeroy and Mervyn says: 'There's a bus driver been shot in Coalisland' and I said to Jim: 'I think that's my da'. We went back into the police station and to the Portacabin that we had out the back. The other two bricks were already back and we were the last ones in. Jim walked in first and I was behind him. Everyone just looked at me and I knew. I knew even before I went into the police station.

Stanley Gordon[6] was in the Ops Room in Killymeal and he arrived out to Pomeroy with Jackie McMenemy.[7] Jackie said: 'Can we have a word with you?' and then he told me that my da had been shot at Artie's Crossroads (east of Coalisland). I asked if he was all right and Jackie just shook his head. He couldn't speak. But I already knew it in my bones from when we had stopped Mervyn. After that, it was just a cloud and it's all vague to me. I know they flew our patrol out to cordon off the scene and they found one of the terrorists lying behind a hedge.

I'd lost my mother just a couple of years before. She died when she was forty-six and my da was only fifty. There were eight of us. I had a brother who was killed in a motorbike accident, so there were seven of us left and I was in the middle. I was twenty years old. My older brother took the two young girls and they lived with him, and me and Billy and Dougie got our own house together. My older sister was married. The family was torn apart. There were several members of my extended family killed by terrorists as well. I was straight back to work a couple of days after the funeral. At that time they didn't give a **** and we were at war. I suppose it's better getting back to work rather than sitting at home dwelling on it. The boys I was serving with became part of my family.

I joined the UDR in '80. I started in Cookstown, then went to Dungannon and I was full-time in B Company. Then I transferred to Armagh Barracks after the amalgamation. I got a medical discharge in '98 but I had intended to do the full twenty-two.

Jay Nethercott[8] again:

As the Company Commander of B Company, the full time company of 8 UDR formed in 1981, I had three platoons under command based in Cookstown and

---

5   Pte Thomas Mervyn Boyd 1935-2018: 8 UDR 1970-92: (R Irish until 1993): Tractor driver for Dungannon Council.
6   CSgt Stanley Gordon BEM 1957-2002: 8 UDR 1976-92: (R Irish until 1999).
7   WO2 John (Jackie) Samuel McMenemy BEM 1935-2020: 8 UDR 1971-92: (R Irish until 1993).
8   Maj William James (Jay) Nethercott MBE QGM 1952-: 8 UDR 1971-87: (5 UDR 1987-9, R Irish until 2000): MID.

James Gibson's Ulsterbus

Dungannon and the soldiers were recruited mostly from East Tyrone. From 1979 members of the Company had attended full time recruits' courses at Ballykinler, my officers were trained at Sandhurst and my NCOs were required by now to attend Regular Army courses. The Battalion had a very effective Intelligence and Search Cell, supported by highly motivated collators from both the part-time and full-time elements.

I had been serving in the UDR since 1971 and had been a part-time soldier with 8 UDR from its formation, serving in K Company based at Killymeal House on the outskirts of Dungannon. I served as a Platoon Commander, part-time with K Company before joining full-time in 1977, serving in various appointments as the Battalion Operations Officer, the Battalion Intelligence Officer and the Company Commander of the Cookstown part-time company, with a full-time platoon under command. This gave me a good understanding of the strengths and abilities of the part-time and full-time elements of the Battalion and I had a detailed knowledge, built up over the years, of operations in the area and an in depth knowledge of known terrorist members from all factions operating in East Tyrone.

B Company was a highly motivated unit, the soldiers and commanders dedicated, skilful and talented and they had the ability to work effectively, in support of the police, within the communities the terrorist exerted control over. The threat was high, a terrorist attack from East Tyrone PIRA was always imminent. The target was usually unknown; anything was possible – from an off-duty attack, to an attack on a Security Force base, to commercial bombings and attacks against patrols.

Guided by the Intelligence Cell, B Company put its effort into Pomeroy and Coalisland, using every skill we had to try and thwart the threat. We were

Scene of James Gibson's Killing

allocated as many helicopter hours as we required, daylight and night time, which gave us greater flexibility and speed of movement.

I was meeting a new platoon commander that day, who was joining us for an attachment from a Regular Army unit for a few months. He had not served in East Tyrone and the plan was that I would take him with me for a week, to meet the police, to show him the area and to help him understand our accent. Even I had to listen hard on the radio during an incident and I was a local! Also a new Regular Army Senior NCO, who was on attachment to the Armagh TCG, was coming that day too for an introduction to East Tyrone.

We had a coffee, introduced ourselves, had a bit of a chat and I gave them both an overview of what we would do on the recce. The plan was to take the TCG car, something different as all our vehicles were compromised, and he would drive. He was in civilian clothes, the Platoon Commander and myself in uniform and armed with semi-automatic pistols and a pocket phone radio on the Battalion net. We headed out to the Coalisland area. It was early afternoon, a pleasant sunny day for a change compared to the gloomy wet winters we usually had. It seemed like a normal, peaceful, rural afternoon, with everyone going about their business and it was a pleasant, picturesque area to drive through. We met up with the platoon deployed on the east side of Coalisland on foot patrol. I chatted with Albert (Dougan[9]), the Platoon Commander, a superb soldier whose opinion I valued highly, and effectively he was my Second in Command. We briefly reviewed our deployment to meet the threat. Our plan seemed sound; Albert had not had any sightings of suspected terrorists or noted anything suspicious. We went on our way, heading into Coalisland, the driver taking my lead – a left turn here, a brief on attacks PIRA had mounted, types of hides used by the terrorists, a suspect's place of work or home – just general terrorist related information, which both passengers would need to learn.

We just had come into the edge of the town when we spotted masked gunmen armed with rifles running to a parked car facing the opposite direction to our car and it took off at speed, heading east. The roads were busy, we had to get turned and give chase. The young Platoon Commander kept a visual on the escaping car as the driver forced our car through the traffic. I had an intimate knowledge of the ground, there was a maze of side roads the escaping gunmen could take and if we lost sight of this car even for a couple of seconds we could well lose the initiative. I could not remember the name of either of the men with me in the car and the radio was not transmitting, ('comms' were always a bit hit and miss with pocket phones in this area). The escaping car turned right, heading south, making for the Washing Bay area where the terrorist would feel safe. Unbelievably, within half a mile, the terrorist car pulled up hard, stopping on the side of the road outside a primary school where children and their parents were getting into cars as the school had finished for the day. We were hard on the tail of the escaping car. 'Driver! Pull in and Stop!' is all I could say as the gunmen exited the car.

At first I thought they knew we were chasing them. None of us spoke; we all wanted to feel as small as possible, or at least I did, as I prepared myself mentally for what was to surely happen and even the pistol now seemed small and inadequate too. But the gunmen were sort of dancing, like a jig nearly, in front of everyone, parents and children. High on adrenalin I suppose. They fired bursts into the air, shouting and roaring in front of the parents and primary school children. It was like something you would see clowns doing at a circus.

I said: 'Do nothing'. It would have been madness to make a move against them with so many children about and we were going to shoot. There would be no holding us back either when it started. Then one of the terrorists lit a petrol bomb to torch their getaway vehicle, threw it into the vehicle and they changed into a dark coloured Ford Escort and with tyres screeching, fled south towards Washing Bay. This in reality took just a matter of seconds. "Driver, Go!" Now a high speed chase was on and we were just about able to stay with the escaping car.

---

[9] Lt Albert Dougan 1957-: (Parachute Regiment 1974-78): 8 UDR 1978-84.

Getaway Car

Although he was masked, I knew one of the terrorists from his size and body shape and could make an educated guess about the identity of another of the gunmen that we were now pursuing. They had murdered an off-duty part-time 8 UDR soldier in the recent past, an easy soft target, and they were vicious killers. I was going to tell my team, we three strangers who had met just a short time before, now working well together, then realised it was irrelevant information for them at this minute and a plan was forming in my head. I knew where we would make our move against the terrorists.

I knew these roads better than the terrorists, every bend, every road junction. We would make our move at a major junction about three kilometres ahead, where they would have to slow down. I talked this plan out loud, giving our driver a verbal brief of the road ahead, fast straights, gentle bends, tight bends, the junction. We saw the terrorist vehicle brake hard and pull in on a sharp left hand bend. Forget the plan, we were nowhere near the junction and the bend in the road was coming up fast. This time it was clear what we would do, pulling up hard within feet of the car. Two gunmen were already out, another man ran out of the hedgerow. We stopped, exited to the driver's side of our vehicle and fired our pistols at the gunmen and the car parked the width of road away from us. The terrorists immediately threw their weapons away; one jumped into the field and the others were into the car, which was at full revs, tyres squealing as they fled, doors open.

No 'comms', weapons at the scene, one terrorist on the run on the ground. We fired more rounds towards him. It was winter and would be dark in a matter of minutes. It was time to get help, and the quicker we got the information out about the escaping car, the better chance it would be spotted. I gave my weapon to the men I was with (I still could not remember their names), told them to hold the scene and I would be back with the patrol we had seen just a short time before. It was a fast run back and I noted the car at the primary school was not on fire, another scene to cordon but the area was deserted.

When you work with soldiers as closely as we did in B Company, there is a bond between you that is hard to explain, you each know what the other is thinking and I found Albert, who had heard me using the car horn SOS continuously till we met up. They dived into the car, as many as it would hold and we went at speed back to the main scene, doors ajar. They never even waited to get the story of what was going on and they had 'comms' on their main radio, which meant we were getting information back to the Battalion Ops room about the escaping car.

The daylight was fading fast and it would be dark in another 40 minutes so we established an Incident Control Point (ICP) at the scene where we had the weapons and an escaping terrorist somewhere on the loose in the fields in the rural area east of Coalisland. Albert deployed soldiers into the fields where the fleeing terrorist had gone, put up some flares and took control of that area. With our 'comms' working, the helicopter moved troops to the ICP. Our focus was to trap the terrorist in as small an area as possible and keep the pressure on, using Nightsun and the heat-seeking helicopter that had the ability to see, with thermal imagery, a human hiding in a hedgerow in the open fields. We had little interest in the abandoned weapons other than securing the scene for forensics and ATO if required. More B Company troops were flown in from Pomeroy. Our A Company, based in Aughnacloy, had a full-time platoon which operated mainly along the Monaghan/Tyrone border area and they were re-deployed forward to Coalisland to assist with the follow-up in support of the police.

John Shackels[10] was the Platoon Commander. He talks first about himself, then A Company in Aughnacloy, and his full-time platoon within it:

I joined the UDR when I was eighteen, in 1972. I didn't join for any great reason, apart from the fact that I love shooting, and I always wanted to be a soldier. I was part-time/full-time in K Company at Killymeal House and I did all my weapon training with Archie Roleston. I was a student at the time at Jordanstown and I didn't get a grant, so I had all the reasons for joining. I worked at the weekend and I got paid!

---

10 Lt John Shackels 1954-: 8 UDR 1981-84.

Then I met my future wife and the UDR wanted me to take a commission but I was getting married and I had just finished university and I'd got a job in Tyrone Brick. 99% of the fellas that I worked with in Tyrone Brick were from Coalisland and they knew exactly who I was. My father had taught most of them (he was Principal of Dungannon College of Further Education), which was a big advantage for me. So I decided that I couldn't take a commission in the UDR and I had to leave. My wife and I both left the UDR in 1976. I worked in Tyrone Brick for a year as Assistant Manager and then I got a job as a foreman with a contractor, Ernest Watt. I went to work in the building industry, a job which took me all over the place. A lot of the people I worked with were from Dungannon, Coalisland, the Lough shore, guys that I knew previously from the UDR.

Well, then Ernest Watt and I had a parting of the ways and I had a young family, so I went back to the UDR full-time in 1979. I did my recruits' course, went to Sandhurst, got commissioned and came back to Aughnacloy (A Company) as a Platoon Commander of the full-time platoon where I stayed until 1981.

I joined the police in 1985 and passed out in late January 1986. I retired from the RUC in 2007. I am very proud of the time that I had in the UDR, both in Aughnacloy and in Dungannon and I'm equally proud of my RUC service. My family have a history of serving in both the RUC and the military.

Aughnacloy was very much a family thing and everybody worked very hard. There were the Crawfords, for example, and RJ Murray[11] who was shot in his car while travelling home with his wife and young baby. If I'd said to RJ: 'Go through that wall', he'd have done it. Many of the guys that I served with in Aughnacloy and Dungannon, I had either gone to school with since primary school, I'd been in the Boys' Brigade with them, or I'd played football against them. Most of the Aughnacloy fellas were part-time farmers. They had small farms where they grew spuds or maybe silage, so at particular times of the year, they had more interest in the farm than they had in being in the UDR. So the Platoon Sergeant, Eustace McKee,[12] and I said to them: 'You will not cut silage on your own. We have four part-time farmers; you meet up every morning and whatever has to be done that day, you do it together, you look after each other. We'll be in the vicinity if you need us, so keep it tight, work together, get

---

11 Pte Robert (RJ) John Murray 1951-: 8 UDR 1971-86: On 26th August 1984 RJ Murray was returning home with his wife, Helen, and their baby, Carrie, when they were attacked by gunmen who stepped out in front of their car. RJ was hit in the head and the car overturned. In the pitch dark and thinking that both her husband and baby were dead, Helen managed to get out of the car and go for help. Due to her courage that day all three survived.
12 WO2 Eustace (Eusty) Wisner McKee 1953-: 8 UDR 1971-92: (R Irish until 2000): MID.

the work done on the farm and get back to the UDR'. I think they probably appreciated that.

My first memories of Aughnacloy were that I arrived on a Monday morning and the guys were out on the ground. There was a landmine on the Caledon road and they had been 'sitting' on the landmine for three days. ATO had dealt with the landmine and as I arrived, two Wessex helicopters came in to take the guys back to Aughnacloy. There is a particular procedure for mounting and dismounting a helicopter. It's Clock 10 to 2. However, the Aughnacloy platoon descended on the two Wessex helicopters like a horde of ants! I couldn't believe it!

The Platoon Sergeant was Eustace McKee, who is a brilliant fella and Roy Weir[13] was our Company Commander. Major Roy Weir was from Dungannon and my grandmother lived beside him in Milltown just outside the town centre. I had known Roy since I was four years old; he was very straight, could take a joke, the life and soul of A Company, and a school principal in his civilian life. Roy ensured everything was properly done. Tasking of our patrol effort was taken from the weekly Battalion Orders Group, our area of operations along the Tyrone/Monaghan border, covering Ballygawley through to the town of Caledon.

There were numerous soft targets living and moving through the patch and it was a dangerous area to live, work and patrol in. When Lance Corporal Cecil McNeill[14] was murdered, my platoon was asked to organise his burial detail. He was a part-time soldier in A Company and we had often provided cover for his route to and from work at an engineering works close to Cappagh. A soft target, he died instantly when terrorists opened fire on him as he arrived for work. There are no words to describe the pain and sense of loss you have when someone from your Company is murdered. Throughout my time with A Company, I never heard one word of hatred or judgement passed against these killers or the communities they lived within.

Our tasks were mostly foot patrols, insertion by helicopter, and we deployed for up to 48 hours. There were many advantages with extended patrols. All the men lived locally so it cut out patterns of movement to and from the base. We had a very close working relationship with the police and played some childish pranks on each other. We drew a truce when they painted our Land Rovers pink, in retaliation for someone tying bin lids to the rear of the Chief Constable's car when he was visiting the base one night.

---

13 Maj Robert (Roy) Howard Weir MBE UD 1946-2007: 8 UDR 1970-87: (6 UDR 1987-89: he was ambushed and seriously wounded outside his company base in Clogher on 7th April 1988): Primary School Principal.

14 +LCpl Cecil William McNeill 1960-83: 8 UDR 1979-83: Mechanical Engineer: Killed 25th February 1983.

Shortly after I was posted to the Aughnacloy platoon, Eustace and I set about getting the fellas in shape. We trained them in weaponry, physical training, mental training, until the following year we went to annual camp at Warcop with the Battalion and Aughnacloy won the platoon competition. I was very proud for the boys, because they had worked their backsides off and it was great morale booster beating all, in particular B Company. On the last Friday of every month we had what we called a 'gripe meeting'. We met in the mess in Aughnacloy, had a couple of beers and invited the fellas to air any grievances they might have. I had put the idea to Roy and he said: 'It's a good idea. Go ahead'. They never had any gripes but enjoyed the beers, a little payback for all their hard work and devotion to duty.

John Shackels then talks about his experience during this incident:

When the IRA murdered Jim Gibson in 1982, in the town of Coalisland, we were on duty in Aughnacloy. My platoon was deployed to the scene of the murder to assist with a follow-up search from the firing point to the getaway route and to protect the scene until it had been dealt with by the police. The place was swarming with people. It was a brutal execution; the bus had careered off the road, mounted a hedgerow and was lying partially on its side. Jim was still lying in the driver's cab when we arrived. A terrible scene for anyone to have to witness.

As the platoon commander, personal example comes into it as well: you just have to do the job and you can't let the emotional bit interfere. That's how I was taught: cut out the emotion and deal with it surgically almost. Do the job, that's it. However, I've been to many military funerals and the last thing that happens is the playing of the Last Post. I just can't listen to that today; it draws on too many sad and emotional times from my time in 8 UDR.

Early in the evening we moved from the murder scene to the B Company ICP, where a cordon was in place and a search operation was in progress. The follow up continued in and around Coalisland, 'helis' were continually arriving with troops deploying to the area, with other 'helis' providing night time search capability and soldiers immediately following up any suspicious activity. It was now dark. Jay briefed myself and the platoon on the operation already under way. We would join the cordon which would continue throughout the night and Albert and I would work together coordinating the immediate follow up to any suspicious activity, looking specifically for the terrorist who had gone to ground and who might well try and make it out of the area under the cover of darkness. Most likely a local from the Coalisland area, the terrorist would know the area very well. B Company were confident the terrorist was contained within the cordon area.

I can remember the bitter cold of that winter's night and in the early hours, warm rations coming out to the troops. What a morale booster a hot cup of tea is when everyone is tired, the cold sapping your energy and alertness and the doubts creep in. Is it all in vain? We all had been on duty from 0600hrs the day before.

Close to the ICP, one of the cordon soldiers, Noel Murray,[15] followed up a noise heard from the hedgerow down in the fields close to the road and using a torch light, discovered a male wearing a combat jacket, hiding in the undergrowth. It was around 0230hrs. The terrorist was caught, arrested and handed over to the RUC.

I radioed back to base that we had arrested the terrorist, a male who would not give any information about himself. The feeling of satisfaction was unbelievable throughout all the agencies on the ground that night.

The Commanding Officer visited us shortly after the arrest. It was a job well done for all involved but we would all remain on cordon as we had to follow up four different scenes at first light. To carry out a search of this area where the terrorist had hidden was now a priority too.

Jay Nethercott completes the account of this incident:

There were no long-range off-duty attacks. They all took place either in or around crossroads, where they knew the vehicle (in this case, the bus) was going to have to stop, they'd be sitting the width of a road away, twelve yards. This was East Tyrone PIRA making a specific point.

There were two priorities for me – the cordon and search of the area the terrorist had escaped to and the car they had fled in. We had to find that car as soon as possible as that would dictate the follow-up to their now abandoned escape plan.

With the helicopter searching the fields, B Company troops were tasked to assist at the scene of a murder the terrorists had carried out in Coalisland against a bus driver bringing school children home. Just a few seconds later, we had spotted the killers fleeing the scene. I noted the information but focused on my two main priorities. John Shackels and his platoon from Aughnacloy carried out this task plus a search from the murder scene to the terrorists' getaway car. We still had no lead on the getaway car, so a section from the platoon flown in from Pomeroy who knew this area very well, met up with John, took his Land Rovers and started a search of the routes where they were most likely to find the

---

15 Pte David (Noel) Murray 1945-: 8 UDR 1971-92: (R Irish until 1994).

car abandoned. Dean McGucken,[16] the section commander, said that he never witnessed a scene like it at the murder of the bus driver.

Albert and John ran the cordon for the escaped terrorist. Everything they requested for this was granted. This still was the main priority and as the winter's night drew in, the bitter cold bit into us all.

At the ICP a couple of hours into the follow-up, the RUC commander for the area came to see me; we knew each other well. He said that he was fully briefed about what we were doing and said he would leave this part of the follow-up for the military but the main reason he had come to see me was to tell me that the man murdered in Coalisland that afternoon was a Mr Jim Gibson. When the police went to inform the family, they found out that Jim's son was a serving soldier in B Company. The man was involved in the follow-up and was deployed on the cordon set up to find the terrorist who had fled into the fields. Our Company Sergeant Major, Victor McNickle,[17] brought Private Gibson to the ICP, where I told him the sad news that his father had been the target the terrorists had so mindlessly gunned down when driving the school bus through Coalisland. Derek was transported back to Cookstown and then to the family home in Coagh. Private Gibson had been in Pomeroy where his Platoon was re-tasked to assist with the follow-up. The helicopter could only take eight soldiers and Gibson went out on the second lift by pure chance. If he had gone with the first lift he would have been with Dean McGucken at the scene of his father's murder.

I knew Jim Gibson. He had served as a part-time soldier in Cookstown and had tragically lost his wife three years earlier. With a young family to look after, he had resigned from the Battalion. Now they were orphans. Private Gibson was only 20 years old.

With a firm cordon in place and B Company deployed, I went back to Killymeal and left Albert and John to oversee the cordon. The weather was atrocious and bitterly cold. At around 0200hrs John radioed in to tell us that they had arrested a man who broke cover from a thick hedge where he had gone to ground close to the ICP. They had found the terrorist. At this stage, I was in Killymeal planning the follow-on operations that we were tasked to do by the RUC. Our Battalion Ops Officer had organised search teams from the part-time companies to deploy at first light, other patrols had to fill in the gaps our deployment into the Coalisland area had created, and we knew that East Tyrone PIRA were capable of further attacks anywhere in our TAOR. I had briefed the RUC detectives on who I believed the killers were and follow-on plans were in progress, which they would lead. There was no sleep that night. I

---

16 WO2 Dean McGucken 1958-: 8 UDR 1979-92: (R Irish until 2001).
17 WO2 Victor McNickle BEM 1943-: 8 UDR 1971-92: (R Irish until 1999).

went back out to the ICP, saw the terrorist who was now in the custody of the RUC, and congratulated the cordon troops on a job well done. The weather was not kind to them and they were there for the duration of this operation, but everyone's spirits were high. The soldiers had done an excellent job.

The various scenes were completed in daylight the next morning. The getaway car was still not found and searches of all garages and out houses continued until, about three days later, a suspicious car in the grounds of a local hotel in Dungannon was reported to the police. The terrorist escape car was recovered intact.

We had failed to hit the escaping terrorist car or any of the gun team when we had engaged them and I have thought about this often over the years. When we came upon the terrorists standing at the back of their car we did not know why they had stopped; it could have been because they saw us following them. In fact they were about to put the weapons in a transit hide on the other side of the road, but we did not know that. The Armalite rifle was clearly visible and the last time we had seen that was at Annaghmore School a few minutes earlier firing on automatic. It was jammed, but we did not know that. As soon as they saw us the terrorists' one thought was to escape, but we did not know that. So the rounds were fired by us getting out of the car, moving rapidly to cover, just trying to put the terrorists off. Time stood still and it all happened it a flash.

Two days after Private Derek Gibson buried his father, he reported back for duty. His family now was B Company, the men he served with. He served with distinction and was with the Company for eighteen years until he was medically discharged, after the injuries he received on duty when his patrol was ambushed with a landmine eventually took their toll.

About two years after the terrorist was arrested for Jim's murder, he was brought to trial. I was called as a witness for the prosecution. The court case was held in Belfast and Albert, myself and the young officer who was with me in the car, attended. We brought Private Gibson with us. Eventually I was called to give my evidence in court, introduced as witness 'C' and the defence lawyer grilled me for a couple of hours. There were a number of East Tyrone PIRA members in the court and they were quite vocal I recall. One in particular glared at me throughout and kept plucking at his jumper, putting the fluff into his hand and stretching his hand forward as he blew the fluff towards me. His way of saying 'I will blow you away'.

When the young officer was called to give evidence he inadvertently used my name in the open court and I got a big cheer from East Tyrone PIRA. Their man was given a life sentence for the murder of Mr Jim Gibson, a civilian going about his normal work looking after the school children from the Coalisland area, and it gave me some sense of peace that his son Derek got some closure for the loss their family endures to this day.

The Commanding Officer at that time writes:

> Much thought had been given to capturing terrorists escaping from an incident on foot. A net had to be thrown around the area very quickly and with very little information to go on. Every minute mattered. Those in the Operations Room had to decide on the size of the net – better too big than too small. They then had to assemble the troops, usually in multiples of 12, and deploy them immediately when they were ready to the net or cordon. They could have been on another task so re-deployment might be quick. However, they could have been off-duty or if, part-time, at work. In this situation speed was all-important and risks were taken so command and control of the cordon had to be established on the ground as soon as possible. Administration too of this large number of men over a long period would also be important.
>
> Many such incidents occurred at night so searching the area within the net would have to wait for daylight and would need more men. In the meantime the terrorists might be tempted to break through the cordon with or without their weapons. So they had to be kept pinned down within the area and this was well done by helicopters such as Nightsun which illuminated an area with a searchlight, or others with sensors that could detect the heat source of a human; the former was more of a deterrent, the latter good for morale because you knew the terrorists were still there.
>
> It was all put into effect in this incident. All four companies of the Battalion and the Regular Company under it were involved in the cordon or in the subsequent search. The weather was atrocious and it was a very long night. I would be very surprised if many did not have doubts on such occasions; I certainly did. However, if there was the remotest chance of capturing James Gibson's killers it would be worth it.
>
> On this complicated and difficult operation the whole Battalion pulled together. A tragedy started it all and then the courage of one man in the Battalion meant the terrorists did not get away as they would have wished. This and the Battalion team effort that followed meant that one terrorist killer faced his day in court.

Retrospective

After nearly three decades the Government declared the Troubles were over, the Regular Army departed, and the UDR disappeared. Few of those who have related their stories would consider themselves winners: a job had been done in that PIRA had abandoned terrorism but normal life was a long way off, and division between the two communities still very wide.

If there were no winners, there were many losers – those who had lost loved ones, those who were mentally or physically injured and their families, and those who had lost businesses or homes. Everyone was a loser because they had endured nearly thirty years of restricted movement and lack of public entertainment, so had a much reduced quality of life.

The twenty years since the Troubles were deemed to have ended have not produced the progress of reconciliation and integration that was hoped for. One reason has been the lack of leadership by politicians and other community leaders. There are some causes for optimism, the small number of non-denominational schools being one. Another is the large number of young people now going to university where they meet those from the other community. Fifty years ago the small farmers of Pomeroy helped their neighbours bring in the harvest with little thought of religious differences. 'Love thy Neighbour' does not allow a choice of who that neighbour can be.

The courage and resilience of these men and women, and their families, needs no further explanation; it comes through loud and clear in these stories.

Some issues do need further clarification, and one is the calibre of the Army issue personal protection weapon. The .22 Walther was chosen because it was light and easily concealed and required little training. It gave the soldier a better chance of escaping when attacked while not encouraging him or her to fight back when outnumbered and outgunned. It was also thought a larger calibre weapon would be attractive to the terrorists and therefore increase the risk of attack. Finally, and arguably, without training a heavier weapon increased the risk of serious accidents. The compromise of allowing those who felt the need for a heavier weapon to buy their own, and carry it, was unsatisfactory because it introduced a number of different weapons for which there was no formal military training.

Another problem was that of looking after those men and women who were considered at high threat when off-duty, and especially caring for them after they had been attacked. There was a view amongst some in the Army and the RUC that such men and women should not be recruited, arguing that it took a disproportionate amount of resources to provide limited cover and that it was immoral to put them at such risk. These people ignored the purpose of the UDR which was to allow men and women to serve in their homeland where their local knowledge could be put to good use; furthermore they had volunteered understanding and accepting the risks.

Providing security advice and training was difficult. It had to be done much of the time in groups and not one-to-one except when the threat was exceptionally high. The inevitable result was that it was dumbed down and lacked focus. For example, telling soldiers that it was inadvisable to hang their uniform on the washing line sounds sensible but if you are living in an isolated house on the front line surrounded by people who are unsympathetic if not hostile and well aware that you are in the UDR it seems less so. Equally, being advised to vary your routes to and from work is hard to criticise but easier for those living in towns: in the country there may only be one practical route without greatly increasing the distance to travel and all that effort could be negated if there is a long driveway from the road to the house at the end of it. In East Tyrone home visits were done as often as possible and, as has been said, when the threat was particularly high. Talking soldiers through their routine at home forced them to focus on when they were most vulnerable and plan the actions they would take if attacked.

Some physical security measures were possible such as flares to call for assistance if the telephone lines were cut, plastic covering for the windows to reduce the risk of glass injuries in an explosion, outside intruder lighting and much else. However, most soldiers were reluctant to have any of the more obvious measures because a siege atmosphere of fear could easily permeate to the whole family.

Operations were mounted to provide cover for those at high risk or isolated, and these would be carried out at certain times such as when the soldier was going to or coming back from work. The problem in 8 UDR was that there were so many soldiers at high threat that defensive operations to cover them and possible mortar attacks on bases and police stations could take all the available resources. Consequently the terrorists could operate freely everywhere else as and when they chose to do so, even attacking these defensive operations. Offensive operations had to be mounted, to control movement, clear routes, gather information, search for weapons and explosives and act as a general deterrent, so a balance had to be struck.

The after-care for soldiers after they had been attacked was very poor, even more so if they had been wounded in the attack. A married part-time soldier who was severely wounded would quickly lose the pay from his civilian job and, as he was unable to carry out his military duties, he would get no pay from the Army either. At a stroke he and his family could be destitute. UDR charitable funds could and did provide short-term loans but they were inadequate: an immediate grant was required removing further stress at such a difficult time – but this was not provided. The Army did eventually step up to the mark by transferring wounded part-time solders to full-time (so paid) until they were fully recovered, and this undoubtedly helped.

There was always the possibility of moving house to a safer area or even out of East Tyrone, and soldiers who chose to do this were given financial assistance. Few did; they had volunteered to hold firm all that their ancestors had passed to them and selling up was equated to giving up.

No-one understood the long term mental effects of such extended operations. Many have written that courage is like an old rechargeable battery. One starts with it full and over time it is used up. Recharging can restore some of that used but never all of it, and each time there is a reduction. There seemed to be two drains on the resource; there was the long term debilitating effect of living under threat 24 hours a day for many years, not just the soldier but his family too. Even without exposure to violence the resource became drained. An incident in which the soldier participated or was the target hastened the process. At the time leadership, discipline and comradeship held men together; today, thirty years after 8 UDR ceased to exist, the long term mental effects are increasingly apparent.

The Battalion existed for 22 years and was on operational service throughout. During that time about 2,500 all ranks (161 officers, 257 Greenfinches and 1958 men including Regulars) served in it and several times that number, their close family members, provided invaluable support. Its success can be judged by the stories in this book as can the price that was paid. Faith, family and friendship; on these three strong bonds, and the support of the community, so much depended.

History should remember these men and women because they volunteered to serve their Country when asked to do so; they knew and accepted the risks, and at the time there was no end in sight to the commitment they were making. These stories tell of their courage and resilience; they should never be forgotten. If their children and grandchildren face a better future, and there is no going back, everyone will have won.

Bibliography

Books & Articles

De Baroid, Ciaran, *Ballymurphy and the Irish War* (Chicago, Illinois: Pluto Press, 2000).

Dingly, James C., *IRA: Irish Republican Army* (Westport, Connecticut: ABC-CLIO, 2012).

Hutchison, W.R., *Tyrone Precincts* (Belfast: W. Erskine May, 1951).

Magee, Gerard, *Tyrone's Struggle* (Dublin: Brunswick Press, 2011).

Magill, '"They wouldn't leave him alone"; The Death of Michael Lynagh', *Magill*, 30th October 1982 <https://magill.ie/archive/they-wouldnt-leave-him-alone-death-michael-lynagh>

Moloney, Ed, *A Secret History of the IRA* (London: Penguin, 2007).

Murtagh, Tom, *The Maze Prison: A Hidden Story of Chaos, Anarchy and Politics* (Hook: Waterside Press, 2018).

O'Brien, Brendan, *The Long War: IRA and Sinn Fein* (Syracuse, New York: Syracuse University Press, 1995).

O'Callaghan, Sean, *The Informer* (London: Corgi Books, 1999).

Oppenheimer, A.R., *IRA: The Bombs and the Bullets* (Dublin: Irish Academic Press, 2008).

Thornton, Chris, et al, *Lost Lives* (Edinburgh: Mainstream Publishing, 1999).

Urban, Mark, *Big Boys' Rules: The Secret War Between the SAS and the IRA* (London: Faber & Faber, 1992).

White, Robert, *Ruari O'Bradaigh: The Life and Politics of an Irish Revolutionary* (Bloomington, Indiana: Indiana University Press, 2006).

Williams, Paul, *Gangland* (Dublin: O'Brien Press, 1998).

Wright, Louisa, 'The IRA's Great Escape', *Time*, 10th October 1983.

Index

8 UDR Names

Abraham, Roberta 107
Anderson, Austin 102
Anderson, Deko 170
+Armstrong, Tim 49

Beggs, Joe 57
Bell, Dinger 48
Benson, Tommy 47, 102
Boyd, George 38, 40-1
Boyd, Mervyn 38, 128-9, 224
Boyd, Wilson 38
Brimage, Trevor 191-2
Brush, Sammy 81, 87
Burnside, Norman 58

Campbell, Ronnie 192
Cantley, Joe 70
Carnegie, Sid 59
+Cooper, Albert 49, 101, 178
Cumberland, Budgie 59

Davison, Florence 46, 52
Davison, Ivan 112
Devlin, Walter 55
Dougan, Albert 143, 227
Doyle, Joan 107

Espie, Glen 62, 66, 88, 200
Espie, Marion 75
Espie, Tom 170

Ferguson, Arnie 161
Ferguson, Helen 61
Ferguson, John 170
Ferguson, Kenny 149, 152, 154, 156, 212
Ferry, Robin 177
Finlay, Tom 149-50, 153, 155, 180, 206-7

Gallagher, Geordie 43, 47
Galloway, David 211-15, 217, 220
Gates, Hughie 43-4
Gates, Tom 187
Gibson, Derek 179, 210, 223
+Gibson, James 221-3, 225-6

+Gibson, Sam 112-3, 150
Glendinning, Raymond 79
Gordon, Dessie 113, 133, 198, 200
Gordon, Ozzie 213-4, 216-7
Gordon, Stanley 141-2, 150, 164, 166, 168-170, 204-5, 207-210, 224
Gourley, Alan 200

Hamilton, Brian 100, 172, 174, 176
+Hardy, John 210-220
Harkness, Allister 145
+Harkness, Trevor 102, 171-82
Harrison, Robert 200
+Henry, Harry 81
Hogg, David 143, 148, 152, 212, 218-9

Irwin, Norman 34, 37

James, Val 185
Jennings, Hugh 185
Johnston, Jack 38, 40
+Johnston, Jimmy 59
Johnston, Robert 36

Kells, Eric 100
Kelly, Franklin 54, 61, 88
Kerr, Joe 120, 184
Kirk, David 186
Kirk, Ned 135, 153

Lamont, Harry 199
Lamont, Jeffrey 199, 201, 208
Lamont, Loraine 199
Lennox, Keith 198

Maginnis, Ken 16-7, 19-20, 27, 29, 48, 81, 84
Marks, Jim 173
Marks, Melvin 171, 174, 176
Marsh, Kenny 101
Marshall, Percy 55
Martin, Archie 76
Martin, Day 76
Martin, Thomas 189, 191, 193, 195, 197
+McCabe, Cormac 111

McCammon, Bob 218
McCauley, Snakebite 55
McCaw, Tony 176
McCollum, Albert 102
+McCreedy, Robert 184
McGucken, Dean 166-7, 234
McKee, Eustace 230-1
McKenzie, Billy 20, 27
McKenzie, Sadie 43, 45-6, 50
McKinney, Tom 43, 46, 50-1, 132, 137
McKnight, Chris 45-6
McMenemy, Jackie 120, 224
McMullan, Tom 187
+McNeill, Cecil 231
McNickle, Victor 139, 141, 166, 234
+McNicol, Raymond 200, 200n
Meenagh, Dorothy 178
Mitchell, Fred 76
+Moffett, Roy 100-1, 104, 161
Monteith, Jim 76
Murphy, Maurice 45, 206
Murray, Noel 233
Murray RJ 230

Neill, David 15
Nesbitt, Ronnie 49, 103
Nethercott, Jay 16-7, 20-1, 158, 163, 170, 179, 224, 233

Patterson, Gary 102, 171, 174-5
Patterson, Jim 167, 223
Patterson, Mavis 51
Pritchard, Dill 143

Rea, Neil 200
Reid, Ruffy 143
Richardson, Raymond 92, 95-7
Robinson, John 190, 194, 210, 218
Roleston, Archie 185, 187, 229

Scarlett, Jimmy 128
Shackels, John 229, 232-3
+Shaw, George 109, 122
+Shiells, Eric 133
Simpson, Aggie 111, 113, 140-1
Simpson, Pal 141
Sinnamon, Eric 36
+Smyrl, Robin 63
Stewart, Bert 102
Stewart, Jackie 45-6
+Stewart, John 49
Stewart, Tom 122
Symington, David 20, 26

Turner, Albert 77, 132, 180

Watson, Carol 106
Watson, Jimmy 143
Watterson, Wincie 199
Weir, Roy 231
White, Chalkie 132, 135, 194-5
Wilkinson, Walter 193
Wilson, David 204
+Wilson, Denis 17
Wray, Winston 28

Other Names

Armstrong, Tony 176

Bell, Thomas 205
Bullock, Martin 211-6

Campbell, Brendan 189, 191-3
Campbell, James 154, 156
Corr, Paul William John 122
Corr, Oliver Alphonsus 113

Donnelly, Gerald Martin 93-5
Donnelly, Thaddeus 188
Doris, Tony 189, 193

Gervin, Martin 189, 193-4
Gildernew, Patsy 130

Hurson, Edward Martin 115, 143

Kilpatrick, Kevin 184

Loughran, PJ 56, 62
Lynagh, Jim 81

McAnallen, Dan 35
McAnespie, Vincent 87, 91
McCrea, Eileen 125
McDonald, Eugene 24, 28
McGeough, Terence Gerard 82, 87, 91
McGurk, Patrick 116, 153
McGurk, Patrick Edward 217
McHugh, Barry 22
McLernon, Brian 188
McNally, Laurence Joseph 93-5
McPhillips, Brendan 122
McStravog, Hugh 188-9
Moore, Dermot 215, 217

Morgan, Seamus 114
Mulgrew, Mark 203, 205, 208-9

Neeson, Terence Joseph 203, 205
Nicholl, Dominic 218

O'Donnell, Ciaran 125
O'Farrell, Sean 195
O'Hagan, Sean 153
O'Neill, Kevin 222

Quinn, Patrick Joseph (k1973) 35
Quinn, Patrick Joseph 94-5

Russell, Peter John 87, 90

Sherry, Peter 115, 153

Vincent, Andrew Hugh 17, 21-2, 27, 29

Places

Annaghmore 101, 221, 223, 235
Ardboe 63-6, 68, 70, 75 77-8, 100, 104-5, 139, 145, 184, 223
Aughnacloy 31, 48-9, 55, 81-3, 87, 90, 111, 117, 159, 184-5, 229-33

Ballygawley 82-6, 120, 133, 164, 214, 216, 231

Caledon 17, 231
Cappagh 32, 41, 57, 88, 109, 115, 133-4, 143, 146, 162-5, 167-8, 179, 182, 210, 212, 231
Castlecaulfield 16, 20, 22-3, 25-6
Coagh 46, 64, 68, 70, 76, 93-4, 102, 145, 147-8, 188-9, 222-3, 234
Coalisland 22, 31, 47-9, 58, 75, 79, 92, 97, 101-2, 107, 109, 112-3, 116, 120-2, 136-7, 143, 149-50, 152-4, 176, 184, 186-92, 194-6, 219, 221-2, 224-7, 229-30, 232-5
Cookstown 31, 35, 40, 42-4, 46-7, 49, 50-2, 55, 58, 62-3, 65, 71, 73-8, 92-5, 97-8, 101, 103-4, 112-3, 130, 133, 136, 139-41, 145, 148, 150, 159-60, 166-7, 173-5, 179-81, 191, 197, 199, 200-1, 203-8, 213, 215, 223-5, 234

Diamond 64, 68-9
Donaghmore 16-8, 20-6, 40, 54-5, 101, 125, 133, 159, 168, 187, 218

Dunamore 130, 132, 138
Dungannon 16-8, 20-5, 29-30, 34-5, 36-7, 38, 40-1, 45-8, 52, 55-6, 60, 81-4, 86, 92-3, 107-8, 112-6, 118-23, 125, 128, 130, 132-3, 135-6, 141, 143, 145, 147-8, 150, 153, 158-60, 164, 167, 170, 177, 179, 184-7, 190-1, 194-5, 199, 204, 206, 209, 211-5, 218-9, 222-5, 230, 235

Eglish 35, 161, 184-5, 217

Galbally 115, 133, 162, 164-5, 168, 171, 212, 218-20
Granville 128, 130, 210-4, 216-7

Kingsisland 187, 222

Pomeroy 16, 22, 29, 31-40, 42, 55, 57, 64-5, 88, 102, 115, 128-9, 131, 134-5, 147, 162, 164, 168, 171-81, 197, 219, 223-5, 229, 233-4, 237

Stewartstown 31, 46, 77, 100-1, 103-4, 133, 191, 193, 210, 222

Washing Bay 191-2, 196, 222, 227